‖‖ ‖ ‖‖‖‖‖‖‖ ‖ ‖ ‖‖‖ ‖‖‖‖‖‖‖‖‖‖‖‖ ‖ ‖‖
✐ **W9-BXV-690**

All of us can recollect times when we have thought that something we had done was so out of character that some other person must have temporarily invaded our body and been the protagonist of such an event. Surely we know that the same phenomenon is true for others around us, especially when they surprise us through their unexpected behavior. But perhaps we should not be alarmed at such irregularities or discrepancies. Perhaps they are not the product of slippages due to fatigue or a decreased ability to control ourselves. Rather they may be signs that we and those around us may be allowing different parts of our personalities, or our selves, to find creative and integrated expression. Indeed, that, in a nutshell, is the main premise of this book.

In *Four and Twenty Blackbirds* Peter Baldwin presents us with a conceptual framework for understanding such seeming discrepancies. Through his "Personae Theory" Dr. Baldwin provides us with a way to understand our multiple selves as well as those of others. These multiple selves are seen as potentially contributing to a whole. People vary in how well they integrate their multiple selves. At one end of the continuum is the person who rigidly strives for sameness and is threatened by any behavioral inconsistency. At the other end are the persons whom we usually refer to as "multiple personalities" and because of the lack of integration among their multiple selves resemble a badly functioning committee. In the middle of the continuum are those who live a fuller and richer life because they allow their multiple selves to find expression within an integrated whole.

In addition to his elegant conceptual framework, Dr. Baldwin also provides us with a vast array of therapeutic techniques that can be used to facilitate the discovery of our selves and aid in their integration. By sharing examples from his own clinical practice Dr. Baldwin richly illustrates the process of Personae Work that he utilizes in therapy.

Dr. Baldwin's book will be helpful to the professional and the lay reader alike. Professionals will derive a theory which is influenced by the works of Erik Erickson, J.L. Moreno, George Kelly, Ervin Goffman, and Fritz Perls as well as a set of techniques highly steeped in the work of Milton Erikson. Lay readers will derive a new way of understanding their own multiple selves in a fashion that normalizes the experience and which encourages them to facilitate their emergence and integration.

A word of caution for the reader. You may wonder why a book written by a single author reads so much like an edited work. The answer is simple—Peter Baldwin has allowed his multiple selves to contribute in their own creative and unique ways. The result is an opportunity to view the thoughts, the professional work, and the many personas of a careful and creative thinker, a master teacher, and a tremendously perceptive, sensitive, and effective psychotherapist.

Joseph W. Bascuas, Ph.D.
Dean, Georgia School of Professional Psychology, Atlanta Georgia

The paper used in this publication meets the minimum requirements
of American National Standard for Information Sciences—
Permanence of Paper for Printed Library Materials,
ANSI Z39.48-1984.

FOUR AND TWENTY BLACKBIRDS

PERSONAE THEORY
AND THE UNDERSTANDING OF
OUR MULTIPLE SELVES

Peter Arthur Baldwin

BRAMBLE ❖ BOOKS

Copyright ©1997 by Peter Arthur Baldwin

All rights reserved. No part of this book may be reproduced in any manner whatever, including information storage, or retrieval, in whole or in part (except for brief quotations in critical articles or reviews), without written permission from the publisher.

For information write to:
Bramble Books, 4001 S. Decatur Blvd., Suite 37-406, Las Vegas, NV 89103

Library of Congress Cataloging-in-Publication Data

Baldwin, Peter Arthur.
    Four and twenty blackbirds : personae theory and the understanding of our multiple selves / Peter Arthur Baldwin.
        p.   cm.
    Includes bibliographical references.
    ISBN 1-883647-06-1 (pbk. : alk. paper)
    1. Personality. 2. Multiple personality. 3. Psychosynthesis.
I. Title.
BF698.B313 1997
155.2—dc21   97-4111
                                CIP

First Printing 1997
1 3 5 7 9 10 8 6 4 2

Printed in the United States of America

FOREWORD

Late in the first chapter of Peter Baldwin's book *Personae Theory*, he reports that many years ago his geometry teacher observed, Peter, you think differently from most of the other students. I don't understand how you think. Believe me you have an interesting mind...that will serve you very well in some career." Now, almost half a century later, in front of a book instead of a blackboard, this is one of the same Peters I know. In the postmodern era, as we grow out of the unyielding requirement for a narrowed rationalistic psychology, we welcome Peter's mind, value the non-linearity, and connect him with the narrative tradition, with Milton Erickson, and other masterful tellers of teaching tales.

Peter is a "strong poet" of the sort whom pragmatist philosopher Richard Rorty (1969), following Bloom and Nietzsche, describes as the cultural hero who has replaced the empirical scientist. Strong poets help us in the "process of coming to see other human beings as 'one of us' rather than as 'them'" through "detailed description of what unfamiliar people look like and of redescription of what we ourselves are like" (p.xvi). This is Peter's kind of truth, one embodied by arraying a "mobile army of metaphors" (Rorty, 1989, p.28) in unusual ways, rather than by argument or data.

Yet this Peter is the same man who has been twice President of the New Hampshire Psychological Association, the person I have known now for more than a decade. We are partners in University Associates in Psychology, P.C., a group practice of professional psychology. In this context, I have been blessed to sit with him and others almost every week since 1986 in peer supervision. Though our languages are different (mine comes from the cognitive inter-personal and constructionist traditions), we have found ourselves agreeing on many things. I have gloried in his stories, been encouraged to bring forward some of my own, and felt supported and heard.

Peter's work and his stories are built at an increasingly well-traveled crossroads in professional psychology (Peterson and Peterson, 1994). As we leave behind the age that idolized the coherent if not congealed self (Gergen, 1991) and feared the painful fragmentation of what used to be called multiple personality disorder, Peter shows us that there are many parts of all of us both in sickness and in health. Led by Jerome Bruner (1990) from social psychology, many are seeing the centrality of narrative to human meaning making. Family therapists (e.g., Lax 1992) and therapists influenced by social constructionism (e.g., McNamee & Gergen 1992) come to emphasize the story and narrative from yet a different direction. Down another road comes the influential anthropologist Clifford Geertz, 1973) of the kind that fills *Personae*.

For many years Peter has taught an elective on Ericksonian hypnosis to advanced students in Antioch New England's Doctoral Program in Clinical Psychology. In the course, always oversubscribed and rated highly, his students spend two and a half hours per week in some sort of joyful learning trance that allows them to experience the examples, cases, and anecdotes from this book and see the world through the eyes and ears of a master therapist. For most of one year Peter taught our colleague group much the same material. We slid into a comfortable trance, found our attention directed here and there, and were refreshed and enriched when we left, realizing our work would be different in some important ways.

Though Peter glories in showing how various sides of himself differ, there sometimes appears to be a reasonably coherent whole person, part master therapist, part master teacher, part story teller, part jokester, and part extremely hard and committed worker. You are about to read a play, a dramatic monologue for a single and yet multiple voices. If you want to, as you read this book, you might find that you come to see this tall man in front of you speaking, white-haired, bearded, a little rumpled, mischievous, sparkling eyes behind trifocals, the hard big hands of a man who keeps a farm and cares for horses, a country New England Unitarian preacher, the universal grandfather and uncle with hearing aids, discursive, digressive, smooth soft voice, always with a bit of humor, patient, knowing the stories you need to hear, seeing the best part of you ...

Roger L. Peterson, Ph.D.
Chairperson, Department of Clinical Psychology
Antioch New England Graduate School
Spofford Lake
New Hampshire

References
Bruner, J. (1990). *Acts of Meaning*. Cambridge, MA: Harvard University Press.
Geertz, C. (1973). *The Interpretation of Cultures*. New York: Basic Books.
Gergen, K.J. (1991). *The Saturated Self: Dilemmas of Identity in Contemporary Life*. NY: Basic Book.
Lax, W.D. (1992) Postmodern thinking in a clinical practice. In S. McNamee & K. Gergen, (Eds). *Constructing Therapy: Social Constructionism and Therapeutic Process*.
Peterson, D.R., & Peterson, R.L. (January, 1994). *Toward an Epistemology for the Education of Professional Psychologists*. Paper presented at the National Council of Schools and Programs of Professional Psychology Midwinter Conference on "Standards for Education in Professional Psychology: Reflection and Integration.," Cancun, Mexico. Revised version April 8, 1994.
Rorty, R. (1989). *Contingency, Irony, and Solidarity*. Cambridge, England: Cambridge University Press.
Sarbin, T.R. (Ed.) (1986). *Narrative Psychology: The Storied Nature of Human Conduct*. New York: Praeger.

DEDICATION

I dedicate this writing to Howard Thurman to whom I went as a college junior, confused in regard to what I wanted to do with my life. Howard was serving as Dean of Boston University's Marsh Chapel. I remember sitting in his office. I loved just being there with him. We could sit in quiet together. He asked me what interested me. I told him about hearing Susan Read in folk concert when I was sixteen and how I had been so inspired by her Child ballads that I had learned to play the guitar and had learned scores of ballads. I talked of my summers working as a hut-man for the Appalachian and Adirondack Mountain Clubs. I shared my supposing for years that I would be a minister. I talked of my enthusiasm for my major studies in psychology. Should I go to forestry school, seminary, graduate school in psychology, music conservatory?

Howard settled back in his leather chair, placed his hands together palm to palm, closed his eyes, and waited. I am aware now that we both entered into trance. "Think of yourself, Peter, as an Innkeeper. It is evening. It is winter and you have kindled a fire so the hearth is a warm place for the gathering. Think of your interests as night visitors who come one by one to the door and knock for entry. There will be visitors, Peter, whom you will find familiar to you in ways you have not shared with me: figures in whom you will come to recognize yourself in various specific ways. When you hear them knocking at the door, welcome them in, draw them to the hearth, attend to their comfort. Introduce them to one another. You will not have to guide them in conversation. They will gradually find ways of conversing with one another. They will welcome you, as their host, into their midst as a matter of course. Remember, do not labor over finding ways for them to be together. Let it happen. You lend a welcome. They will grace your dwelling."

TABLE OF CONTENTS

INTRODUCTION

My Name is Legion

In Mark's account of Jesus (Mark 5:2) he tells of an encounter between Jesus and a wretched man who lived among the tombs. Asked his name, the man replied, "My name is Legion: for we are many." The commentator (Interpreter's Bible, 1953) of this passage puts the man's statement into words we can understand today: "There are many persons in me, pulling in opposite directions, many clamorous voices in the town meeting of (my) mind, no gavel in the hands of an effective chairperson."

A town meeting with an absent or weak moderator can be hell. With a good moderator, a town meeting can go well, can be a lot of fun, can get mighty colorful! The same applies to the town meeting of the mind. Suffering and fun are both possible. Many people with whom I work as a psychotherapist observe that all their experience of "on the one hand and on all the others" amounts to hearing from a number of personas, sometimes all clamoring at once, each calling for attention and response. And this can be hell. Sometimes it isn't hell at all! A lot of the time coming from several places at the same time within one's own mind adds spice to life. Most people find they can identify themselves as a troupe of characters, a cast composed of principal, supporting, and bit players. Moreover, the character who plays a bit in one scene, may be a principal in another.

Now I pay attention to every person as a group. And, as a result, I find myself (and my friends and clients tell me they find me) far more alert and responsive to what is happening. Life is a queer

1

business for all of us. With every turn of events, in every situation something different is at stake, something different is expected of us. Over the course of each day we are engaged in various dramas. Five hundred years ago Desiderius Erasmus (Hudson, 1941) put this very well.

> If a person were to try stripping the disguises from actors while they play a scene upon the stage, showing to the audience their real looks and the faces they were born with, would not such a one spoil the whole play? And would not the spectators think he deserved to be driven out of the theater with brickbats, as a drunken disturber?…Now what else is the whole life of mortals but a sort of comedy, in which the various actors, disguised by various costumes and masks, walk on and play each one his part, until the manager waves them off the stage? Moreover, this manager frequently bids the same actor go back in a different costume, so that he who has but lately played the king in scarlet now acts the flunky in patched clothes. Thus all things are presented by shadows; yet this play is put on in no other way.

In the newspapers, over the radio, in day to day conversations, references are made to "personas." These references do not seem to have to do with people's whimsical impressions of one another. Something more noteworthy is being pointed out, something peculiarly interesting! Reference is being made to a character self projected by someone in public before the public eye. I endorse the observation that personas are central to being simply and authentically human. While it is possible for the reader to infer from Erasmus' statement that masks hide or distract from our "real" identity, I propose that masks provide appearances by which our "real" identity can be inferred. Helen Harris Perlman (Perlman, 1968) writes:

> Persona is the Latin word for the masks used in the Greek drama. It meant that the actor was heard and his identity recognized by others through the sounds that issued from

the open mask mouth. From it the word 'person' emerged to express the idea of a human being who meant something, who represented something, and who seemed to have some defined connectedness with others by action or affects. (We still use person to connote this: we say of an infant who begins to show signs of awareness of self in relation to others, 'He's becoming a *person*.' A person makes himself known, felt, taken in by others, through his particular roles and their functions. Some of his personas—his masks—are readily detachable and put aside, but others become fused with his skin and bone.

In the service of illustration, I offer a cameo account of one client's personas, and some points that develop from it.

Kesstler, identifies himself as ten principal characters [personas]. He is:

David —a social hedonist who does not enjoy being alone. He initiates or is responsive to pleasant gatherings of men and women who enjoy interesting talk, good food and good drink. He loves and feels good being loved.

Beatle —likes to organize, spends hours alone sorting out miscellaneous nails and tacks, nuts and bolts. For Beatle it is better to be fastidious than to complete a task. His absorption with minutiae protects him from thinking about his inadequacies.

Melvin —a dark hedonist and recluse. He drinks alone. He resists compromise. Melvin can remain mute for long periods of time, and he indulges himself in resentments, including resentment when others don't approach him.

William —is profoundly idealistic. He rallies behind and champions causes. He delights in intellectual wrestling. On an antagonist's scent he is capable of brutal ferocity, running in form from rude crudeness to gracious, witty, and subtle irony.

Skipper —is footloose. He is the principal keeper of a touring van, ever ready and prepared with a full tank of gas and larder for departure at a moment's notice. When his host body is on the road to one of William's appointments, to Beatle's clean-up-the-mess somewhere, or to one of David's social gatherings, Skipper will grab the mike, as it were, and say: "Let's just keep driving. Anywhere will do. Let's just keep moving."

Fred —performs services for the company, will take on anything, wants to be seen as important and loyal.

Michael —is disdainfully clammed up, or, he may snort from the cover of an audience when the pompous trip themselves up being too clever for words, misusing a Latin phrase, for instance. Michael has the effect upon others of making them feel they are subject to a grand inquisitor. "Michael is born of frustration, and when I come out of being Michael, I am shaken and weakened."

Stanley —the revolutionary. There is nothing gracious, witty, or sophisticated about Stanley's manner. Rather, he's caustic; he does not mince words and is devoid of polite manners. While he is not an alcoholic, he does drink, and if anyone suggests he should not, Stanley's triggered off. "I'm entitled not to be told what to do or not to do. I won't be leaned on by anyone!"

Ken —the product of elite schools and old family wealth. Ken is committed to proper appearance, good form, and amiable manners. It doesn't matter very much what is happening so long as good form is being observed. Ken wants to be loved, approved of, and he works hard to please, to appear attractive, and to avoid being disapproved of.

Shirley —verges on being goody-goody, on being limitlessly solicitous and protecting toward those on the brink of calamity or who look as though they will severely harm themselves. Shirley emerges as a response to presented fear and abject frailty.

I gave this Introduction, including this listing of personas, to Kesstler to check for accuracy and to reconfirm his permission to share his experience with others. He took the list home and left it where it was clearly available for others to read. His wife picked it up. He had not shared the names of his personas with her, and he wondered what she would make of what she was reading. When she was finished, she looked at him, looked back at the material, and said: "Why, this is you, Kesstler! It is, isn't it! I recognize you in every description. They are all you! Only, one is missing! Your warmth and loving. That's what is missing."

When I saw Kesstler the next week, he appeared delighted with his wife's validating recognition. And he was curious over her observation that one persona was missing. Exploring this together yielded rich findings. David's loving, while a delight, lacks depth and commitment. Shirley's generosity lacks equanimity and simple, unconditional mutuality. Ken's attentiveness features fear and form. "As a matter of fact," Kesstler observed with an attitude of great tiredness, "It's increasingly difficult for me to achieve a semblance of love and intimacy relying upon Ken's way of trying to win attention and avoid disapproval.

"The missing persona is *Kessey*. When I was a child, I couldn't quite pronounce my name. I called myself Kessey. My father picked up on that and called me Kessey in an affectionate way. He was not very demonstrative, but I remember how he'd blow my hair all a tousle! I feel his warm breath right now. Kessey is my child-like loving warmth."

With these very different selves discerned and named, confusion is reduced and self-management is enhanced.

In realizing an integrity among the many that compose each of us, we are capable of experiencing ourselves and being experienced by others as multi-faceted characters. And while it may be the fate of each persona that she or he will not prove master of the fate of the whole person, that she or he will not get their way in every way all of the time, neither is it the case that any persona need be butchered.

Theoretical Bearings

Erik Erikson wrote of the various selves making up the composite self, and of the healthy "I" capable of speaking with reasonable coherence out of many diverse aspects of Self. I will be referring in specific from remarks he offered in his *Identity, Youth and Crisis*.

I am intrigued by and indebted to Julian Jaynes' notion of the analogue "I". For me, Jaynes' observations advance the body of thought in regard to the nature of self that comes to us from Husserl,

Heidegger, Binswanger, and Gordon Alport. The self is an illusion, an illusion that is conditioned by our introjections of others' projections upon us and by our adaptive and creative wit.

Central to this essay is the notion of "true self" as pure potentiality. The meaning I assign to "true self" evidences my profound indebtedness to Logo-therapist Viktor Frankl and philosophers' philosopher Frederick Ferre. I have read from both of their works and from each I have learned so much through our personal encounters.

J. L. Moreno distinguished among somatic, social and psychodramatic selves, and developed a therapeutic approach featuring the notion that human beings are best understood in interaction with others, that we are actors who are behaving most authentically when engaged in spontaneous encounter with others in scenes of critical importance. My conception of personas corresponds to Moreno's psychodramatic selves; each is a discrete alter ego.

Sigmund Freud alluded to the division of self into the central self which is powered by pregenital and genital sexuality on the one hand, and on the other, the self that emerges as part of the ego related to the outside world. I feel that my indebtedness to Freud is expressed by my supposing that our personas function in the service of our primitive, intrapersonal developmental stories and in the service of our adaptive encounters within social dramas.

W.R.D. Fairbairn, Melanie Klein and others building on Freud's theoretical foundation developed object relations theory. Two exponents of this body of theory interest me in particular: Mahler and Winnecott.

I am indebted to Margaret Mahler's contributions to our understanding of symbiosis, separation, and individuation during the course of middle and late infancy. Her findings add clarification and detail to Moreno's discussion of somatic, social, and psychodramatic selves. In detailing how the mother facilitates or frustrates the small child's hatching out into the world, she captures for me in a powerful manner how each of us from a very early age perceives the world as we are prompted to do.

D.W. Winnecott elaborates upon Mahler's studies in his discussion of true and false selves. One of his patients coined the expression "caretaking self." I believe that each of our personas is a caretaking self, each reflecting features of our integral (or true) Self as well as features or characteristics assumed for the sake of camouflaging the true self in order to protect it. Here we have an adaptive caretaking self." I believe that each of our personas is a caretaking self, each reflecting features of our integral (or true) Self as well as features or characteristics assumed for the sake of camouflaging the true self in order to protect it. Here we have an adaptive development serving both assimilation and accommodation. The severity of falseness of the persona as caretaking self depends upon the extent of what one has to do (i.e. accommodation) to get what one needs (i.e., assimilation).

Murray Bowen's discussion of undifferentiated family ego mass and Margaret Mahler's discussion of symbiosis dovetail. Furthermore, Bowen's concept of the basic and negotiable selves corresponds to Winnecott's notion of the true and caretaking selves respectively. Bowen's techniques in family therapy apply in teasing personas out of a snarled composite self, identifying agenda among the personas, alerting to collusions, bringing secrets out into the open, and facilitating functionally adaptive teamwork.

My interest over the years in George Kelly's psychology of personal constructs (which I suppose was triggered by my previous indebtedness to the Meditations of Marcus Aurelius), led to interest in the thinking of Erving Goffman. Goffman's *The Presentation of Self in Everyday Life* and other works feature the dramaturgical perspective on human behavior. I engage my clients in a social learning exercise *a la* Goffman when I invite them to suppose that all the world is a stage; when I ask them to identify pleasant and unpleasant scenes; and when I encourage them to name the coping, thriving, and playful characters they recognize they can assume. From the point of view of this valid if insufficient perspective, we are not human until we learn to behave. Human behavior is invariably symbolic and socially meaningful. "I act, therefore I am." And to act is to perform before physically present as well as imagined audiences in the theater called community-living. Audiences define reality and norms; they clarify acceptable and insupportable standard deviations from the norm; and they provide feedforward and feedback that shape the form and manner of our subsequent behaviors.

Goffman's emphasis is interpersonal. I have appropriated his principles and apply them to my clients' intrapersonal cast of personal characters, fostering in them increased awareness and capacity in living effectively within themselves and in the world.

While in the process of developing this work I became familiar with the pioneering work in ego-state psychology by John and Helen Watkins of the University of Montana. Their response after reviewing this essay proved deeply heartening. And then to read John Rowan's *Subpersonalities*, and to find in his book many more theoretical foundations for my thinking is gratifying.

Frederick (Fritz) Perls and other theorists within Gestalt Therapy note how typically fragmented, split up, and scattered most people are due to frightening experiences in life and our inevitable failures of nerve in staying in the present moment and place while whatever is happening runs its course. We run for cover, scatter and hide parts of ourselves, even "disappear" parts of ourselves. The objective of Gestalt therapy is to facilitate persons' becoming aware of their splits and fragments and lost parts, to re-own and reintegrate all of their parts into a functioning whole.

Prominent among the influences upon my thought and practice have been the contributions of Milton Erickson, M.D., and his principal colleagues and students. The following perspective evidences how Ericksonian thought has served to influence a weaving together of these theoretical frames.

Living Hypnotically in a Hypnotic World

The student asked the Master: "What is the first principle guiding one's way into wisdom and enlightenment?" The Master responded: "Increase and sharpen your awareness." The student continued, "What is the second principle?" The Master added: "There is no second principle!" The principles and practice of Gestalt Therapy proceed from this single premise: that growth, that health, that healing, that wholeness for a person, for a local community, and for all the world generates spontaneously from deepened and sharpened awareness.

Understanding the various forms of awareness as Minding, there is conscious and non-conscious minding. Every cell of the body carries the entire genetic code, receives and transmits information, and contributes via feedforward, feedback, and adaptive initiatives to the natural and social environment. Mindful conversation occurs constantly within the community meeting of our multiple personas and between and among all the intelligent tissue centers composing our body-mind-Self. Conscious minding amounts to a remarkably useful if relatively modest facet of our overall minding. Put another way, *conscious awareness plays an exquisitely valuable if quantitatively minor part in our total minding.* What a blessing that we are spared being consciously attentive to all of our learning experiences, all the information we have accumulated, all the night and day dreams we have generated! Best that the great store of information and experience we have accumulated is filed in the unconscious back of our mind. It is best that the great number of completed and incomplete gestalten are not immediately available to conscious minding. How good it is that in the hypnotic state referred to as therapeutic trance we can access rich minding resources within the care of supportive and competent company.

Perls and company observed that all proprioceptive thinking is fantasy, that "reality," however variously defined, is imaginatively constructed. However fiercely people claim hold on undeniable truth, final and conclusive truth eludes human minding. So called theoretical truths are forever subject to question and revision. I endorse the notion that all ideas evolve into definition accidental to ill or well informed mind-play. We conduct our lives in association with and informed by ideas that command our attention. We are each of us fascinated with, enthralled by, fictions held solely or collectively. Collective cognitive imperatives are simple and complex notions that command social order and social activity. Social collectives, this is to say communities, states, peoples are held in thrall by images and notions. Being fascinated prompts thoughts, feelings, and action congruent with the image-object of that fascination. Being fascinated is living hypnotically! Living hypnotically is enthralled living, living entranced by images, idiosyncratic or shared notions, that command the attention and engage individual and shared resources in action.

The word trance can apply to a pattern of thought and/or behavior that is compelling for an individual or group. Hence we can talk of a person's or group's trance life. There can be healthy or unhealthy trance lives. An unhealthy trance life features an individual's or a group's repeating over and again disastrous patterns of thought and behavior. Like the mythical Ouroborous (serpent) constantly fascinated by and consuming its own tail, such a person or group is recycling its own old damaged and damaging tale. When, on the other hand, we say to or about someone that they are thriving, it is clear that they are living a creatively adaptive trance life. The word trance can also apply to that state of minding where one is accessing deep, unconscious minding. Therapeutic hypnosis is an intervention modality engaged to enhance a persons' access to rich deep minding awareness and resourcefulness.

Living hypnotically in a hypnotic world means that we live alone and together informed by realities we have dreamed up and by which we have become enthralled. Whether we survive or thrive depends upon whether the realities we dream up, and the trance lives we engage in are informed by valid and sufficient awareness of and attention to everything that is happening within and around us.

The Chapters, Topic by Topic

This essay has evolved over a period of fifteen years from a brief report to colleagues at a meeting of the New Hampshire Psychological Association in 1979 to this larger piece.

Chapter One offers an overview of what follows, and suggests implications Personae Theory has for individual testing, social responsibility, and psychotherapy.

In Chapter Two I advance the notion that all human behavior is performance, and that all the world is a stage. I treat personality as comprised of multiple sub-selves, this is to say personas. The experience of "I" as in "I am" is defined in terms of *"I" as form* and *"I" as process*, the former signifying the analogue construct within which are subsumed a person's personas integrated or in disarray, the latter signifying the vincular or meta self, the pathfinding and group facilitating component to personality.

In Chapter Three I propose that True Self is pure potential, and that self actualization occurs as potential becomes evident in the process of being. Story is introduced as the tale that prompts and offers direction to performance, and relative to story, how personas may vary among themselves in language and dialect. Consideration of story directs our attention to the noetic facet to human being, this is to say our absorption with identifying and realizing meaning in each of our lives. I proceed from this base to differentiate between intimate and public personas.

Chapter Four outlines the process objectives in personas work. This chapter features the craft of identifying and attending to the play of personas in our own experience of ourselves and others. And Chapter Five offers an illustration of the inter-dynamics among personas.

Chapters Six and Seven focus on the therapeutic process, featuring the engagement of client and therapist in a process of heightened imagination or trance.

Chapter Eight serves as an epilogue. This concluding chapter begins with a theoretical precis of Personae Theory as closely argued and illustrated in Chapters One through Seven. And then this precis, reflecting the mind of the author-as-theoretician, is followed by several meditations that draw the reader into the mind of the author-as-artist. Chapter Eight might just as well have served as the first chapter as it offers the clearest statement of Personae Theory's central principles and draws the reader into the kind of hypnotic minding that opens attention to the play of personas.

In "Minding" the Way You Read

Colleagues have encouraged me to say a word at the outset about my writing style. What follows includes scholarly reflection, autobiographical anecdotes, fragments from my clinical notebook, and poetic cameos. Each of these modes, all of them weaving together, while at times disconcerting, even perturbing, necessarily belong together within the tapestry of report and rumination upon the content and process of human behavior. This essay in several voices illustrates Personae Theory by its literary style. Had, for the sake of precision, one persona written it, clarity in all of its textures and colors would have been sacrificed. The reading of this book will prove most interesting and fruitful if you, the reader, fancy you are "reading aloud," as it were, to the company of your own personas.

As a school teacher welcomes thoughts and impressions from members of her class as she reads aloud, attend to the variety of responses and associations generated in your own minding as you journey through these pages.

References:

Goffman, Erving, *The Presentation of Self in Everyday Life*, Doubleday, NY, 1959

Hudson, Hoyt Hopewell (Translator), *The Praise of Folly*, by Desiderius Erasmus, Princeton University Press, 1941.

Interpreter's Bible, Vol 7, p. 715.

Kelly, George A., A *Theory of Personality; The Psychology of Personal Constructs*, Norton, NY, 1963.

Perlman, Helen Harris, *Persona, Social Role and Person*, University of Chicago Press, 1968, p.4.

Rowan, John, *Subpersonalities; The People Inside Us*, Routledge, London, 1990.

PART I

CENTRAL THEORETICAL PRINCIPLES

1

Openings

Implications of
Personae Theory

This essay represents an opening, an enlarging upon what has come to my attention, how I live and work with what has become clear to me and the many who have shared with me. The word persona is a latin word that means mask, the sound that comes from behind the mask, with mask and sound creating together a dramatic character part in any given scene.

Discovering Personas

Eighteen years ago a client in his first meeting with me set the stage for our work by asking: "Can you understand from the outset that I experience myself as several, that I do not speak with one voice, that I will talk of the same event from very different angles?" This was the first time anyone had spoken to me in such a plain and matter of fact way of personas. As I recall, I did not experience myself as surprised. I suppose I was ready to have the obvious pointed out for me. My work with this man prompted me to see if others might be bringing the same question to my attention in subtler ways. I found that they were. I discovered that with only a minimum of explanation, many clients responded naturally to the idea that we are each of us several. This signifies that existing, that being, for each of us, means that "I am" is the same as the "We are" of my several voices in concert or in disarray.

I engaged the interest of several colleagues in addressing the implications of various observations offered by Erik Erikson concerning multiple selves composing human personality. The paper I prepared for this occasion marked my first effort to set forth in writing my report of clinical findings on multiple selves. Bit by bit, that first modest piece has evolved. After four years had passed in this process, I read a piece by free lance writer Peg Boyles (Boyles, 1984). What a thrill to find another person having set down precisely what I was reporting from my clients!
Boyles writes:

The most important lesson I have learned in forty years of living is that I am not a unitary person, but rather a motley collection of fairly disconnected selves, each with its own pressing agenda. My use of the singular,—upper case personal pronoun "I" is the height of presumption—I use it out of habit and in respect of convention. But in fact, "I" is always the dominant persona of the moment, whoever has struggled temporarily into the driver's seat. Understanding this about myself has greatly helped me tolerate the foibles and inconsistencies of others.

For me, the fundamental task of life is to track down these various inner selves, observe them, get them to acknowledge one another's presence, establish communication networks among them, assign appropriate work to each, and finally achieve consensus regarding our mutual direction.

From this perspective, "I" becomes a goal, a model, an aspiration, as in "If thine eye (I) be single, thy whole body shall be full of light." Until then, I have learned it is prudent never to assume that some major decision rendered unilaterally by the persona of the moment is going to be received enthusiastically and accepted by the others.

Among my many complex, quite individual selves, I have observed that some enjoy the limelight, clamor for recognition, love center stage. They talk a lot, make plenty of noise, and often embarrass themselves attempting to speak for the rest of us. Others work their way subversively, preferring the cover of darkness.

This piece by a person I had not met and who knew nothing of me or my thinking, offered sufficient support to my claim that my work consisted primarily of reporting a common story shared by many clients. While I had made no attempt yet to publish on this subject, I was sharing portions of my writing with Antioch New England colleagues and students. From these faculty and student colleagues I have received consistent and mounting support. Each has added clarity to what has now become a shared task. Here is free verse from a student reflecting upon personas.

a persona is
a core attitude
accompanied
incarnated
in posture/gesture/tension/pressure
all constellated in an image-in-mind/body
an image of a person
a who-i-am
known within
and projected out
into the world of how do you do
so nice to see you

Sybil
(a woman who is 16 separate people)
is but the extreme
of what we all are
(in part)
a series of personas
more or less

distinct
separate
autonomous
an intertwined collage of images
amongst which
we shift and switch
sometimes with great rapidity
sometimes staying stuck in one
for long periods of time.

Personae build around a core
growing in time
through steady accretion
of new experience
of new layers of meaning.

Their composite collage of images
is never still
alliances form and dissolve
individuals rise to prominence
dominating the daily stage life of their carrier
while others may find their expression in the
world of dreams
or rest content for a time to be of subtle
influence
through alliance with the more preeminent
characters.

—Victor Novick

We are everyone of us more than meets the eye.

In the mid-sixties I was employed by the Unitarian
Universalist Association of Churches to work with its
highschool youth across the continent. Participation in the
local group occasionally featured attendance at regional
weekend conferences, a high point in the experience of
many of these young people. The single most frequently
recurring account of the value of these weekend experiences by these young participants was: "There I can try out

being different selves as I search for who I am." There at
these weekend gatherings young people offered one another room to try on and try out varying ways of appearing
before one another.

A week-long Continental Convention drawing participation by over two hundred representatives from local,
federation, and regional memberships occurred at Ithaca
College. The convention was in crisis with the college
officials within two hours of the arrival from all points of
this mass of raggle-taggle scruffs. The Ithaca College
administrators were horrified by the young people's appearance. The youth won a by-the-skin-of-their-teeth
reprieve from being summarily evicted; the convention had
twenty-four hours to prove itself a responsible presence on
campus. Six days passed. At the close of the convention the
college officials offered: "We have learned from you that
appearances are not necessarily a reliable measure of the
persons behind the appearances. Your programs were
substantive. You are a remarkable group. We have learned
much from you. There was something about the whole
thing that obviously prompted us to tolerate your occa-
sional outrageous antics. But do go somewhere else next
year! Some other college ought to have its turn!"

Behind the prankster costumes and performances in the case of each
young person were other character selves who did not escape notice
by the Ithaca people.

How would it be otherwise? It is absurd to suppose that any
given person who reaches the advanced age of six has assumed or
is rehearsing only one character role! By six we are already each one
of us a travelling road show, a troupe of characters: some self-cast,
some set-cast by others molding and sculpting us as they see fit in
scenes they are attempting to control.

By the age of six, my client Liz was already into a long
run experiencing herself as playing pretty Barbie to her
sugar-daddy father, helpful Eve to her mother, scratchy
Cathy to her sisters, smart Jane to her teacher, with walk-
on performances in all scenes from time to time by withdrawn

and unaccommodating Denise, absent-minded Abby, pure-in-heart Katie, forlorn-and-tearful Julie, and-free-spirit Lilith. Each of these characters personified the mood changes and varying frames of mind by which she experienced herself and was experienced by others. The control that others introduced by way of various forms of positive and negative attention greatly affected the spirit of her performances. As others employed manipulative strategies, Liz incorporated these manipulative skills, coping as best she could in avoiding stress and securing pleasures through her character performances. When a given character performance displeased any of the major figures in her life, their common complaint to her was: "Snap out of it; you are not being the Liz I know (and want to meet). Go out, and come in again (as the Liz who pleases me)."

Liz illustrates the observation that each of us is more than meets the eye. There is a strong element of paradox to this! Liz's many-faceted selves are available to the discerning eye, the eye free from selective attention and inattention. It is the conventionally conditioned, the normalized eye, which fails to make these distinctions.

In presenting Liz's personas I have touched upon developmental issues deserving comment. Each of her personas has emerged in play and/or work within the context of critical periods in her developmental journey. Each feels and has the feel of being older or younger than the others. Each sees the world and life through different eyes. Their way of thinking about good and bad, of making ethical decisions, the pleasure they seek and the pain they strive to avoid in the moment all varies. And while some personas have emerged as natural appearances of her natural self at play in the world, others have assumed characterological forms tailored to meet the terms of others she has learned she must please or tame in order to survive, to get along in life well enough.

Personae as Natural to Personality

I recognize the validity of diagnoses of multiple personality as a disorder, explaining multiple selves through dissociation. And I recognize the validity of diagnosing multiple personality as a feature of borderline personality, explaining this development as the splitting of ego states, each personality vying for and seizing hold of conscious attention and coping activity. And yet I find that the attention given to multiple personality in current clinical literature has about it a catastrophic mentality, and tends to neglect reference to "natural" play and healthy creativity in the human psyche in favor of "normality". This attention to dissociation and defensive splitting as causes for multiple selves is valid but insufficient. It offers only a part of a fuller explanation. Personae Theory, as an expression of humanistic psychology, offers a fuller explanation as it reflects upon human behavior from "natural" as well as "normal" conceptual images of what it is to be human, and thus includes play as well as pathology in discussing the origin of multiple selves.

On Natural and Normal Play

A distinction between the "natural" and the "normal" is central to the meaning of "play". Here are some anecdotes that capture the essence of the playful frame of mind:

During the summer following his first year of graduate studies in Theology, Robert's parents drove to Brewster on Cape Cod to attend the opening performance of Ruth Gordon's autobiographical play *Years Ago* in which Robert was playing Ruth's father. At the reception following the performance, the Consulting Director, Mr. Latham asked Robert Edgerton's father what he thought of the production. "Why, I think it was great, and I found my son Bob big as day all the way through his performance." Mr. Latham responded: "Mr. Edgerton, I do the same when I'm visiting my grown up children where they are living now. I look for what I can recognize as familiar about them in order to reassure myself that I still know them. You came looking for Bob, and you found him. Please don't be offended. As I haven't been looking for anything in particular about Bob, I probably see far more in him than you do. There's far more about him than probably meets your eye."

Liz's many faceted selves and the far-more-about Bob than his father recognized in his son's performance are available to the discerning eye, the eye free from conventional, normal selective attention and selective inattention, the eye open for adventure in the as yet uncharted strange wilderness extending beyond what each of us already knows in one another.

> I used to bar visitors from my small, experientially engaged graduate class sessions in order to protect the small group sharing from the inhibition that typically occurs in the presence of a stranger. Now I welcome the presence of visitors *for their strangeness.* Strangeness is in the eye of the beholder. The strangeness with which unknown visitors are beheld brings to the attention of class members the strangeness, this is to say the vast uncharted wilderness that each of us tends to ignore in one another while we concentrate on the familiar we have come to trust and to which we have come to play.

When questioned as to what they have been doing with the other kids all Saturday morning, little children tend to say: "Nothing! Just fooling around." Explaining would be talking about, and talking about is not the same at all as what they were doing. That is, unless the talking about becomes play in and of itself. Asking strangers what they like doing rather than asking them what they do produces interesting results. If the strangers do like to fool around they will hear you asking how they like to play. If they have really heard the question as you have asked it and don't feel comfortable fooling around, if they can't find an escape hatch, they may translate your question into the question they are more comfortable with, "What do you do?" and respond to you by identifying themselves in terms of what they do in life.

> Fathers' Day was scheduled in the third week of kindergarten. Playground time had begun as fathers arrived. The children were at play; fathers gravitated toward one another, formed a circle, and proceeded to introduce themselves to one another. Each detailed who they were and what they did. The children played around us. One father after another

was teased away from the circle into play with his child. Even so, fathers asked their children to name those with whom they interacted. The children didn't know names very well yet. And it didn't matter. They were just fooling around!

Children enjoy fooling around, and in fooling around with one another they create their own experience. In their play they use what is available: palpable materials and interesting ideas. Culture is commonly shared significant information. Play is conversation; conversation is playing with information available at the time, information mutually meaningful among the players. In their play they make information available to one another meaningfully. They take the culture apart and play with it together. Playing becomes one play after another, sometimes one play within another play. Participants take turns playing different parts. Figuring themselves out from all the modeling and all the cueing to which they are exposed, first mimicking and then internalizing, they explore optional leads as to what/who/how they can be, what/who/how others they can be, and what/who/how they want to be. Children tend to be freer than supervising adults from needing to know clear outcomes. Surprise is delightful. They like to play new parts in novel ways. Why settle for knowing one game? Why stop after learning one song? What's the point of playing the same part every time?

Normal behavior is behaving consistently and predictably. Natural behavior is playing with all the possibilities in all possible ways. The best thing is to be able to live naturally, knowing how to perform normally from time to time when behaving normally proves interesting for the time being and situationally useful. Representational theater involves playing in character as cast and keeping to the assigned script. Improvisational theater allows actors to shift character parts and to adlib. Say that the cat is the controlling presence of a supervising agent or agency; when the cat's away, the mice come out to play.

Human beings seem inherently and paradoxically inclined to safety and adventure. We want to be safe enough as we pursue adventure. Rock climbers playing together want to know that everyone is afraid enough of what they are doing to act prudently, not so afraid that they will freeze, just afraid enough to enjoy the exhilaration of the adventure. And fear of this kind is a delicious excitement.

We engage in a whimsical game; we tend in our culture to prescribe when and how adventure is to occur, and, curiously, we play behind our own backs. We place limits on adventuresome behavior by organizing the forms we allow it to assume. We have established conventions by which adventure is to occur. We want adventure to be ruled by authorized codes of conduct and scheduled as organized outings and sporting events, seemly courting, socially acceptable enterprise, entertaining theater sponsored under appropriate auspices. And all forms of adventure must work well without evoking disturbing surprise. Strangeness and the weird are normally looked upon askance. Nonetheless, human playfulness, however subject to even well-intended restriction, inclines to expression, oftentimes masked by gestures in conformity and compliance.

In a culture that prescribes centralization and unification of personhood, we engage together in a marvelous prank. We are each one of us many in one body, and yet play at being one-in-one. we wink at each other in our pretending to be one-in-one even as we come at one another from the side and from all directions in brief asides and many voices. We agree to a rule that we are each one of us one. And we consent to the additional rule of being unaware of the rules by which we play! We are comfortable, or at least feign comfort, in our unattending, in our illusion of unawareness.

The Emergence of Personae
Out of Play and Out of Struggle

Personae figure in and come from different scenes in a person's odyssey; some are happier than others. When people are asked to share memories from the great variety of scenes in and out of their homes, in and out of school or work, across the years of their lives, they typically locate happy and unhappy situations, safe and unsafe scenes, circumstances in which they feel they have been at play and others in which they have suffered and labored to survive. And they are able to see quite clearly with which scenes each persona is predominantly associated. They see more clearly now how some personas have emerged quite free to enjoy life and work playfully, while others have emerged with defensive coping as their characteristic attitude and manner, since for them questions of survival have overshadowed prospects of thriving.

Personae Theory, then, extends beyond classical views of multiple personality by recognizing personas as natural to personality. In a given person, therefore, one or more personas may be creatively playful and free from neurotic features; others may be neurotic, others character-disordered, still others profoundly disturbed.

Many character selves can emerge out of the process of playing with culturally available expressive motifs or they can be idiosyncratically invented out of one's own creativity. These personas that issue from healthy play are direct expressions of the true Self engaged in the world.

For example, my persona David was inspired by David Edmunds whose forest ranger lodge sat half a mile down trail from the Adirondack Mountain Club's Johns Brook Lodge, where I was Director when I was seventeen. Being in the mountains with David as mentor offered a natural, pleasant deepening and broadening of my joy at being in the mountains and forests. He was a kindly mentor and nourishing older friend; he opened my eyes and guided me in altogether welcome skills of forest and trail life. That my wife and I now own and manage a registered tree farm offers natural fulfillment in my persona David's life.

Other personas emerge out of anxious effort to fit and function in the scenes into which we are thrown, scenes in which we are stuck because that's how things are, like being born on a farm or the inner city or polite society. A personal case in point comes to mind.

However grateful I may feel in a number of ways for the advantages that have come with growing up a faculty brat at Phillips Andover Academy, the dyslexia that prompted my placement at Eaglebrook School for Boys for the eighth and ninth grades, and the subsequent four years at Andover produced my persona Alan. People speak of finishing schools for young women! Alan, a very decently finished character, is ever anxious over appearances, proper manners, being seen as well connected, noted as succeeding, and so forth. He does not play naturally. However well camouflaged his anxiety of the moment, anxiety fuels his efforts to accommodate and please gracefully so that he secures and preserves an attractive place in the picture.

Still other personas may develop out of a division or splitting of felt inclinations into characterological polarities. Erik Erikson observed that each human being's first and most important developmental task in life is to come to terms with their experiences of trusting and mistrusting life itself and the people with whom they share life, most importantly mother and father! The most desired developmental outcome of struggling with experiences of trusting and mistrusting, according to Erikson, is an attitude of fundamental trust tempered by a good nose for the untrustworthy. If a person's life experience has proven sufficiently disturbing, he or she may not be able to balance the trust and suspicion they experience in the scenes defining their life or the major figures in their life. Such a traumatized person may fail to develop tolerance for ambiguity, sufficient equanimity in the face of a scene or of a person being a mixture of trustworthiness and untrustworthiness. Their solution may be to split good and bad, trustworthy and untrustworthy, safe and unsafe into radically contrasting polarities, and to cultivate within themselves characters that reflect this splitting, this polarization. My client Kesstler, mentioned in the Introduction offers a clear example of this splitting.

Kesstler has identified eleven principal personas of which two, Shirley and Melvin, offer themselves as clear examples of polar splits. Shirley verges on being goody-goody, on being limitlessly solicitous and protecting toward those on the brink of calamity or who look as though they will severely harm themselves. Kesstler sees Shirley as having emerged as a response to presented fear and abject frailty. Melvin is a dark hedonist and recluse. He drinks alone. He resists compromise. Melvin can remain mute for long periods of time, and he indulges himself in resentments, including resentment when others don't approach him. Note that Shirley's and Melvin's attitudes toward the world and other people are laden with projection. In Shirley, Kesstler incorporates his deep seated desire to be rescued; in Melvin, he incorporates the fear that he is loathed by those from whom he has most needed nourishing attention.

In our work together, Kesstler and I were from time to time struck with the pathological appearance of one or another of his personas. We also found that within certain contexts, and when personas were balancing one another in productive interaction, every one of his personas evidenced features of human creativity and mental health. Likewise, in my work with Liz, while her nine principal personas were each capable of contributing to neurotic and character disordered problem solving modalities by which Liz as a person could be summarily characterized, each persona was also capable of personifying very positive and healthy attributes of full human creativity and wisdom. I conclude that personality organization needs to be considered in terms of the dynamics figuring among personas within context rather than apart from the existential situation.

On Story as Informing Performance

Story determines how we perform. Both Adolf Hitler and Martin Luther King were superb actors. Each commanded a charismatic hold on his audience. Hitler's and King's performances were prompted by Story: Hitler's by a vision of Aryan triumph, King's by a vision of beloved community binding of all peoples. We commonly ask one another: "What did you do that for? What's the story?" And the inflection with which we ask these two simple questions marks bitter anguish or wondrous appreciation. I am intending a clear difference between Odyssey and Story. The former amounts to the dramatic account of a person's life journey, however inspiring in its revelation of lessons well learned and quests fulfilled. The latter represents a paradigmatic tale that determines the fundamental attitude of a person, that provides the basis for collaboration or disarray among personas. One person's story may be a common story simply accepted by blind faith, another person's story may emerge idiosyncratically out of the stuff of her or his experience.

By way of an example, I share the Story of my mentor from earliest childhood, Howard Thurman. The dedication he wrote for his autobiography (Thurman, 1979) captures his Story:

> "To the stranger in the railroad station in Daytona Beach who revived my broken dream sixty-five years ago."

There was no eighth grade in public schools for blacks in Howard's Florida youth, hence no need for high schools in most communities. If you haven't graduated from eighth grade, how can you expect high school? Now the principal of Howard's grammar school recognized his brightness and tutored him in eighth-grade subjects. The principal of the white grammar school to which Howard's principal took him for examination confirmed that he had earned matriculation into high school. I quote now from his autobiography:

> There were only three public high schools for black children in the entire state of Florida, but there were several private church-supported schools, the nearest to Daytona Beach being Florida Baptist Academy in Jacksonville. A cousin who lived in Jacksonville told my mother that if I enrolled in the academy, I could live with him and his wife, doing chores around the house in exchange for a room and one meal a day.
>
> When the time came to leave for Jacksonville, I packed a borrowed old trunk with no lock and no handles, roped it securely, said my good-byes, and left for the railway station. When I bought my ticket, the agent refused to check my trunk on my ticket because the regulations stipulated that the check must be attached to the trunk handle, not to a rope. The trunk would have to be sent express but I had no money except for a dollar and a few cents left after I bought my ticket.
>
> I sat down on the steps of the railway station and cried my heart out. Presently I opened my eyes and saw before me a large pair of work shoes. My eyes crawled upward until I saw the man's face. He was a black man, dressed in

overalls and a denim cap. As he looked down at me he rolled a cigarette and lit it. Then he said, "Boy, what in hell are you crying about?"

I told him. (To which he resonded:)

"If you're trying to get out of this damn town to get an education, the least I can do is to help you. Come with me," he said.

He took me around to the agent and asked: "How much does it take to send this boy's trunk to Jacksonville?"

Then he took out his rawhide money bag and counted the money out. When the agent handed him the receipt, he handed it to me. Then, without a word, he turned and disappeared down the railroad track. I never saw him again.

I knew Howard Thurman well from my earliest childhood until his death. I see this story implicit throughout his odyssey; I see implicit the boy ever questing and I see in him the stranger lending to the mending of broken dreams. In his last letter to me in response to my letter telling him of my transition into the practice of professional psychology, he wrote: "You have my blessings, Peter, as you devote yourself to assisting persons as they break free from their inner incarcerations."

My personas do not perform willy-nilly, prompted by whatever play is in progress. While each persona is infected by her or his own deep story, however sacred or profane, and while my odyssey has certainly featured scenes, sometimes entire acts, when the one or the other persona has led the others in some merry chase, there is one deepest structure story that is more compelling than all the others, one most fundamental story that ultimately subsumes all the others. I call it the Fable of the Night Visitor.

When I was seventeen, I was physically ill in dismay over my mother's unrelenting emotional illness. Her illness could be defined as the fevering of her soul, wracking her mind and body. In a fit of utter frustration my father had, against doctors' objections, taken my mother out of hospital. Now she was home, and miserable. There appeared to be no end, no respite, no help, and no solution to her misery. A very old friend of my family — a most remarkable spirit

—arrived one night on short notice from San Francisco. He asked to use our home as a base camp while he talked before various gatherings in the Boston area. Seeing how my mother was, he cancelled or postponed two days of meetings, and he stayed with her undisturbed through the days and deep into the night for two days. When he left, she was different. There appeared a qualitative difference about her, a transformation of some kind. Psyche is a Greek word meaning soul, spirit, "the vital principle of corporeal matter..." My mother, had been deeply affected by a minister to the soul, the man I came to think of as The Night Visitor. Subsequently, she sought a doctor of the soul and found an excellent psychotherapist. She engaged fruitfully in psychotherapy for over six years. My mother's change upon the departure of our guest of two days was immediately apparent and heartening. We knew upon Howard Thurman's departure from our home that the mending of her soul's struggle had commenced. Six years later, when she terminated psychotherapy, she also completed graduate school, and began a rich career as a gifted psychiatric social worker.

This is the story that possesses me. And I am inspired by this story to be an apprentice night visitor and to lend to the mending of broken dreams.

Now, with an understanding of how Personae Theory has emerged and evolved, we may consider the implications these findings have for individual testing, for the study of social psychology, for matters of personal and community responsibility, and for the practice of psychotherapy.

Implications of Personae Theory in Individual Testing

Western culture places great emphasis on consistency, predictability, structure, and control. By the time a young person approaches twenty, she or he is expected to have realized what is called identity. However variously a young person may experience himself and be experienced by others from scene to scene, accommodating to cultural expectations that he prove recognizable as the same person by whatever account may prompt conscious and unconscious deception of self and others.

This has important implications for so-called individual testing, whatever the testing is intended to yield. There are disparities among personas relative to psychosexual, psychosocial, and cognitive and moral development. Examination of personas indicates that they differ from one another in right- and left-brain orientation. They do not share the same memories, and as they recall a given event, they report upon the event differently. Our findings indicate that personas bring differing characterological orientations to problem solving and vary in regard to extroversion and introversion. Their existential orientations in regard to natural, social, and inner worlds tend to vary. Who, then, is being tested?

It is commonplace to hear someone say, "I'm not going to mention any of this to George while he is in his present frame of mind! I'll wait until he is in a place where he can listen to what I have to say." This way of thinking so clearly implies the play of personas in everyday situations and also opens up questions as to people's performances when being examined. According to systems theory, family members are targeted on the unconscious level of family interactions to perform various errands and tasks, and to assume various roles within the family system. Similar activities and operations occur intrapersonally among personas. Thus, one persona may be assigned to serve as the examination victim or buff. The lecturer who calls for comment following a presentation does well to refrain from accepting the first comment as representing the position of everyone in the audience. Some people must say something, sometimes whatever enters their mind. Others who are used to speaking right up may overstate their case as much to twit others in the audience as to engage with the speaker. Still others are mullers, sometimes very thoughtful mullers, who may be shy as well, and who may decide not to say anything at all.

This perspective invites fresh ways of considering so-called anomalous data in a subject's test performance. Therefore, one possible diagnostic ramification might be that instead of allowing anomalies in a subject's testing performance to prompt a classification of characterological disturbance, the anomaly or anomalies may be regarded as indicating the existence of one or more than one camouflaged persona. Peg Boyles speaks clearly to this point:

> Among my many complex, quite individual selves, I have observed that some enjoy the limelight, clamor for recognition, love center stage. They talk a lot, make plenty of noise, and often embarrass themselves attempting to speak for the rest of us. Others work their way subversively, preferring the cover of darkness. (Boyles)

This invites investigation as to the basis for the camouflaging; does it occur as a feature of the dynamics among personas, or does it occur because one or more are *personas non grata* in the family or subculture?

Resolving questions as to whether a testing anomaly indicates characterological disturbance or camouflaged personas may well require attention to the participants' performance in everyday life scenes. Not all personas are present and accounted for in every scene. (1) Not all personas are available for testing. (2) Also, the thinking process of some personas is not revealed by conventional testing protocols. Here follow examples of each of these observations.

> (1) A client, thirteen years old, Alvin, received dismal marks in school. Testing data reflected a greatly disturbed person of uncertain ability, certainly scant achievement in normal terms of achievement. I proposed to Alvin that he was emulating Thomas Alva Edison. I had learned first from his mother, then in extensive conversation with Alvin, that he had read everything he could find on the life of Thomas Alva Edison. Alvin protested that he did not emulate Edison, that he was inspired by Edison. I insisted. Alvin matched my proposal with the null hypothesis that he was not emulating the life and accomplishments of Thomas Edison. In due course he conceded. He had to his own satisfaction and mine failed to prove that he was not in remarkable detail following Edison's life, step by step. Reading and absorbing issue after issue of *Scientific American*, with three patents pending, absorbed in scholarly

reading, he was, after the example of Edison, the bane of teacher after teacher. Now he was expelled from school altogether. Like Edison, he had no close friend. He acted out, beat on his little brother, loathed wasting time on sleep, was enthralled with intellectual puzzles, did not communicate well on paper. I liked him. Having failed to prove he was not emulating Edison, he resolved he would follow Edison step by step, and had to believe he was going to succeed ultimately. Alvin's persona, Alva, did not announce his presence in school. Although Alvin's testing results may very well indeed suggest characterological disturbance, they also failed to identify the Alva I knew well outside of the school setting. No doubt Alva kibitzed as he slipped into the testing process here and there, thereby providing what appeared anomalous scat which the testing psychologist was apparently loath to identify as significant.

(2) Psychologist Jean Houston has written (Houston, Dromenon) about Billy, an elementary school boy whose problem solving outside of school failed to reflect in either classroom performance or in school sponsored psychometrics. In school he tested about 85, which is below normal intelligence. While visiting in Billy's home, Dr. Houston observed Billy's attempts to measure the area of the basement family room, a room defined by several corners. Following his mother's instructions to figure the area by following the instructions his teachers insisted upon, Billy's solution made the room out to be the size of a football field. Then, when his mother invited Billy to solve the puzzle his own way, he "shut his eyes, and made little rhythmic movements with his head as if he were listening to an inner song. After which he jotted down something on the pad, closed his eyes for some more internal business, opened them, jotted something else down, and gave (his mother and Dr. Houston) the correct answer." Dr. Houston asked Billy whether he was thinking in pictures when his eyes were shut. "'Yes,' he nodded, 'but it's other stuff too …When I close my eyes to figure something out it's like a cross between music and architecture.'" Dr. Houston took

him to a nearby university and administered a standard I.Q. test. His score was 85. Dr. Houston reports:

> I then told him that we would take another test but this time he was to use his imagery and musical thinking to answer the test questions. "It's not allowed," he complained. "I'm the one who is giving the tests, Billy, and I say that it is!" "O.K., but you've got to change the way that the test is given," he said. "You will have to ask those questions so I can answer them by doing the special kind of stuff I do in my head." "Then you will have to help me, Billy," I responded. "We'll have to redesign the test together." And that is just what we did. Together we took each question and wherever possible translated it into a visual form and even sometimes into a cross between music and architecture.

Dr. Houston reports that even where his answers proved incorrect, the process of Billy's thinking evidenced remarkable creativity, brilliance, and originality. And he tested, following this method, at an intelligence quotient of 135. Dr. Houston adds that "The baffled (university) psychologist who scored both tests said it was unique in his experience." I read Jean Houston's account as raising the possibility that Billy passed the problem solving activity from one persona to another, from a persona identified by others and himself as learning-impaired to a persona who dropped out of school when no seat was included for him in the classroom. I am aware that this is pure speculation, though sufficiently plausible. I am also aware of how Billy's story parallels one of my own personal stories.

> My right-brain oriented persona, George, who was clearly if only fleetingly recognized by one of my high school instructors, came into his element in two courses in college, then prominently in graduate studies where creative thinking was featured. My dyslexic persona, Bagweed, corresponds with Billy's learning-impaired persona. Would

that a Dr. Houston had come into my life when I was in elementary school! As it turned out, I did enjoy the happy experience of having geometry teacher, George Sandborn, effect essentially the same results. He commented after closely observing my performance in solving abstract geometrical problems, problem solving I could not consciously account for in a step by step manner, "Peter, you think differently from most of the other students. I don't understand how you think. Believe me, you have an interesting mind. My bet is that some day you will like your mind, and that the way you think will serve you very well in some career!" Apparently the day dreaming in which I was engrossed through grammer school and into high school, that prompted my teachers to observe that I had a problem keeping my mind on classroom instruction, that raised serious questions as to whether I would be able to complete high school, amounted to absorbtion in untutored, right-brain skills building. I infer that this mental activity was the business and play of a persona who chose to be named George, in honor of the math teacher who found him out!

A few years ago, one of my graduate students, whose dyslexia interferred with her capacity to write acceptably, reported to me, after handing in a very well written course paper, that she had heard me mumble to myself, "For all I know, she may have a persona who is not dyslexic," and that she experienced a strange mental shift while typing at her word processor two weeks later. When she read the print-out of her paper, she did not recognize the writing style!

I find that personas do not engage in every scene. Further, I have learned from clients that even in scenes in which the same personas appear, the constellation among them—the influence and interdynamics among them—shifts categorically and noetically. Even when the same personas are present and accounted for across scenes, the performance varies in ethic, form of thought, motivational objective, and story line. Therefore, replication of testing a person over time, by the same tester or by different testers in essentially the same setting, may establish reliability, of that testing in that setting! But the validity of the testing results may not extend to other settings in which other personas may be available, and in which the dynamic among personas and the significance of the situation for the person may prompt very different performance.

Identifying the person as a group of personas opens up very interesting questions in regard to testing of all kinds.

Implications for Social Psychology

The personas perspective also opens up questions regarding social psychology. Social psychologists examine both how an individual may be attitudinally disposed to behaving in particular ways socially, and how social situations prompt individual social behavior. Both frameworks deserve attention. Examination of social behavior from each of these perspectives becomes all the more intriguing and rich in material as we allow for the play of personas under examination.

I recall a lively exchange with my father during Chicago's Mayor Richard Daley's administration. I complained that Daley wasn't concerned with environmental matters. My father scolded me for my sweeping judgment: "Peter, you have no idea what is in Daley's thinking." I responded: "It is by a person's behavior that we know him. By his record in office I judge him as lacking in commitment to environmental concerns." I am the wiser today. My indictment of Daley was valid *and* insufficient. A person's observable action initiated by one persona or by a coalition of personas may not represent the position and wishes of several other personas. Onlookers present while Kitty Genovese was stabbed to death reported afterwards that their inaction did not reflect their "true" colors. When this perspective is applied to the study of the interaction among family members, it corrects for overly simplistic assessments of the role or roles each family member plays in the system. Personae Theory prompts reconsideration of time-honored and time-worn assumptions in the study and treatment of social behavior.

Implications for Social Responsibility

What of law and order? Doesn't this way of thinking offer people license to say: "I can't be held responsible for what one of my own personas did!" If we permit ourselves to suppose that not every persona showed up at the wedding and walked up the church aisle, doesn't this perspective offer license to act out, to excuse ourselves at every turn? I infer that this concern derives from the value our culture sets on unification and mastery, a corollary of this principle being that it is good to be able to "nail down" problems. However laudable owning that "the buck stops with me," this claim figures as but one facet of a larger picture in which all personas share responsibility for means and ends.

Presuming personality to be unified offers comfort to the simplistic notion that accountability can and should confirm mastery over self and situation. The Quaker practice of proactively "awaiting" the "sense of the meeting" offers a superb illustration of an alternative model: the decentralized, nonequilibrious conception of process featuring continuous becoming. When a Meeting of Friends is functioning at its reasonable optimum, it fosters common respect for every member's point of view rather than actively striving for resolution through the controlling interest of a majority. Ghandi committed himself to practicing law in such a manner that adversaries could emerge from struggling with each other in dignity.

Similarly, Erik Erikson (Erikson, 1964) differentiates between morality and ethics, the former amounting to conformity to the strictures of inherited mores, the latter reflected in thoughtful responsiveness to creative problem solving in each novel situation, with cultural mores considered but not mindlessly heeded. Recognizing one's Self as several by no means legitimates license and the careless blaming of an "out of control" persona for actions dismaying others. It must also be recognized that one persona holding out against all the others may prove to be the one voice crying in the wilderness on behalf of reason and responsibility, a dissident relegated by the others to solitary confinement, a prisoner of conscience, perhaps even a victim of physical and psychological torture. I underscore how each person as a community within one body must be held responsible for action and inaction. However illuminating the insights provided in studying the Kitty Genovese incident, each non-acting witness to her murder was morally and ethically disgraced.

Engaging in Self responsibility thus calls for community action. And the "town meeting of the mind" may be conducted according to Parliamentary Procedure, the dictates of the mightiest, or the way practiced by Friends. I endorse the Friends' way as it integrates most creatively with forms of group work that have been developed over recent decades by social and behavioral scientists. As personas vary in regard to moral development and values perspectives, attention to and effective work within the community of the mind invites patient and careful process, process rarely implemented effectively by the might of the one or the might of the majority.

I offer these preliminary thoughts by way of opening up discussion concerning the ethical ramifications of recognizing personality as comprising personas interacting with one another in encountering life and solving problems.

Personae Theory and Psychotherapy

I conclude with the matter of psychotherapy, and with what Personae Theory opens up in the therapeutic process. Psychotherapy informed by Personae Theory can sometimes assume elements of surrealism. The familiar becomes *strangely* familiar. Stretching the point occurs to make the point. Reality is treated in caricature. Attending to the surreal involves paying attention to what underlies "real" appearances as in the presentation of what is real through fantastic imagery, through "mental free association." A realistic portrait represents an appearance *qua* the appearance, the appearance as a photograph would offer. A surreal portrait on canvass, clay or in bronze would include the artist's impressions of the subject's personality features underlying surface appearance. In attempting to convey what is on my mind in this regard, and as I come to the end of this chapter, I will engage now in the surrealistic.

Attending "realistically" to what my client offers is a leftbrained process in which I either reduce client statements to a simplistic account of troubling issues, or I define the significance of what is presented by casting the client's statements in broad clinical generalities. This way of thinking is linear and prompted by clinical conventions. I am thus searching for clues in the client's presentation that offer me information as to where the client is on the map within territory familiar to me. Once I have located these clues, I can assist the client, so I must believe, out of trouble.

Attending "surrealistically" to my client and what my client offers amounts primarily to a right-brained process in which I permit myself to be moved over and away from myself, drawn out, entranced by the other and what the other is doing, and engaged in the client's manner of thinking. Psychologists talk of the creative process involving at least in part the productive regression of ego functioning in the service of the unconscious.

Let this concept serve as a metaphor for the therapist joining with the client. A daydream from a therapy session comes to mind: I "awaken" to the realization that I am in a room with people I do not know. I am wondering what they are doing together. I sense that what they are doing and what they are talking about, while deliberate and conscientious in spirit, is camouflaging a deeper unconscious intentionality. I am mindful of Dr. James Mann's working assumption that the client's presented focus, however sincere, is never the troublesome central issue. I suspend judgment, distract myself from working too hard on recognizing what is going on in terms of my own mental frames of reference; I surrender the nerve center of consent to letting what is going on "get to me;" I deliver myself into what is happening; I "get into the spirit of the party," and let what is happening employ, work with, the mental images available within my right brain bank. The enlightenment that occurs "comes to me" the way a verse occurs to me spontaneously in my automatic writing.

Now I can apply left-brain thinking to what I have been experiencing to identify affinities between the story that has emerged out of my engagement with this other person and the stories that person shares about others.

The surrealistic feature of this process occurs both in the mental activity involved while joined with the client in predominantly unconscious play, and in the mixture of left- and right-brain interaction. How can I convey this experience?

I share with my client from the outset of our work together the dramaturgical notion that all the world is a stage, that human encounter in its many forms amounts to "living theater," that my role is as fellow actor and consulting director. I make as clear as I can that by director I mean facilitator rather than manager. As director I am the active, enquiring audience who moves back and forth from off to on stage, attending, engaging, attending again. As audience I ponder upon what I see and hear, I join the actors in their composite and personas forms in the midst of the action, at times impersonating one or another of their personas. I engage in asides to phantom fellow audience, speaking from audience to the actor or actors on stage, request re-plays, prompt re-framings of story options explicitly or implicitly apparent in the action.

I begin as audience listening to the client "on stage" briefing me on problems, or more actively, as the first appearing persona anguished over problems. There's a twenty-question sense to how I inquire non verbally and verbally to what is presented before me, not twenty questions in its most stylized form: I am not limited to questions, and more times than not my gestures are in the form of inquiring statements rather than as questions.

Engagement with my client is similar in some respects to the exercise of writing. Right now, as I am writing, I am searching in my writing for what it is I am wanting to convey. I know the message is within me to share. I could simply sit quietly and await an emergence into consciousness of the statement fully formed in final draft. Better that I engage actively in a stream of minding relative to the intended focus: What Personae Theory opens to the nature and process of facilitating psychotherapy.

What of my own personas in this process? I am conscious of my writing activity. What flows onto paper comes from unconscious activity. My personas are attending to me-the-writer/recorder from behind one-way glass. They see me. I do not see or hear them save when one or another comes through into consciousness with an image or idea. They are kibitzing in the writing activity.

Marcel Marceau is looking down at me through his picture on the pitched roof wall in my A-frame loft study. And from beside him a woman from whose head are springing pictorial images of her twelve discernable personas. I project onto Marceau; I gather from the woman. There we have it! The psychodramatic encounter that occurs in the psychotherapeutic encounter invariably involves projection and gathering on the part of therapist and subject.

In some presentational improvisational theater situations, actors invite audience to engage with them. Don't you have to loosen up, be a little giddy, relax caution to do that? Yes! You do! You have to be a little crazy, you have to drop being earnest, you have to be playful, to do personas work. It requires fooling around, the way children often characterize simply playing, very often in relation to dreadful issues.

Personae Theory opens further ways for therapist and subject to meet in dramatic encounter for the sake of enhancing the act of being in the world.

References

Boyles, Peg, *New Hampshire Times*, June 9, 1984, p. 24

Erikson, Erik, *Insight and Responsibility*, W.W. Norton, NY, 1964

Houston, Jean, "The World of Imagery," Dromenon, Vol II, No. 3-4, pp. 17-23

Thurman, Howard, *With Head and Heart*,Harcourtg Brace Javanovich, NY, 1979, pp. 24-25.

2

Behavior as Performance, By a Cast of Many

- All human behavior is performance, and all the world is a stage.

- There evolves in every one of us over the years a number of selves, distinct ego-states, psychodramatic characters composing each of our personalities.

- "I" *as form* identifies my entity as the one-who-I-am. "I" in this sense of the word is composed of a number-of-me, evidenced in my speaking on the one hand and on the other in response to something that is happening at the moment. And then, given what is happening in the moment, having given voice on the one hand and on the other, "I" speak in one voice. "I" speak in one voice variously textured and seasoned by the play in varying measure of each persona.

- "I" *as process* indicates my keeping in touch with, and my capacity to integrate and mobilize my various voices. This process was evident in the play of the various forms "I" assumed as I wrote of "I" as form.

- The word "I" carries a double significance: "I" is who I am, and "I" is how I am doing with myselves. As to "I" as who I am, "I" is my analogue Self—the "that but not that" Who-I-Am. Understand this statement in light of a Hindu assertion that there are nine hundred and ninety names for God, and that every name of God is "that but not that," that God can be described only by analogy. Now, as to "I" as how I am doing with my-selves, "I" is my Vincular Self in process, pathfinding, self integrating, self managing. My vincular activity consists of my working with the ambiguities and mixed feelings I experience within myself in such a manner that I am respecting everything that is happening within, striking bargains within, orchestrating and managing outward performance that has meaning for myself and for others.

- Persons evidencing extreme single-mindedness on the one hand, and on the other floridly chaotic splitting among a number of personas manifest mental illness at the two poles of a mental health continuum. Optimal mental health figures around the center of the continuum.

Everyday Life as the Performance of Living Theater:

We may be born Homo *sapiens*. We are not born human. Being human is behaving in human fashion, performing well or badly in a manner and according to manners distinguishing one as human rather than like "the lower animals."

While human and simpler animals interact through significant signing as they engage in cooperative, adaptive activity, humans have invented and share in mutually significant symbol systems that inform their performance in encounter with one another. Humans do not even have to be in one another's physical presence in order to be performing before one another. We are able to *imagine* being with one another. Even the human recluse's activities constitute human behavior to the extent that their patterns of activity prove meaningfully recognizable to another who happens by unnoticed. Human behavior is featured by operational, semantic, and narrative significance. And all human behavior either implicitly or explicitly involves encounter with other humans. All human behavior involves performance in reference to other performers, whether the other performers are on stage or in the audience, and whether the other performers are literally or figuratively present.

"All the world is a stage."
"The play's the thing."

The theater of everyday life engages each one of us in character parts, in unfolding re-presentational or presentational, improvisational story. Pure re-presentational theater is characterized by rote delivery of a set script painstakingly rehearsed such that every move on stage is repeated, performance after performance. our lives follow fairly regular routines. We know there are patterns to our lives. However much we may suppose each day is a new day, task follows task in a more or less predictable fashion, and in performing these tasks, we fall back on familiar ways of talking.

Presentational, improvisational story involves spontaneity, ad-libbing. Performing comics talk of routines they have memorized which they bring with them onto stage. Playing the audience, their ad-libbing embellishes upon and livens up lines they would otherwise have to slog through before a "dead" audience. The ad-libbing, the improvisation, breathes life into the play, brings life into the story line. Improvisation invites surprise. Our friends and family know and anticipate what we are likely to say in almost any familiar scene. When we change our line, improvise, they don't know whether to be delighted or dismayed. Sometimes we lose track of the issue we are agonizing over when our antagonist refuses to say the lines we are wanting to hear.

Imagine yourself on stage. What have you done in imagining this? Have you fancied yourself in a particular kind of building, one with rank upon rank of seats leading down to the base of a stage, which in turn is framed—by a great arch? Did you go to one side of the stage and walk up the steps onto the stage? Or did you imagine yourself in the kind of theater in which rows of seats form a sickle-like semicircle two thirds of the way around a raised platform in the middle of the room? It does not matter which way you have imagined this setting. The important points are the spaces. Most people have seen street theater, where a band of players have, by suggestion or with the simplest physical devices, marked off an area within which its performance will take place. The two spaces are the stage and the audience areas. And within the stage space there are indicated, once again by suggestion or device, a stage front, back-stage, stage right, and stage left. Players use these spaces within the stage area as statements. For instance, you have heard the expression "up-staging" someone. This means that someone has thrown another player into his shadow. This can mean a stepping in front of the other, drawing audience attention away from the other player.

Upstaging uses stage "space" to make a statement. Plays are always performed before an audience, whether the audience is really there or imagined as present. I remember venturing as a teenager into a hot, city night spot. And, when I saw what was going on-stage, I may even have been overheard by someone near me muttering to myself; "If my mother could see me now!" Well, I was clearly imagining her there observing my performance in walking into such a place! Even imagining someone seeing and hearing us makes what we are engaged in theater. Erving Goffman has written about all of this in great detail, and makes very interesting reading in his book, *The Presentation of Self in Everyday Life.* Being selfconscious means being audience-conscious. Being self-conscious amounts to what we are thinking and how we are feeling about the audience reaction. One of the basic disciplines of the able actor is reading, sensing, audience reaction.

All behavior is performance. Essential to being socialized is the necessity to become adept actors and an adept audience. Theater

School for everyone begins at home in the first year of our lives. People bending over us in our cradles and playpens, holding us on their laps, playing with us on the floor, are urging us to join with them in conversation. They listen to the sounds we make, smiling every time we make a sound that comes close to a word they recognize. They make the sound we have just made, bringing the shape of the sound closer to how the word is supposed to sound. They do the same in response to our random facial expressions, the gestures we make with our hands, the attitudes we strike with our bodies.

In saying that all behavior is performance, I am defining "behavior" as mutually significant social interaction. Idiosyncratic verbal and non verbal gestures, however meaningful to the subject producing them, do not constitute behavior unless these gestures carry at least minimally corresponding significance for some member of the audience before whom the subject is appearing.

The big people in our lives engage us in drama class most of the time they are with us. They want us to learn how to interact with them in forms appropriate to the scene they fancy we are in from moment to moment. They make soft, applauding sounds if we lie still and let them change our diapers. They cheer when we open our mouths to the "airplane" full of strained peaches! As toddlers we are placed on stage with other toddlers and instructed in how to observe the space assigned to us. Through this training we learn how to recognize stage right, stage left, up and down stage. We learn to wait in line and to wait until it is time for us to say our lines. Then, when we know how to say lines that relate meaningfully, to the assigned action, we are placed with another young child, and we are coached in playing together with the same play materials. we learn to move from parallel play to playing together. These times of permitting ourselves "to be done to" without struggle are the first theater lessons that lead to later engagement in the performances called "the attentive student" and "the good patient."

By the time we are five we are engaged in advanced theater games in which we interact in roles like playing school, performing character parts in simple stories. At this time, children will complain about having to play with a child who doesn't know how to play. More times than not, what they are complaining about is that the child doesn't know how to play parts. To play one part, a person has to know at least the rudiments of playing every part. This is a cardinal feature in theater; characters have to understand other character parts in order to perform the one in which they have been cast. This understanding evolves through and is the result of the process of socialization. The ultimate end of all socialization, which includes all forms of instructive interaction as well as preschool, elementary, high school, vocational training, post-secondary, as well as graduate and post-graduate education, is the establishment of *homo sapien* persons as human beings engaged in at least civil, hopefully distinguished, performance in the process of society.

From the time we are very young we learn to perform before the physically present audience including sub-audiences within the total audience, and we eventually begin to perform before imagined audiences. Imagined audiences include our own persona selves, our peers, our personal friends, family figures, figures in civil and moral authority, and groups to which we aspire. We attend to the actual or imagined responses of audiences for prompting and approval. As audience we attend to how we are being identified and perceived by actors about us. And as we respond to their performance we become audience-actors to the players-audience.

From very early on we alert to how, in this Punch and Judy world, there are many *dramatis personae*, characters we can imitate to start with and then incorporate within our personal repertoire of acts. The character parts that work well for us become part of our personal story. The study of families and the generational and trans-generational stories that come to light from this study makes clear how children are systematically, whether wittingly or unwittingly, prompted to develop competence as specific kinds of dramatic characters. We see how they are also prompted as well to enact portions of the ongoing family story. An example of this comes to mind.

> I was engaged at the request of a high school adminis-
> tration, with the consent of the parents, to work with a
> family in regard to the outrageous behavior of the middle
> child, Shelly, the only daughter. The rest of the family
> "behaved well" and were, along with the school personnel,
> at their wits end to make heads or tails of the girl's conduct.

Early in our consultations, it became apparent to me that the girl herself was unable to account for her antics. There was nothing she did that was illegal or grossly offensive. She simply shocked everyone and kept everyone's attention on her to the neglect of others. During one of our sessions, I very nearly missed attending to one family member's reference to Aunt Libby. This was the first reference to an Aunt Libby. I knew nothing about her. I sensed a hint of outrageousness in the tone of voice of the family member mentioning her. Without repeating the content of the aside, I asked each family member to take a minute or two to put together their individual version of the story of Aunt Libby. Before asking each in turn to share their story, I urged everyone to preserve their own version, to disregard disparities, and to repeat in their own fashion what others might have covered before their turn. I began with the daughter. She had very little to say and she did not appear to be withholding. Even when others urged her to say more, supposing she knew much more, she claimed she had said all she knew. The composite made Aunt Libby out to be the black sheep of the family in her generation and captured to a "t" the character this young woman had been enacting. No one had considered the connection between her and Aunt Libby until this moment. The girl was stunned by the connection. The moral of the story, as family members put it together was that it was convenient to have one person act the fool and black sheep. It helped others know how not to behave and it served to provide each with a sense of their own propriety and social acceptability. As a result, this young woman confirmed how she was at one and the same time bored with convention and disinclined to play stand-in for someone else for the convenience of the family. She served notice that while she was now intent upon keeping track of her own life, she intended to make her mischief character work in her interest. This insight offered a useful basis for therapeutic work in which the family now engaged.

This account also indicates how an individual's incorporation of a dramatic persona involves existential story.

While we develop common social roles in the service of gaining command of complex skills, dramatic personas emerge out of story-oriented dramatic interactions. And, although many of us share dramatic personas akin to one another, (i.e. I may have a mischievous self akin to the young woman's Aunt Libby), our counterpart personas are at most only akin. There is only affinity between them as their stories inevitably differ in some ways.

Attention to story will be offered in Chapter III. For now, we turn to the nature of personas as selves within the multiple Self.

Each Person is Multiple, Male and Female

As I reported in Chapter One, people with whom I have worked tell me that they experience themselves and are experienced by others differently from scene to scene, in different locations, within the different contexts and situations that make up their lives. Each of us is a cast of characters. However well we conspire with one another to cover up this fact, the contrasting ways in which we conduct ourselves demonstrate that each of us is a collective of emergent personas.

It is helpful to envision, within the skin-envelope of every person, many voices, a society of the mind, multiple selves. We are every one of us a multiple personality. In our thinking we are a town meeting of the mind, a community of male and female denizens, dwelling more or less in harmony. Frightening, celebrated cases of Eve, Veronica, Sybil, and many other flamboyant examples of "split" personalities are caricatures of how we all are. These cases parallel communities plagued by deeply split, neighborhood enclaves that act independently and oftentimes at cross purposes with one another. Healthier, more smoothly operating communities featuring informal and formal cooperativeness among subgroups correspond to healthier minds.

I am now going to introduce the issue of gender and personas, followed by an account of how personas emerge from the cultural setting.

Gender and Personae

I have come to recognize that each one of us has male and female personas composing the company that is represented by the name by which we are identified. Biological differences between males and females, while predisposing males and females in various ways, do not even begin to figure as significantly in determining characterological differences between males and females as does socialization, the systematic molding of the minds and conduct of persons by a society to share common norms. The separation of the sexes characterologically is not biologically inherent to the species homo sapiens. It has emerged as a cultural invention.

Actor James Stewart and actress Linda Hunt are role models who shatter characterological stereotypes. In a television documentary on Stewart, his contemporaries characterize him as a feminine hero, a person who allowed qualities in others to come out, who conveyed the sense that he was capable of decisiveness without need of displaying brutal forms of decisiveness, who while distinguished for his leadership in armed combat never proved combative, who cherished and cared for all persons in soft and nourishing ways; Jimmy Stewart has proven a person integrating features traditionally associated with maleness and femaleness without the machismo associated with the John Wayne image. Linda Hunt's portrayal of a male figure in the movie, "The Year of Living Dangerously" demonstrated, and her National Public Radio comments upon her performance in that role made clear, that maleness and femaleness, characterologically speaking, are available to every person, that femaleness and maleness are distinctive to personality rather than to the body in and of itself.

Great playwrights give strength to Personae Theory, which accounts for how they could achieve their literary efforts. American dramatist Eugene O'Neill's portrayals of men and women have been recognized as brilliant psychological studies. Audiences and readers have found themselves stunned by the way in which O'Neill has found them out and presented them and their experience of themselves on paper and in theatrical performance. Actresses today claim that they are compelled by the figures he has sketched and the lines he has offered them for performance. O'Neill's plays are timeless. There is an amazing and remarkably powerful force informing O'Neill's renditions. Eugene O'Neill exudes a personal and psychological "knowing" enabling him to project onto paper, and to project through actors and actresses in the performance of his works, how it is to be a human male and how it is to be a human female. In other words, Eugene O'Neill introduces himself to us through his drama. Eugene O'Neill introduces himself in and through the characters he portrayed. Speaking of O'Neill, Linda Hunt made clear that there was far more to his introduction of female characters than good lines produced by a man with a good ear for dialogue, by a man of empathic imagination. She indicated that in reading O'Neill she encountered female personalities coming out of O'Neill the person.

O'Neill's character portrayals harken back to the male and female voices within himself. That actors and actresses find themselves compelled by the male and female characters offered in script after script by gifted playwrights attests to the same truth inherent in all gifted playwrights. It follows that either playwrights are living entities different in kind from the rest of us, or that all of us share in the same truth. I presume the latter alternative. While males and females, physiologically speaking, may not be able to share literally and specifically in every kind of experience, they can indeed share empathically in the variety of human experience. To share empathically is to be available, to be responsive to, to share meaningfully and productively in relation to what is happening for a person of the other gender, granting that the differences in the "chromosome wash" peculiar to males and females precludes identical experience.

From Appropriated to Emergent Identification of Personae

It's not at all unusual for kids growing up to latch onto and copycat others they want to be like, or whose example impresses them as worth following. Adult musicians, artists and apprentices in other trades immitate the craft and manner of those they emmulate, with some remaining carbon-copy-like all their lives and others gradually feeling their way and coming into their own. Personas evolve similarly, through a process of copying and inventing. My client, Mike, offers an excellent example of this process.

Mike's behavior during the course of the first session caused me grave misgiving. He was off-the-wall, and going through one change after another. The first question to explore was whether there was any coherence to his acts at home and in public. In the service of this exploration, I asked him what movie actors or historical figures he experienced himself as from episode to episode. He was quick to identify a number of remarkably contrasting character parts. I asked his wife to confer with us in regard to the validity of his associations. She confirmed his identifications. With these in mind he was able to organize and make sense, albeit disturbing sense, of what had been happening with him from day to day. I invited him to observe during the next week the various personas he found himself assuming. He returned the next session greatly interested and reassured by how much he saw. He recognized how he was in effect behaving like a one-man travelling theater troupe assuming character parts on the spur of the moment according to various internal and external cues. Along with knowing the character parts, Mike had a good appreciation for the audience reaction typically evoked by each part and was now noticeably frightened by the trouble his performances had recently been producing. Eager to win favorable audience reaction from family, and neighbors, and equipped with fresh insights and heightened awareness in regard to his "performances," Mike was now able to manage vastly increased self-control.

Before continuing with the account of Mike's story, I will underscore the matter of appropriated, as distinguished from emergent, personas. Mike's case illustrates each in turn.

Some people appear to get along by imitating people they admire. Others appear to behave like birds of the same feather. And a few appear to act like their own selves. Worded differently, cult and fan club members emulate their idols. People who like to keep within their own set, that is being like those they like who in turn like them. Some persons, while inspired by those they admire and indebted to fellows with attitudes and manners complementing their own are ultimately true to themselves. A continuum figures between the adaptive extremes. Appropriation of personas from available cultural character models represents adaptation at the former extreme while unselfconscious self-actualization represents adaptation at the latter extreme of the continuum. At this latter end, personas have blended together, their sharp delineations have faded, resulting in the actualization of creative self-management and productivity in the present from moment to moment.

By way of exemplifying all three adaptive categories along the continuum: among a band of clowns, one may discern those who mimic great master clowns, others who fool around together, and the few who, while clowns among clowns, are nonetheless the first and only of their own, unique kind.

Emergent, idiosyncratic, psychodramatic personas figure about midway along this continuum. Their adaptive features bear resemblance to cultural idols, associate far more intimately with specially significant personal acquaintances, and are distinguished by the signature or marks upon them of their own unique, personal, existential life story. Back to Mike's example.

Each of Mike's appropriated, first-order personas carried the name of an available cultural personage. His performances from moment to moment were his representations of their acts variously adapted to the situation and audience of the moment. In contrast, his second-order personas, whom he discerned as emerging out of the stuff and business of his own personal stories, bear the names of personal acquaintances or are nicknames of his own invention. Mike originally identified himself as:
—Jack Nicholson as McMurphy in One Flew Over the Cuckoo's Nest,
—Al Pacino as the Godfather,
—Marlon Brando in Streetcar,
—Woody Allen in Annie Hall,
—Rod Steiger in almost anything,
—Rob Reiner playing Mike Stivik, social worker son-in-law in All in the Family, "Meathead,"

—Leonardo DaVinci, and,

—Spencer Tracy as Spencer Tracy.

Personally idiosyncratic personas may become evident in some cases at the very outset of the therapeutic investigation. In Mike's case two years lapsed between the identification of his appropriated personas role models and our discernment of his personal life story emergent personas. This two-year lapse becomes understandable in the context of two of Mike's many stories.

The first story tells how, when Mike ran away from home when he was about twelve, no one chased after him. When he returned home of his own initiative after a few days, he was greeted with some such comment as, "So! You came home!" The second story relates how his father, who thought his enlisting in the military would make a man of him, could not bring himself to write to his son while Mike was in combat in Vietnam. Back home, Mike's comment referring to how no mail from his father "Didn't exactly help," was met by his mother with the explanation of how, time after time, his father sat as if paralyzed at the writing desk. It may well be that the single, most telling statement Mike allowed over the years in psychotherapy was, "I have no self discipline! I need to be found out!" Given past stories of rejection and de-valuation, it is not surprising that Mike longs for and revolts against being chased after and found out. (Nor is it surprising that he has sought family among "street people.")

With time, however, Mike began to "uncover" his own personal-life-story-emergent personas. Mike's street life fostered within him the emergence of two predominant ego-states, that is to say, two distinct and principal personas: Dietter-A.C. and Geno-D.C. I'll not detail two other street personas: Gunter and Guido. Drawing from his family of origin experience, there emerged Evans, Armando, Pussy Cat, Bumpa, Doom, and Jeff Davis.

Fancying Mike to be looking over my shoulder as I write, I hear his sharp exclamation over my listing Armando among those emerging from his family experience. Armando is also the name of a man with whom he apprenticed, a most remarkable jack-of-all trades person. And so I say to Mike looking over my shoulder: "Mike, there was a lot of Armando, I'm sure you'll remember telling me, in relation to your father when you were a young man working for him at the shop on vacations. He was altogether different at home. But at work you really liked him and busted ass for him!"

In brief, Mike's emergent personas are:

—Dietter-A.C.: counterpart to Jack Nicholson's McMurphy, by and large in control and full of fun, easy and bright, used to be scary until he was "caught" in various ways. No longer scary for Mike;

—Geno-D.C.: counterpart to Rod Steiger, turned in on himself, out of control, has the addict's personality features,i.e., feels cheated and entitled, only interested in himself. When he is frustrated he goes berserk. Like a three-time loser.

—Evans: counterpart to Spencer Tracy, inspired by his (Mike's) maternal grandfather, very centered. Mike supposes he was into being Evans when he stepped off the plane from Nam and greeted his family at Logan Airport. Very controlled, as when he asked his girl friend to marry him and her parents for their blessing to marry their daughter. Very calm as when at nine he helped his brother extricate a finger from a machine and later saved the life of a kid at a picnic.

—Armando: counterpart to Jack-of-all-trades Leonardo DaVinci, the name appropriated from a man Mike apprenticed with at work some years ago. As Armando, Mike has great pride in the cleverness and quality of his work. He can remember details having to do with work projects and recall these details for long periods of time. Calm and philosophical. Savors quality. Enjoys the intrinsic value of craftful work.

—Pussy Cat: disarming man-boy-child who learned from his father how to mollify angry women after he's been running crazy. Here is a piece of Woody Allen in *Annie Hall*.

—Bumpa: a not quite as smooth and sophisticated as the Al Pacino version of Godfather, inspired by Mike's paternal grandfather. Talking about this grandfather he recalls how Grandfather Bumpa tolerated bullshit and kidding, grossed out his own wife, teased younger women with patriarchal arrogance, dished out good times, promised protection but could capriciously betray. There was the time when Mike as Geno retaliated against one of his Bumpa grandfather's betrayals by leaving his grandparents' mansion in ruin after a surreptitious teenage party when the grandparents were absent. Hence, Mike's Geno and Bumpa provide for an unstable internal state given their dynamics in relation to one another.

The identification of these features of Mike's composite personality have produced in him considerable satisfaction over gaining a vastly increased sense of intimate self revelation, even though the complexity and ambiguity produced by such a self understanding does occasionally produce anguish.

A persona dramatically presents one of one's ideas about life and one's own being. Optimally, when all of one's specific ideas integrate coherently and one is embodying self-comprehension, one is virtually unselfconscious: one needs not be conscious of personas. Awareness of and attention to personas fades as one is fluidly absorbed with and adaptively engaged in the present moment. When I can say, to use an everyday expression, that I have some idea about what I am about, I am confirming for the moment that I am collected. We are all familiar with this second common expression. It is usually used when a person appears in disarray. I recall all too vividly times when someone has urged me to "collect myself." Personae work assisted Mike in collecting himself, which in turn contributed to his being able to manage himself from scene to scene in the theater of his everyday life. Let us turn now to a close look at what it means to experience one's self as "I." "I" has the double significance of representing I-as-form, and I-as-process.

"I" as an Analogue I-as-form:

However many voices contribute to who a person is, each of us represents a company of characters as One, and thinks in terms of himself as the subject of the experience, "I", and the object of the experience, "Me."

"I" is an analogue for, not identical with, the personas. The everyday, commonplace claim by any of us to being "I", and meaning by that word anything more than a reference to a physical body represents a leap of faith, faith in the credibility of a remarkable notion! The assertion that "I" will be present and accounted for where I'm scheduled to be is open to question. Maybe I'll be there only in body; perhaps I'll be distracted. Who's to know what I will be like? Maybe something will have happened between the setting of the date and the actual meeting which will alter who the "I" is who arrives.

"I" is pure symbol. The "I" is the reference we employ for a traveling road company, a cast of characters composing our adaptive styles. Each of us is our personas. Erik Erikson (Erikson, 1968) writes:

> "I" is nothing less than the verbal assurance according to which I feel that I am the center of awareness in a universe of experience in which I have a coherent identity, and that I am in possession of my wits and am able to say what I see and think. (p. 220)
>
> What the "I" reflects on when it sees or contemplates the body, the personality, and the roles to which it is attached for life ... are the various selves which make up the composite self .... It takes, indeed, a healthy personality for the "I" to be able to speak out of (many diverse) conditions in such a way that at any given moment it can testify to a reasonably coherent Self. (p. 217)
>
> While...ego ideal could be said to represent a set of to-be-striven-for but forever not-quite-attainable ideal goals for the Self, ego identity could be said to be characterized by the actually attained but forever-to-be-revised sense of the reality of the Self within social reality. (p.211)

In contrast to experiencing one's self as coherently gathered together is feeling lost and confused, feeling at the mercy of situations, suffering profound embarrassment over the incongruity of how we are from scene to scene. *This* is to suffer identity diffusion: to experience one's self as fragmented, as uncentered, as falling apart within. [With] identity diffusion…a split of self-images is suggested, a loss of center and a dispersion…(i.e. a) falling apart within itself." (Ibid, 212)

Sometimes people feel together, all of one piece, integrated. At other times they feel lost, confused, depressed, frightened and angry. Paying attention to another person assuming she or he is a single-minded entity is like assuming an audience of two or many more as being of one mind. It is better to be with and respond to persons in the manner with which one joins a group.

People typically assume a whole different frame of mind when they are in a group than when dealing with just one other person. Now that I am more often paying attention to others in much the same way as I pay attention to a group, I'm less prone to getting confused and frustrated by contradictions, ambiguities and the play of ambivalence in what they have to say.

"I" as Process, as Vincular Self in Process

Each persona is an adaptive response to one's environment. People, from the time they are very little, are trying on and trying out all sorts of ways of being. Identity diffusion has for some theorists signified the unfortunate condition in which a person has not yet decided who they are once and for all. I offer a revision of the term, suggesting that identity diffusion ought properly to be employed to identify the degree to which a person's life is characterized by dysfunctional anarchy among the personas, when they are in an uproar. Identity integrity, on the other hand, reflects effective commmunication and cooperation among personas constituting the community of the mind.

In order to secure and sustain integral community of the mind, in order for a person to secure and keep their collective wits about themselves, they must of necessity be able to understand and follow their own game, play by play. I will proceed now to move to the heart of the business of selves command first through imaginative and then through theoretical reflection.

How do we keep things straight? Say you have turned on your car radio, and tune in to a baseball game in progress. What's happening? You know baseball. If you didn't, the play-by-play account wouldn't make any sense. You do know the game! You know there are nine players on the field. You see in your mind's eye the layout of the playing field. You know that for every player on the field there's at least lone fellow team member on the bench. You know what the team's "bench" means. You know that a team member on the bench can, if instructed by the team manager, substitute for a player on the field. You also know about the other team, that not every player on the other team on their bench is "in the game" and on the batting order. While you know that "team" means a single entity, you also understand clearly that this single entity is composed of many members, each a player personality. Driving along, listening to the sportscaster, because you know the game, you know the difference between when the sportscaster is filling time with sports trivia and when he is reporting what is happening on the field. You aren't thinking about every member of each team as you are driving along, listening to the game. Your attention is directed by the play-by-play account of what is happening. And in paying attention to the play-by-play, you keep on track of what is happening, disregarding distractions.

Each of us has, as it were, a sportscaster in our head bringing us the game play-by-play. This is how we keep track of what is happening in the various sports arenas of our lives. This is not strictly the case! For some, their sportscaster tends to get lost, misreports calls and decisions, or confuses trivia with the action story. I will elaborate upon this notion of the sportscaster within each one of us as one feature of our vincular self, our personal group facilitator, our pathfinding self. I hasten to observe that while the radio sportscaster is not engaged in the play, the vincular self is party to and actively engaged in the game.

Most every one of us suffers moments when we can't get a purchase on what's happening, when we wonder what others would think if they asked us how we are and we couldn't for the life of us say. There are times when we feel all sixes and sevens, half a bubble off plumb, a hub deep in the sand, with one oar out of the water, like the lights are on but nobody is home, one brick short of a load, not playing with a full deck, slipping away from the dock, off to the races, going north on a south-bound lane, having lost a few shingles in the big blow. At times like this our situation may not be as serious as it seems. Good teams can fall apart, can lose it for a spell, the team members despairing over ever "getting it together again!" or, we as the audience may become confused speaking of ourselves as composed of a squad of personas players trying to follow what our internal sportscaster is or is failing to report.

In my first session with Mike, I urged him to observe himself in performance, to characterize contrasting performances in terms of culturally available figures he believed he was behaving like. In encouraging Mike to observe himself and track his selves I was prompting his vincular process, his ability to oversee and facilitate his personas in performance. In further work with Mike, we teased, out of the play of his life, nickname counter-characters for these initially appropriated character designations, and examined how he came to conduct himself in one scene or another behind the mask of each of these characters.

Lewis Thomas, author of *Notes of a Biology Watcher*, writes about his multiple selves in *The Medusa and the Snail: More Notes of a Biology Watcher* (Thomas, 1980). I include here some excerpts from his piece entitled "The Selves":

> There are psychiatric patients who are said to be incapacitated by having more than one self...People like this are called hysterics by the professionals, or maybe schizophrenic, and there is, I am told, nothing much that can be done. Having more than one self is supposed to be deeply pathological in itself, and there is no known way to evict trespassers...
>
> I am not sure that the number of different selves is in and of itself all that pathological; I hope not. Eight strikes

me personally as a reasonably small and easily manageable
number. It is the simultaneity of their appearance that is the
real problem,...

To be truthful there have been a few times when they
were all there at once,...What do we meet about? It is hard
to say. The door bangs open and in they come, calling for
the meeting to start, and then they all talk at once. Odd to
say, it is not just a jumble of talk; they tend to space what
they're saying so that words and phrases from one will fit
into short spaces left in silence by the others. At good times
it has the feel of an intensely complicated conversation, but
at others the sounds are more like something overheard in
a crowded station. At worse times the silences get out of
synchrony, interrupting each other; it is as though all the
papers had suddenly blown off the table.

We never get anything settled. In recent years I've
sensed an increase in their impatience with me, whoever
they think I am, and with the fix they're in. They don't come
right out and say so but what they are beginning to want
more than anything else is a chairman.

The worse times of all have been when I've wanted to
be just one. Try walking out on the ocean beach at night,
looking at stars, thinking, 'Be one, be one.' Doesn't work,
ever. Just when you feel ascension, turning, wheeling, and
that whirling sound like a mantel clock getting ready to
strike, the other selves begin talking.

Whatever you're thinking, they say it's not like that at
all.

The only way to quiet them down, get them to stop, is
to play music. That does it. Bach stops them every time, in
their tracks, almost as though that's what they've been
waiting for. (pp. 33-35)

Lewis Thomas' solution of turning on some Bach is not so very
different from some mom throwing her hands up in despair and
putting on the TV to quiet down her klatch of brawling kids and their
playmates! Only, I suspect Thomas' inner crowd all prefer Bach to
a cartoon show.

Roberts Rules for parliamentary procedure serves as a standard device to insure that just one person talks at a time and keeps talk on the subject. It also provides a control over helter skelter argument. When members of a group hurt enough because nothing is getting done and it looks like they're going to be lost when they see that no one's likely to get their way the only way they want it, and that only wheeling and dealing is going to get everyone a little of what they want; when they see how one or two unbridled members do all the talking and that those who don't get in on the decision-making and don't like the decision can sabotage the whole business by and by, then they are ripe for effective leadership and a sensible way of doing business with one another.

The Vincular Self

The word vinculum derives from the latin word vincere, to bind. Webster offers three applications: (1) a bond or union; particularly, in algebra, a bond or straight mark placed over several members of a compound quantity, which are to be subjected to the same operation; (2) A string or band of muscular fibers; a frenum; (3) The juncture of the two pedal tendons in some birds.

The activity attending to and attempting to manage one's various personas with more or less command is vincular activity. The vinculum, or vincular self, is the persona that arises as leader among equals, absorbed in a very special task/role: the pathfinder, participating in that which is being observed and facilitated. Depending upon its strength, it binds together the various facets of an individual's personality. If a person experiences him or her self and/ or is experienced by others as functioning like five, eleven, or more players lacking all semblance of teamwork, such a person is devoid of a managing vinculum or meta-self. If a person behaves like a team rigidly bound such that no member can move out of step with the others, she or he is crippled by excessive vincular over-power. In other words, the meta-self is tyrannical. These contrasting modalities are akin to committees or task forces cursed by leaders who are either excessively permissive or excessively controlling. The ideal calls for a vinculum or meta-self team captain who inspires colorful idiosyncratic initiative by team members capable of playing together.

My thinking in this connection is informed by that of Julian Jaynes (Jaynes,1976). I see in conscious reflection only a special sort of thinking, useful only some of the time as one improves upon one's operations and facilitates productive developments in the interplay among one's personas. This conscious process enables one to go non-conscious once more.

The meta-self, the Self, the Vinculum is what Julian Jaynes talks of in terms of an analogue "I" and metaphor "me". Self is a metaphor, a story-in-time-and-space-personal-daydream.

This line of conceptualizing is compatible with and elaborates upon Gordon Allport's definition of one's *Proprium*, one's phenomenal character within which is subsumed all of one's ego-skills, self-identifications and alienations, self-worthing, self-extension, striving, and knowing. It adds to Allport's notion of attitudinal dispositions, the recognition of personality as composed of a number of discrete personas, (what D.W. Winnecott's patient referred to as "caretaking selves"). And one's vincular or propriate Self amounts to one's emergent functionally autonomous servant-leader of all of one's constituent selves.

I first encountered the notion of vinculum in an unpublished paper shared with me personally by Network therapist Ross Speck. He identified vinculum as the bond connecting persons in Nexus, a closely bonded sub-population within a social network. You can't see a vinculum. You infer it by evidence of bonding. The same applies to personas and the vincular self. we become aware of behaviors which suggest a personality construct among constructs. While all individuals evidence extrinsically culture-appropriated and/or intrinsically person-specific personas, not everyone evidences the development of a vincular self, which is to say vincular behaviors.

By way of example, in May of 1958, Charles De Gaulle accepted President Coty's request to form a new government for a France on the brink of civil war. In addressing his fellow countrymen over the radio, De Gaulle declared: "Je suis La France. Je suis l'image de La France." Charles De Gaulle offered himself and functioned as France's "I", as France's vinculum. Charles DeGaulle could only continue in office as "La France" so long as the French ruled France through him. Some people exist with virtually no ring master, no vinculum. These live like Luigi Pirandello's *Six Characters in Search of an Author.*

Full vincular effectiveness requires four capacities. We must be able (1) to identify ourselves in terms of some existential life purposeful story. Whether the story is idiosyncratic or common to that of many others does not seem to matter. What does matter is whether the story is internalized and intrinsically authentic. (2) And we want to be clear in regard to life values and able to differentiate among these values in terms of superordinal and subordinal importance. (3) We must be able to step aside from ourselves and see ourselves in perspective. And (4),we must be able to orient ourselves contextually, consider immediate and long term objectives,and draw upon accumulated experience and skills to realize these goals.

Persons lacking vincular strength appear at the mercy of pressures from within and without. Vincular capacity runs along two strength-dimension continua: from weak to strong and from brittle to pliable. The foremost functions of the vincular or meta or propriate Self are those of the effective group leader: to facilitate among group members clarification of the central and peripheral values in which all have investment in varying degrees of interest and disinterest; to manage and make effective use of emergent conflict among members in regard to styles and objectives; and, to support members working cooperatively toward the realization of common well-being. The integrating vincular self can suffer over the profound awareness that personas "know" things he or she does not know. He or she can worry that the personas are irresponsible, that one or another or all of them are not devoted to the common good; or, that unless controls are imposed, confusion at least, disaster at most will follow.

This happens. Debilitating neurotic conditions and psychotic episodes mark a failure of the group process. If the vincular Self is underdeveloped, overly controlling, exhausted or shattered, uproar and mayhem can follow. Individual personas evidence the employment of "favorite" mechanisms of defense in the service of problem-solving strategies. Some, though not necessarily all, personas may behave neurotically, and neurotic conditions often vary among an individual's personas. When vincular process is lacking, organized, creative, adaptive functioning may give way to individual persona neuroses.

I close this discussion on "I" as vincular activity with some illustrations.

—Some years ago I served as director of a summer institute. All of my staff and I were scheduled to arrive a day early in order to attend to last moment details and to galvanize ourselves as an effective team. Upon my arrival, I was met in the parking area by two Associate Directors. Despite previous agreements, and flying straight in the face of what they knew were my leadership needs, they announced that they had to be away from the center that evening, and, "Wouldn't I like to go with them!" Their performance at Fox Hollow Folk Festival, scheduled two days earlier, had been rained out. Their performance was re-scheduled for later this evening. What was I to do? As angry as I was, I loved them, and I knew they were bound to behave in character with their cardinal interests. I recognized the limits to my power and abandoned an attitude of controlling. I went with the happening. While all of the staff were stirred up, the stress provoked among us a creative, interdependent dynamic that ultimately served us all and served the institute as well. This story offers a paradigmatic model for dynamics that occur intra-personally among personas and between personas and the vincular self.

—I founded a double quartet in my first year in college, remained leader for another year without election, and was elected in my third year. When I appeared flattered by the election, the other participants counseled me to cool it: "We elected you, Pete, because we know you well enough to run the group through you." Such a leader, to serve must be able to manage episodes of loneliness and despair even as he or she may enjoy very special moments of privileged accomplishment and appreciation. In the healthiest and most whole state, the vincular self behaves as servant-leader.

—Some colleagues stopped by my home without warning, hoping to find me in. I was down in the meadow being predominantly my persona David, burning brush. David's history was one of gradual emergence as I caught being-in-the-woods-fever from my dad. By seventeen, I often fell into a mood in which I'd rather be alone in the woods and mountains than with people (my forest ranger friend named David excepted). I had my reasons for preferring meadows, mountains, streams and woods to people. As the years passed, I became more at home with others again. But that's not my persona David's story. That's more the business of some other personas. My colleagues stopped in without warning. Their experience of me where we usually spent time together led them to assume that I would be the same at my home. What they didn't know or pay attention to was that I was featured by a different constellation of personas at home than where they usually saw me.

The "I" they thought they'd find wasn't home. They entered the house at my wife's bidding and asked if I was home. Carolyn looked at them doubtfully and suggested to them not to count on it. As these folk wandered down the meadow toward where I was attending the fire, some struggle occurred within me. David wasn't very pleased to see company approaching, but, being shy, probably wouldn't on his own have been impolite. Harry, who doesn't feel any need to be polite and who doesn't take crap from anyone and who felt like watching over David, insinuated a shadow of a scowl onto "my" face and added a gruffness to my voice. Some of the others fell into line, because they couldn't see any chance of getting Harry to back off. They rationalized ways of supporting the act. The visitors picked up the attitude and wandered back up toward the house. They were still there when I arrived for lunch. My vincular self, (I remember clearly how I experienced myself thinking and talking like a news commentator,) simply told the visitors how things were, that I wasn't really home the way I supposed they'd have expected. I silently asked Harry to back off for a while, and managed to urge essential personas to stage a minimal show of the "I" they were used to. The visit wasn't wonderful. It could have been worse! This example illustrates "I" as form as well as "I" in vincular process.

The Mental Health Continuum

Sing a song of sixpence, pocket full of rye.
Four and twenty blackbirds baked in a pie.
When the pie was opened, the birds began to sing.
Now wasn't that a dainty dish to set before the king.

What do you fancy this verse means? Don't you suppose it's a riddle? And isn't any given personality a riddle? I think so! I number myself among those psychotherapists who find that whatever issue or issues the client may present as their principal focus it rarely proves to be the central issue disturbing them.

I often invite new clients to exchange riddles with me. And when we have each "stumped" the other with a riddle, I urge us to suffer together the "not knowing the solution to the other's best riddle," and to let the suspense we have generated together sharpen our wits. We then attend to the concerns the client introduces in session as symptom-clues to the nature and solution of the deep-story-riddle or riddles that have brought her or him into psychotherapy.

I am wondering if in the four and twenty blackbirds nursery rhyme the king's cook is a person's deep minding, conventionally referred to as the unconscious, presenting for the king to consider consciously the realization that he has a number of voices that can flock together or fly away in all directions. I wonder about the six pence and the pocket full of rye. Is this line simply nonsense? Not necessarily! I don't know. I keep wondering.

BLACKBIRDS features the premise that no one is of "one mind." Sick or healthy, everyone of our minds is a pie, fully or half baked, nestling a flock of alter egos, or personas, which are natural features of personality development. The way these personas work and play together defines a -10...0...+10 mental health continuum. Persons evidencing extreme single-mindedness characterize pathology at one end of this continuum. Floridly chaotic splitting among personas characterizes pathology at the other end of the continuum. Profound single mindedness as pathological follows from remarks above having to do with the downside aspects of conventionality and normalcy. Optimal mental health is therefore characterized by clearly multifaceted persons who experience them-selves and are experienced by others as interesting, productive, and fundamentally happy. And all of us experience moments clearly plotted along this continuum.

Performance involves personas of a qualitatively different kind from the *intimate* personas I have thus far considered. There are also public personas in evidence. Performance is inevitably informed by story. Moreover, language and dialect deserve careful attention as they season story with accidental and deep cultural and subcultural meanings. Finally, all performance, and the stories that inform performance, is staged, whether deliberately or spontaneously, in order to realize the fullest possible life. The next chapter takes up these matters.

Reference:
Erikson, Erik, *Identity, Youth and Crisis*, W.W. Norton, NY, 1968, pp. 211, 212, 217, 220.
Jaynes, Julian, *The Origin of Consciousness in the Breakdown of the Bicameral Mind*, Houghton Mifflin Company, Boston, 1976.
Thomas, Lewish, *The Medusa and the Snail: More Notes of a Biology Watcher*, Bantam, N.Y. & London, 1980, pp.33-35.

3

THE TRUE SELF, STORY, AND THE PUBLIC PERSONA

We can characterize human existence as performance in a world in which everyone is engaged in living theater, in which all the world is a stage. In this context, we become human as we learn to interact with others in mutually meaningful ways. We engage in character roles with one another as allies and antagonists, scene after scene, in the plays that constitute life odyssey.

Social roles are distinguished from psychodramatic roles, the former including performances as customer, patient, employee, the good host, and so forth; the latter involving character portrayals such as comprise the cast of a play or novel. Over the course of our lives, there emerges in each one of us a cast of male and/or female psychodramatic character selves which we call personae, or personas. The manner in which any of us portrays social roles is "seasoned" by features of one or another of our personas.

While social role performance is prompted by situational context, performance by our personas in full view or by subtle suggestion is prompted by story. Story, as a vision of possible dramatic developments along the way toward an anticipated outcome, informs performance.

But story is not behind everything; story hearkens to a yet deeper truth at the very core of all human behavior. Each one of us participates in the full range of human potentiality available through our genetic inheritance. We are variously endowed genetically. For each of us, our true Self is pure potentiality. How this true Self is expressed in particular ways depends upon the stories in which we participate and the stories we create through which we become Self-expressing.

And with this chapter we come to the matter of the Public Persona, the presentation of Self different in kind from intimate personas. While intimate personas are character roles that have emerged from playing and coping in scene after scene in everyday life, public personas are theatrical inventions, character creations drawing from features of intimate personas intended to impress the public. People may have command of more than one public persona. It has been my experience that when a renowned public figure, a person who is known to the public primarily in terms of his or her public personas, enters into psychotherapy, they appeal directly or indirectly to the psychotherapist to meet them at the interface of public and intimate personas so as to get to problems producing failure in public performance and failure in realizing deep personal satisfactions.

The True Self as Pure Potential; Self Actualization as Wholeness in Process

Each of us is more than meets the eye. Eighteenth century German philosopher Immanual Kant used the word "phenomenal" to refer to the objective, external appearances we perceive with our common senses. Someone smiles at me. The smile is a phenomenon. I have to guess what is behind the smile. I consider what is going on between the two of us. I take into consideration the situation, and everything that we are doing together, and guess there is mocking or there is kindness behind the smiling. I am searching for the mental attitude behind the observable gesture. I look beyond mental attitudes for the person behind appearances. We commonly talk of wanting to meet the person behind all the appearances. We talk of a person coming into their own, coming into their fullness. When we think of what it is to be a human being, we are not simply thinking of being human, we are considering the being whom we are getting to know. Kant wrote that we are each of us phenomenal and noumenal. And by noumenal, he meant that each of us is a noumenon, the inherently real self, the self-in-itself behind all appearances, the object of purely intellectual intuition, an existence we imagine, a significance of someone or something we infer to be beyond external appearances. We meet each other in the process of our being, in the process of our being together.

God is defined in Western thought as ultimate Holiness, with "holiness" deriving from the word wholeness. Consider God as participating in process, place God at the end rather than at the beginning of process. As we consider God as within and as the realization of the process of Being, we, in like manner, can see personal wholeness as the actualization of potentiality.

"True Self" is pure potential latently inherent in genetic and cultural information which in active transactional and transformational process can become evident. True Self as pure potential is a concept which can neither be verified nor validated. It can neither be proven nor disproven. We infer the existence and significance of true self as an act of intuition on the strength of process outcome. True Self is a noumenon, an existence we imagine. Immanuel Kant as well as British and New England Transcendentalists embraced this mode of thinking. I find this view is implied in God's response to Moses before the burning bush: "I am." As in the Aramaic, from which this saying is translated, it is a language without verb tenses, "I Am" is also "I shall be." Thus God said to Moses, "I am Who I shall be."

Proteus was a sea god, the son of Oceanus and Tethys. Proteus was famous for assuming various shapes. From Proteus we employ protean to describe ". . . one who, or that which, assumes various forms, aspects, or characters: a changing, varying, or inconsistent person or thing." (Oxford English Dictionary) I am proceeding from the view that personality is protean, that our personas in active, observable play constitute our phenomenal reality, and that our "True Self" constitutes our noumenal reality. Further, when all personas are in harmonious cooperation in the fulfilling of our potentialities, we are realizing existential reality in self actualization.

We ask ourselves, "Who is such and such a person?" If we arrive at an answer solely on the basis of appearance, solely in terms of a person's presentations of their integrated Self or presentations of their personas selves, we make a judgment as to the phenomenal reality of that person. If, on the other hand, we proceed beyond appearances by intuitively inferring story figuring beneath or behind or beyond appearances, if we seek story accounting for appearances, we are seeking through story the deeper noumenal reality of the person.

To understand who each of us is, we attend to every form in which our protean phenomenological reality presents itself, and assume an attitude of receptivity to what we are experiencing, such that through inference and intuition we may apprehend our noumenal reality, that kind of reality which has stimulated mythic poetry, story, and song throughout human civilization. According to this view of being and existence, each one of us is more than the number of our parts, deeper than the specifics and particulars of our resumes. We attend to both dramatic and subtle presentation of personas in verbal and non-verbal behavior and in interpersonal behavior in order to assess how a person negotiates with others and to discern signs (or clues, traces, symptoms, shadows and so forth) of something far deeper and of far greater significance than the behaviors in and of themselves deeper even than story.

A clearer grasp of this Kantian philosophical perspective on the nomenal and noumenal aspects of Self may be realized through the following literary and clinical accounts.

Nikos Kazantzakis, in his book *The Rock Garden*, has his principal character visiting with the keeper of a rock garden in Japan. As I recall, the gardener says: "I arrange my rock garden to match the composition of my life. Some of the substance was there from before my beginning. It is given and I have shaped it according to my pleasure. I have incorporated into this space some substance that comes from other places. Some substance that was given, I have removed and disposed of. Each stone and each growing thing in my garden is a phenomenal representation of the various aspects of my living and my being."

There are three levels to my rock-garden-being-in-the-world. My various performances comprise the outer level. The stories and convictions that I treasure most dearly, and that inform my performances comprise the middle level. What of the deepest level? That is beyond words or concrete representation, but it is there. Have you had the experience of swimming in water and moving in and out of cold spots? Beneath these cold spots are springs. Beneath the symbolic garden, are the well-springs of noumenal wisdom. Tending the rock garden, evokes the middle garden which, in turn, evokes the deepest sources and design. I cannot find access to my deepest self by deliberate effort. In tending my garden as a matter of daily devotion, it happens that, from time to time, I come to see clearly what was always implicitly there. Tending my garden is a highly hypnotic experience!

Here follows an example of how I have translated the rock garden metaphor into group hypnotherapeutic exploration.

A drawing or enlarged photograph I place before the attention of a group moves one person to joy, another to sadness, another to anger, yet another to indifference. When I remove the picture from view and ask them to describe the particulars of the picture, their accounts are essentially the same. However, the picture, bringing to mind for each person a different story context, affects individuals variously. Now we share stories and in doing so are involved together at two levels: the first being the more or less commonly perceived picture and the second being the deeper story level. Moreover, something else begins to happen. Each story touches an even deeper place. We have moved, each in his or her own manner, from the phenomenal to the semantic to the noumenal. What group members saw in common and the idiosyncratic stories evoked by the

picture, represent the first and second levels of significance. The process of telling the stories stimulated
intimations of that reality which is meta- or sub-phenom-
enal.

Let's see how experience of personas relates to this line of
thinking.

One day in therapy session, my client Persephone, who
over the weeks had been intensively absorbed with her
personas, observed how she supposed her personas were
specific appearances of archetypal dynamisms. I shared
with her the rock garden paradigm. She reflected upon this
in relation to her experience of her personas: "The hold
upon me of the first level appearance and the second level
significance lessens as I experience the third level to which
the first and second levels allude. Actually, the personas as
figures fade and that's all right." I see this occur as persons
gain access to the heights and depths of their being. Even as
they continue to explore their life experience with reference to their personas, their attitude toward the particularness
of personas alters.

Persephone continued: "I feel resistant to coming to
session. Why not? It is frightening to look at the demons.
They are named but still there. The illusion of Self is
difficult to de-create. Ha! the Jungian connection!"
Persephone proceeded to talk about the extremes in the
postures and expressions of one and another of her personas
and how each helps secure balance and limits. "I'm deeply
affected by flowing water, which I see as the symbol of
energy, moving over fixed elements such as rocks changing
in appearance from moment to moment. The striking
appearance of energy in the water flowing or splashing over
a rock comes from up-stream. I see this sharply defined
figure as a phenomenon." The inflection with which
Persephone uttered the word phenomenon moved me to
suppose she meant by phenomenon "striking" and "strange".
"And when I can see the phenomenal in my pain, the
experience of pain changes. And then the particularity of

the specific persona loses its hold. This is sort of an out-of-body release, a 'Piss-ant' posture in the midst of catastrophe. All this talk is a gesture toward experiencing belief in freedom from hell in life."

I find it paradoxical that the word *phenomenon* can denote not only external appearance available to common senses, but also strange and striking appearance. It is with "strange" and "striking" that I am interested here. Persephone said: "When I can see the phenomenal in my pain, the experience of pain changes." She observed this against the background of Jungian thoughtfulness. When the energy-water comes from the source-upstream and curls around, flows over, splashes upon something she is looking at represented symbolically by a rock, which, in turn, may represent Persephone or her pain,…she is "deeply affected."

The therapist's task is threefold: to watch with the subject for first-level appearances in the form of personas in performance; to facilitate the clarification of the second-level stories; to honor each persona's story as a conduit through which third-level illumination, healing, and empowerment may be evoked. In this fashion phenomenal and noumenal realities may yield to the existential realization of the person's actualization.

Story

The Role of Narrative in Story

Excluding clinicians committed exclusively to symptom relief and/or the modification of specific problem-exacerbating behaviors, psychotherapists of virtually all schools of thought look with their client at Story to see how a person's story has gone wrong. What clinicians look for and how they attempt to aid clients may vary remarkably. Still therapists from every single orientation recognize Story as the primary interest: personal, cultural, sub-cultural, ethnic, neighborhood stories, . . the one, the other, and sometimes all interwoven one with the other.

The appropriation or fabrication of story affords each person a working grasp of his or her experience of instantaneous being-in-the-world. Story captivates one's experience - one's being in solitariness and/or with others. Deep story will enhance or impair experiencing, savoring, and expressing the joy of being alive. Satisfactory story provides focus and framework within which and through which ontological angst and ontological guilt play into constructive and sensitive productivity. Efficiently sufficient story illuminates and directs our way through our own-world, our world of experience with others, and the world of our experience in relation to nature as a whole. Working with clients amounts, in large part, to joining with them within their own stories: stories which have not sufficed; stories of lostness and/or disaster; stories viciously circling in on themselves crying for new information. Harmony or dysfunctional stress among personas can result where congruity or incongruity occur among their stories.

Fathoming latent, nonconscious story is the most delicate clinical work. People don't have to be conscious of story for them to feel at home with themselves, to enjoy a sense of well-being or to feel a wreck. It is when people find themselves in difficulty, and do not know why they are in trouble, or why they feel terrible even though everything that is happening has the appearance of going well, that conscious and nonconscious stories invite scrutiny.

The following accounts offer illustration of these points.

—Frank's wife has filed for divorce. He cannot understand why and doesn't understand what she means by what she says is wrong. Both she and he, when first married, lived according to the old, conventional storybook marriage and embodied the family in which the husband worked hard to support the family and the wife nurtured the children, kept house, and waited on her husband. After several years she fell into profound depression and did not know why. More recently, picking up on many women's reappraisal of their dignities and interests, she sees some of the current books on women's and men's issues as written for her. Frank doesn't know what she's talking about; it doesn't make sense to him given how he understands the old book. But his story is not working. It has failed. And, he is a wreck. He can't work, can't do anything, shifts from blustering to pleading and then back to blustering. He can't understand her language. He can't look at the new book as he is still clinging to the old story. My heart goes out to him! I personally like the new book and I realize the depth of grief he is going to have to go through to let go of the old, standard story in which he has invested so much.

—Frances at eighteen suffered a schizophrenic break. She was part of a symbiotic family story which did not equip her to live independently. When she left her West Coast home for college on the East Coast she fell apart. Her collapse was precipitated by her parents' separation. Her sustaining story was about love in the family and everybody being together. Cut off by thousands of miles, having to take care of herself, hearing that her parents were headed for divorce left her bereft, without a center, without ego. She was lost, had lost her way. In being lost, she lost her being. When little children see their parents deliberately withholding eye contact for an extended period of time, they may panic; existentially they-are-not unless they are being watched over. Frances, being lost, panicked, lost her bearings, was without a map. She was nowhere once her story was shattered. Her situation was far more critical than that of a boy separated from his parents at a Montana Rodeo-Carnival. The boy was able to tell the police that his family had a trailer in a trailer camp in the city. Scared as he was, he knew his family was not lost, nor was he in fact! While separated and scared, he knew all was not lost. He simply needed comforting and assistance. Losing one's corner-stone story leaves one stricken and bereft. The basis for saying who-one-is falls away. To get well Frances had to find a new story through psychotherapy.

These examples as I've written about them make no mention of personas. I have found that each persona has her or his own idiosyncratic story. This being the case, why does psychotherapy so often go well when both psychotherapist and client have proceeded on the assumption that personality is discretely unified, that each of us has one self? It is my assumption that therapists and clients have unwittingly addressed the concerns, the joys and sorrows and wounds, of the several personas. It is a common occurrence that with family, multiple family, network, and small group therapy, work with one member has beneficial effects upon the others. We frequently find when group members are invited or moved to comment on how another's work has affected them, they share how, vicariously, they felt the work was theirs as well. The individual who was working frequently responds that he or she drew great support from and was affected by many unspoken and spoken promptings from the others.

However, it does not always prove to be the case that all the individual's personas get into the one act. Case histories reveal how often the therapist's supposed treatment was nearing termination when an unexpected issue arose, one quite different in kind from previous issues. I infer that personas have been standing in line, as it were, for their special chance, their turn to work with story and stories.

Now I want to sharpen our focus on the fact that story informs performance, and that story engages audience participation. When I turn on the television, and find a program in progress, I want to know what's behind the action. Because I don't know the story behind the English game of cricket, I may fail to follow the action on the television screen. Maybe a sportscaster will fill the viewing audience in on the story. If I tune in on a drama in progress, I may see if I can pick up on the story line. Until I get the gist of the story, anything I see and hear that makes any sense to me will be limited to the action of the moment. As discerning story behind what I am viewing affects whether or not I wish to play the role of audience, so story informs whether I engage and how I engage with others in dramatic encounter.

While much of how we conduct ourselves from day to day is prompted by the fulfilling of our plans and personal objectives, not everything we do can be explained in terms of our own stories. Sometimes we awaken to how we're performing a stand-in part in someone else's story. For instance.

—A lawyer in therapy wanted to understand why he found himself incapable of setting limits on the time he surrendered to a woebegone client who teetered on the border of becoming a "bag lady" law practice client. He fancied himself in command of at least as much capacity for decisiveness as the next fellow, but with her that capacity just wasn't available to him. He gathered from others that she had run through every other attorney in town, and in relatively short order, exhausted their sense of *pro bono* responsibility. How, then, was it that he could short-change others on time they deserved not to mention neglect the demands of paperwork on his desk and sit for long periods of time attending to her until she chose to leave?

Once he figured out how she and he were probably serving as stand-ins for one another in their life scenarios, he began to experience some relief from his compulsion to accommodate to her directions and promptings. He saw her as marginally surviving and became conscious of how uneasy he was that should he turn her away, pushing her to take care of her own business, she might suffer an emotional collapse, perhaps even commit suicide. There was something about her that prompted him to think about the story of his mother who was precariously "on the edge" and the memory that he had served his father with a cold silence-treatment for six months before his father committed suicide—a story that continues to haunt him. He doesn't want to play any part in contributing to another calamity by careless neglect or abandonment. As for his part in her play? He pieced together a credible scenario in which she called for a character who, out of personal guilt, would give her all the time and attention of which she felt deprived throughout her life and with whom she could re-stimulate her image of herself as a victimized and ineffectual person. They made a great match! It came as a sobering thought to him that his existence with her was like playing a part in someone else's dream.

Not every story is available to objective observation or even consciously available. When any one of us reports that we have been wool-gathering, there is the possibility that we have been engaged in a private drama located within our own, personal wake-state dream world. And, oftentimes, when we are asked to account for where we have been, we have already forgotten. Furthermore, sometimes we are hardly, if at all, consciously aware of the dream-making as it occurs. Some personas exist almost entirely in this dream world. These are phantom or semi-phantom personas and they engage in phantom stories. The following incidents offer illustration.

—A client and I exchanged greetings and took our usual seats. Looking at me in a friendly way, he asked me how I was. I debated with myself for a few seconds. "He's my client, I should tell him my father died four days ago? How can I not? My withholding would be written all over my face. He is also a clinician and doesn't miss much." I told him. He responded sensitively. Silence. As I sit here, I see in my mind's eye the two of us getting up and hugging. I'm sitting in my chair and seeing very clearly the two of us on our feet and my welcoming a loving hug! Now, I, in fact, get up. He follows suit. We hug. Seated again, I say to him: "Well, it took us long enough to catch up with the hugging. Just think. We might have missed out on what was happening." He responded that he understood perfectly. He, too, had seen the hugging in his mind's eye. Actions occur one step behind, oftentimes only a few hundred milliseconds behind our perception of how we are about to act.

—I was joined early the next morning as I breakfasted at a local diner, by a friend who was acquainted with Personae Theory. He asked how my own travelling road show was doing. We chuckled and enjoyed one another's company. "I have a curious story for you," he offered. "When I went to therapy the other day I reached for a check that I had folded and placed in my shirt pocket earlier in the day. It wasn't there! I couldn't believe it. I searched in my jacket and throughout my pockets. It wasn't there. I swear I remember writing out the check after dressing that morning, tearing the check out of the checkbook, folding it, and placing it in my pocket. My doctor and I talked about it for a bit and then went on to other things. That evening, when I returned home, I found my checkbook on my dresser with the check made out and still in the checkbook. And yet I had this altogether vivid memory of tearing it out of the check-book, folding it, and placing it in my pocket. How can this be?" I said to him that, of course, there was no way I could know how come, but that I had a theory of what might have happened. "Is it not possible that one or another of your personas never signed up for the therapy hitch? That he or she didn't like anything about the whole show? Is it possible that one of your personas, another one, is sympathetic with the notion of therapy for you-all, but does not feel that you can afford it just now?" My friend grinned, and indicated that I was right on target. Then, I added, "After you finished writing out the check, one or more of your resisting personas did a sleight-of-hand trick on you. What I mean is that they distracted you in some fashion from acting on what your check-writing self saw you were about to do, that is, removing the check from the book, folding it, and pocketing it." I shared with him my hugging scene as I have related it. My friend understood the concept, noted the pertinence, and supposed my interpretation to be valid. Of course he had torn the check out of the book and placed it in his pocket! This is by way of saying that he saw himself doing it. The missing element was that he was distracted by resisting personas from catching up in phenomenal behavioral fact with what he had seen himself doing.

—Persephone's son and only child is seventeen. She talked of how fine she finds him. She sometimes wonders these days about another child, the meaning for her of having a daughter, of how birthing and nurturing a daughter now, seventeen years after her son's birth would mark a third major life chapter for her, the first chapter being their own childhood experience, the third carrying the opportunity of freeing herself from the haunting of that childhood by sharing with a daughter a healthy relationship.

The incidents of the phantom hug and phantom check had occurred within the twenty-four hours preceding Persephone's talk of a daughter, and were fresh in my mind and I shared these stories with her. She appropriated for herself the relevance of the notion that phantom behaviors have a substantive reality. This meant for her that even thinking about conceiving and nurturing a daughter into healthy maturity constitutes substantively real experience, a commanding story, in somewhat the same fashion that dream-work is real and can add to one's therapeutic progress and personal growth. A parallel occurred to us. One need not leave ones seat, mount the stage, and engage with actors in the play for the play to stimulate cathartic, not to mention abreactional, release and beneficial result. If one is absorbed in the play, one is existentially on stage, is with the actors, is party to the unfolding drama, one with the actors, a phantom player. It is commonplace for a member of the audience to say how she or he took the play to heart and will surely not be the same for having been there.

The Role of Language and Dialect in Story

Language and dialect are as important as is narrative to story.

—About the fifth week into the Fall semester at New England College, a delegation approached me after the class in Introduction to General Psychology. "You are new on campus, Professor Baldwin. No one knows you. There's talk among the students. We are not satisfied that you are for real. You sound phony." I asked them what it was that I was doing that seemed phony. "One minute you talk like you are proper Bostonian, then it sounds like street talk, then you sound like a New Hampshire native." I asked each one of them where they came from and if they'd moved often. It turned out that everyone of them came from a single subcultural background. "Where do you come from?" they asked me. "From three subcultures, three places," I replied. "I am upstate New Hampshire. I am Andover Academy where my father taught. I am south-side inner-city Chicago, where I lived enough years to have been encultured there. My language is me, we agreed together. I am where I sound from, where I talk from. We all appreciated this sharing. Next class session we reported our exchange to the rest of the class.

Our personal reality is more than phenomenal appearance, more than meets the eye. We are all that we imagine. We are forever running away from or hurrying to catch up with ourselves. Oftentimes, we are existentially in more than one place at a time. Our voices in the moment, how we sound to ourselves and to others, may offer clues to "where we are." For instance.

—June, 1982: My father slipped away into death early evening, a week ago Friday. Saturday and Sunday I spent with mother and knew I was in shock and hence numb to the deepest grief. I steeled myself on Monday and Tuesday while I saw patient after patient in my Keene office. I teared at the wake Tuesday evening, was in a fog, though I wept, at the funeral. Thursday and Friday, I steeled myself once again in order to conduct therapy at my Gilmanton office. Beginning just before dinner on Friday, one week following my father's death, I began to crumble. Every little thing that went awry sent me further into dismal distress. I unconsciously projected my sense of having been abandoned onto ready targets. I was inconsolable in my determination that friends were deliberately leaving me in the lurch. At 3:30 a.m. I was wakeful and morose. My wife urged me to breathe evenly. She was noting how shallow and irregular my breathing appeared. I could not seem to help myself. "I forget to breathe," I nearly whimpered. "You are sounding like a big baby," she finally complained in exasperation. "Which persona am I dealing with?" I could not answer though her question struck me as very important. I both resented and very much respected her question. I began to settle down. Sleep came. It is morning now and I am writing, I recall how I was talking. She was correct. I did feel and sound like a big, upset baby. I know now it was Pete at seventeen, neither child nor adult. When I was seventeen, my mother was in the hospital for months, my father with her over the weekends, my brother away in college. I was alone much of the time, a day student at

Andover trailing after and hanging on at the periphery of peer groups. I felt abandoned, hurt, in chronic grief, suffering spells of diarrhea for weeks on end. That night, a week after my father's dying I was Pete at seventeen. I know this to have been the case, largely because of the sound of my voice: a baby's voice in a big body, a big baby voice.

—My client Elizabeth had been reared in Colombia throughout her childhood. She was Colombian. Now, years later she was an American and spoke only English with her English-speaking husband. Their marriage was suffering some marked stress, and insufficient explanations for all the felt stress led them into group therapy. They were stuck and confused. I invited Elizabeth to talk with her husband of her life, her joys and her sorrows and to do so in Spanish. She looked at me with consternation. "He won't understand a thing I say! He doesn't know Spanish." "Go ahead anyway," I prompted. "Try the experiment." She poured forth for ten minutes becoming more and more animated. She wept and laughed and scolded. When her husband was invited to share what he heard and saw, he observed with astonishment that he saw and heard her as never before. He stopped thinking about how he didn't understand her words. He was now seeing and hearing a beautiful, more full, rich, amazing, many-featured human being. "There's so much to you I have never seen before." She looked at him with great intensity and said, "English is my second language. I forgot to remember this years ago. English is your language. I meet you and live with you within the confines of your language. In leaving Spanish behind, I leave much of my life behind. I can only pack a little of myself into the English bag. So much, so many of my possessions are left home, left behind, left scattered about. I now know that I must retrieve myself. I love you. I accept that even were you to learn Spanish, Spanish would be your second language. You and I can live richly where we can, where we are able to meet. I see now that as I cultivate Spanish-speaking friends, I can be much more of myself. Is that O.K.?" That was O.K. with him.

In a later chapter I will offer in more detail the account of how Persephone was prompted to become conscious of her black persona, Vicky, and her white southern belle persona, Charlotte, as she herself sensed a subtle flavor of black southern accent in her tone of voice as she, as vincular self, reviewed her therapeutic progress. *When I speak of one's language being one's self, I am referring to idiom, accent, tongue, and non-verbal style.* A case I will refer to later will offer an account of a woman with a four-year-old battered persona whose stark terror is now able to be met and eased by her ten year old confident babysitter persona. As each of these personas presented themselves in session, it was strikingly apparent that the former was verbally mute and dramatically expressive nonverbally, while the latter spoke verbally a mile a minute.

—When Joy was asked in therapy group where she came from, where she spent her early childhood, she found ways of slipping out of answering. The day came when the group confronted her with their impression that she appeared frightened by the question. They didn't assault her. They said it was her business; their business was to be clear with her about their experience of her running away from their question. Joy panicked, and stayed with her fright. Her voice changed dramatically. None of us had guessed that Joy had come from the South, and yet here we were hearing a rich, Southern country dialect we could hardly understand. Joy was raised in a Tobacco Road novel. Fright, shame, earthy humor, stark ferocity were all interwoven in her twenty-minute soliloquy about her early years. She was sweating profusely, laughing and crying. As the weeks passed, Joy retrieved a self which she had in shame and terror locked away. I do not recall precisely how she finally put in words her feeling toward her share-cropper family self. However, her message was, "My language is me." I must credit psychiatrist Beulah Parker with this line that served as the title of her book reflecting upon her psychotherapeutic work with a disturbed adolescent. [Basic Books, 1962]

—George lives in a New England country village. He joined the ongoing Gestalt group because he was searching for an answer to a nagging question about feeling at home with himself. He said he was born and raised in England. That interested me personally as I'd been a graduate student at the University of London. Week after week passed. George participated actively. I was struck especially by George's recurring references to Tolkien's Hobbit stories that feature quest and home themes. I asked George one evening to lead the rest of us on a fantasy tour to his home in England. He accepted the request as a pleasant whimsy. Home proved to be East London. With each passing minute, George fell further into Cockney. At one point I sensed embarrassment on his part over hearing the sound of his own voice. He accepted my nudging to let go his hesitance. In a little while, it was as if he had forgotten we were his companions. The notion of himself as tour guide fell away. He became absorbed with where he found himself in East London. He became possessed by old story, and tumbled upon a critical unresolved conflict having to do with his relation with his family of origin there in East London. During this group session and several thereafter, George found it imperative to re-engage his Cockney dialect and invoke a sense of the London setting in order to move toward and realize a resolution of his inner conflict. After this experience, he reported feeling very much more at home with himself in New England.

We are, each of us, unfolding story. And, we are, each of us, many voices.

The Public Persona

A public persona is the enactment of an image an individual accepts or has cultivated to represent how he or she wants to be thought of and treated by the general public. It consists of her or his own name-brand public character role, his or her most invested-in self-object, his or her principal *raison d'etre* before the general public. A public persona is different in kind from personal psycho-dramatic, caretaking selves appropriated from the culture's stock of characters or emergent selves idiosyncratically intrinsic to an individual's personal story.

A person may cultivate a public persona in order to be connected and identified with something far greater than his or her mere personal self. The public persona can protect off-stage life and private time from public invasion. The public persona may protect a person from the public's discovering that there is little to the person behind outer performance. And, or, engaging with others as public persona befitting the situation may provide assurance that the person is appearing as expected.

Marquis *Who's Who* lists personages. A personage is an individual's established public persona. Preparing, updating, repairing a resume is in effect touching up one's makeup, one's public persona. If we enclose a photograph with the resume, we add all the more information to our audience, on the basis of which they develop an image of how we wish to be seen by the public.

To ask the audience how they see us is to invite self disclosure. We rarely ask! You wonder how I can say such a thing? Aren't each of us constantly wanting to know others' impressions of us? More times than not, it is approval we are seeking. Approval at best, permission to continue as we are if we can't win approval, forgiveness for being as we are at the very least. Early in his ministry, people came to Jesus and asked him who he was. They asked him if he was the one that John the Baptist said would come. Jesus replied by asking: "Who do men say that I am? This story is a projective. Each of us is free to interpret, to infer, to assign to Jesus' question whatever appeals to us. I like his response as it represents for me a person's recognition that each of us is in part how we are seen. Each of us is, in part, the picture of us that other people have in mind. I am probably less able than my public to account for my public persona. I am not nearly as aware of who and how I am as those before whom and with whom I present myself. When, therefore, I invite and open myself to the impressions of others, I avail myself to self disclosures.

A person's public persona appears like, but is not the same in kind as, an intimate persona. Both are illusions suggested by the attitudes struck by the individual. In the former case, the impression is fostered to surround and camouflage the private identity of the individual. In the latter case, the impression is fostered to draw out and reveal facets of the individual's personal identity. Let me illustrate.

—Elizabeth Taylor filed suit to block completion and release of a film about her, claiming that she is her own industry and that only she has the right to suggest and profit by the image her name connotes. She apparently wished to have surrounding her and protecting her privacy, a public image of her that suited her own purposes. This corresponds in kind to the person who carries a turned-on transistor radio cassette player everywhere he goes down the street, in the subway, or up a mountain. The music produced from his radio cassette player provides a costume-in-sound, an informational bubble surrounding him. This "costume" identifies him-as-person with the message conveyed by the sound-costume. The costume distracts him and his audience from what lies beneath the costume. His personal anonymity is secured!

—The Wizard of Oz (Baum, 1899) offers a paradigmatic account of the public persona:

> Presently they heard a Voice, seeming to come from-somewhere near the top of the great dome, and it said, solemnly, "I am Oz, the Great and Terrible. Why do you seek me?" They looked again in every part of the room and then, seeing no one, Dorothy asked, "Where are you?"
> "I am everywhere," answered the Voice, "But to the eyes of common mortals I am invisible. I will now seat myself upon my throne, that you may converse with me." Indeed, the Voice seemed just then to come straight from the throne itself: so they walked toward it and stood in a row while Dorothy said:
> "We have come to claim our promise, O Oz."
> "Dear me," said the Voice; "how sudden! Well,

come to me tomorrow, for I must have time to think it over."

"You've had plenty of time already," said the Tin Woodsman angrily. "We shan't wait a day longer," said the Scarecrow.

"You must keep your promises to us!" exclaimed Dorothy. So he gave a large, loud roar, which was so fierce and dreadful that Toto jumped away from him in alarm and tipped over the screen that stood in a corner. As it fell with a crash, they looked that way, and the next moment all of them were filled with wonder. For they saw, standing in just the spot where the screen had been, a little old man with bald head and wrinkled face, who seemed to be as much surprised as they were. The Tin Woodsman, raising his axe, rushed toward the little man and cried out,

"Who are you?"

"I am Oz, the Great and Terrible," said the little man, in a trembling voice, "but don't strike me! Please don't! And I'll do anything you want me to."

"...I have been making believe. . . . I'm just a common man."

"Doesn't anyone else know you're a humbug?" asked Dorothy.

"No one knows it but you four—and myself," replied Oz. "I have fooled everyone so long that I thought I should never be found out."

—Michael is a certified public accountant. I met him in 1960 when he was a patient in a hospital. He was committed after trying to get to the President in the White House. All he wanted to do was appeal to the President to do something about all the terrible problems. He approached the White House guard and said he wanted to see the President. Asked who he was, Michael replied he was Michael. When the guard asked him who he thought he was to walk right up to the White House expecting to see the President, Michael drew upon the authority he associated with his name. Roman Catholics and persons acquainted with the wonderfully rich story connecting by name each plain person, through saints, angels, and heavenly figures, to divine grace will appreciate how Michael's sense of personal authority reached into the very center of divine authority. "I come as a messenger. My name is Michael. I have my name from the archangel Michael who bears important messages." In the secular world of associations, we identify ourselves by degree, position and association. If he had said he was a Ph.D. from the Massachusetts Institute of Technology's Institute for International Affairs he still would have been refused entrance. However, what he would have received would have been bemused respect and a firm referral to the appropriate appointments secretary. Michael acted in accord with those who gain respect. His associations simply did not fit the scene.

"So you fancy yourself the archangel Michael!"
"Sort of! I was given his name. The archangel is with me. May I please see the President?"

"To walk right into the White House, Mister, you have to be somebody very big, mister. And if you think you are an archangel, Mister, you don't belong here. Come with me!"

And that marked the beginning of Michael's journey to the Massachusetts Mental Health Center. I-am-the-archangel-Michael-with-me was Michael's public persona.

Most people can understand how a famous figure may cultivate or accept a public persona as a continuation off-stage of an on-stage celebrated performance. And, despite attending disdain, most can understand how an imposter may be preserving a semblance of personal dignity by perpetually carrying on an act. What is most difficult to understand and to cope with is a person who virtually never relates to others, including intimates, save through a public persona. Such people suppose they are being their non-public selves. Those well acquainted with them experience them as being their public selves. When an individual thinks he or she is being "plain folk"—informal, immediate, intimate, available, and open—

and others are experiencing them as behaving as a public persona, stress arises. We may say of such a person, "She says a lot, supposes we know her well, but we actually know very little. She is so full of her manner."

I am reminded of what Dr. Elvin Semrad (Rako, 1980) of the Massachusetts Mental Health Center used to say, "I've always thought that some of the things people suffer most from are the things they tell themselves that are not true."

Through psychotherapy, we can come to see more clearly how we accept and make up stories for and about ourselves; how we wear our stories in our manner; and, if we have forgotten, how we can learn once again to let go of the act and simply be with ourselves and others.

I do not recall whether it was R.D. Laing, Ram Das or someone else from whom I learned the following thinking exercise. I ask you, "when we drop our masks, when you and I let go of any notion of time, of history, of task, story, and place, then what remains between us? What is left? Nothing! No-thingness, pure happening. As Martin Buber would say: We are I and thou. We are experiencing Encounter, Communitas. Anthropologist Victor Turner defines communitas as characterizing pure, undifferentiated encounter among people. It is only when we begin to do things, to organize, institutionalize, rubricate our being together that communitas fades and we have community. And the more complex we become, the closer we approach a rigid state of affairs. Through effective psychotherapy we can learn once again how to let go of the act and simply be with ourselves and others.

The following anecdotes illustrate the emergence and dramatic performance of the public persona.

—In talking about one another's public personas, a wife and husband in couples' therapy recognized how, while each individual's intimate, emergent, psychodramatic personas contribute to the public persona, the whole is greater than the sum of its parts. This is not unlike the impression created by a company of dancers. Understanding the impression the dancers have created together defies reducing the total act to the contributions of individual dancers. Similarly, adept group facilitators are well aware of how from time to time a member may say or do something that is speaking for the group. Each intensive group becomes a lively, transpersonal, existential entity in and of itself. This wife and husband know one another's private life personas well. They also see how each is something different in kind out in the world. They are aware of how they get into their public characters gradually. There are certain moves each attends to in preparing themselves mentally for going before and engaging with their publics. They recognize how when one phones the other at their out in the world places of work unexpectedly they will get the public persona voice-and-manner of the other. One says to the other: "When you've left the house for work and then return because you have forgotten something, you are not for a moment, upon your return, as you were when we were together before you left. I know better than to say anything to you that is very personal. And, during the day, if I need to be in touch with you personally, it is best to leave a message for you to return my call even when we could in fact talk immediately. It is better to provide space so each of us can, if possible, sneak out for a moment to talk personally."

—Jacky at twelve years old projected a public persona of one fated always to be an orphan-ward of the state. As much as he claimed wanting to be adopted, every time he and his current foster parents became close he'd "behave like a pain" and then ask welfare to take him away. Through psychotherapeutic exploration Jacky came to see that while he recognized rationally that his biological parents were altogether unfit to live with one another and care for him, he was, nonetheless, loyal to the daydream that a boy is entitled to a mom and dad who like themselves, love one another, and cherish their son. Jacky suffered most from this daydream story he kept telling himself semi-consciously, a story that was true in heart and false in fact. One day when Jacky saw that I was looking for a pen, Jacky drew a very handsome one from his shirt pocket. I commented on what a fine pen it was, and he said it belonged to his foster father, and that carrying his foster father's beautiful pen made him feel important. I shared with him how maybe that breast pocket was also close to his heart as was his foster father's pen just as his foster father was becoming close to his heart. Jacky and I talked about the daydream to which he had been loyal for so long at the cost of every new chance for an adoptive home. As he let go of an old true to heart story and reached for a more reasonably available story, his air of being a hopelessly homeless orphan fell away.

As psychotherapist, I am a living camera constantly snapping candid impressions. I see with my eyes and my mind's eye. I hear with my ears and my mind's ears. How the other person is has impact upon me viscerally. My body is a lens and film. I am somatically affected by the person with whom I am in encounter. With the other's consent share many of my snap shots. And the sharing fosters self disclosure.

Paradoxically, as I am open to seeing myself through others' eyes, as I am open to how others see me, I am freer to see myself with my own eyes. Let me illustrate this point.

—I recall listening to a graduate intern's report of his clinical progress and noting how relaxed and clear he appeared to be. Everything seemed in order. I began to suffer a terrible stomach ache. I supposed the problem was mine, something I'd eaten or some piece of my own personal work. I decided to tell my supervisee that I had a stomach ache that had come on suddenly. I asked him if he was sitting on something he wasn't talking about. He thought for a moment, then stared at me, then burst into tears. My stomach ache began to abate. There was in fact a terrible piece of business going on in his life that he had tucked away so carefully that in coming into my office he'd forgotten it for the time being. My sharing candidly with him prompted clear self disclosure. What I felt was a way of seeing. And, my seeing brought him back to himself.

—A colleague and I talked about these concepts the other day—this business of public personas and the therapist's part in helping persons to see themselves. He shared a story with me about a priest with whom he worked as therapist. My colleague told me of the very touching moment when the priest, in the manner of a simple, non-public, person said: "I see now how, in becoming more and more the priest, I abandoned myself. Now I have recovered the lost heart of my self. I guess I am just an ordinary catholic. How good it is to have found my way home."

—A personal anecdote offers a hint of what public persona signifies. My grandfather received a gift of a vintage velvet, silk, and satin smoking jacket from a dear old friend after the death of her husband. Such a distinction! Such quality and style! When my grandfather passed away I inherited the jacket. I donned it one New Year's Eve and sported it as casually as I could manage. I felt as elegant as I appeared. After about an hour into the party, one of my friends instructed me to take it off: "O.K., Peter, time to take off the smoking jacket and join the rest of us." It became clear to me that this jacket prompted me into embodying a public image of aloof elegance. My friends experienced me as elegant if, out of touch. I didn't know I was out of touch. I assumed I was with them. I was not! Prompting me home was relatively easy. All I had to shed was an article of clothing. When, however, the wrap is an air a person assumes by habit and is as invisible as the Emperor's new clothes, the chore of fetching him home may be more difficult.

—I recall being fetched home. In 1959, my first clinical supervisor sidled up to me in the hospital coffee shop, ordered a beverage, and without preliminaries concluded in his gravely deep southern inflection: "Well, Mr. Baldwin, it must be an awful burden you drag behind you." I asked him what he was talking about. He responded: "All those national and international famous people who visited your childhood home year after year. I would think that would make a boy feel he had to amount to something awfully big to mean anything worthwhile. It just makes me feel bad to think how hard it must be for you to suppose you can be plain folk." My clinical supervisor spotted through my name-dropping behavior an indication that to be noticed, verified and validated, I had to be a personage worth noting, note-worthy in public to the public. This supervisor fetched me home *to be*, simply to be, first and foremost, a plain folk intimately able to know myself simply, and accessible to others wishing to meet the person behind the mask.

Weaving the Threads Together
Through the Story of a Dying Young Man

Everybody who knew David had always known that he was The Sick Kid, and in the privacy of neighborhood homes, people talked of him as the poor boy who would die young. Incurable heart disease. Inoperable. Now, in college, he was in his last year of life.

Home for the weekend, he told his father he thought he had better see a psychologist. "I'm withdrawing a lot. I don't want to spend the little time remaining withdrawn into my own room. Maybe a psychologist can help me stay interested in life, in the time that remains. Arrangements were made for him to consult with me.

We explored his feelings of sadness and of resentment. He recognized that his energy level was affected by his illness and his depression. How to minimize the draining effect of feeling depressed? He was taking two drama department courses, one in directing. His interest in theater was rapidly dissolving; he didn't feel much like attending class sessions.

"When I couldn't participate in sports, I became interested in the drama program at school. This was in the sixth grade. Theater became my primary interest. Now I realize that all my absorption in plays was an escape from reality. My life has been featured by escape. Now I am dying. Escaping from moment to moment into the world of theatrical fantasy seems so stupid."

I reported an incident to David that had occurred in the hour before I met with him. My office is on the third floor of an old mill. The first two floors constitute another world, quite separate from and very different in atmosphere from the third floor suite of offices I share with colleagues. Below us is a marketplace, a very attractive shopping mall. The corridors are for all the world like narrow streets off from which sit shops to the left and right. As I had some free time, I had gone to a ground level news shop for the morning paper. Having made my purchase, and in the mood to enjoy the street scene, I walked through the marketplace in a leisurely manner, watching people. In talking of this to David all I had to say to him was that I had gone to the Marketplace in the last hour for the morning paper, and had engaged in an interesting scene on my way back. Here's how my report continued:

"And so, David, there I was, walking through the Marketplace, taking in the people, when I witnessed a remarkable scene between a mother and her son. I figured him to be about twelve. They were standing just outside of the door to a clothing shop, leaning toward one another in muted fury. You know the Norman Rockwell scenes? Yes? Well, they were Norman Rockwell figures in the flesh. Here was street theater, and I stopped to take them in. I just gazed at them the way pedestrians tarry to watch the action when a company of actors and actresses do street theater. I couldn't hear anything either was saying to one another, though I could see they were screaming in one another's faces. Tight, muted screams, as I said. What a show! It was fantastic. They offered a gripping tableau.

The mother saw me first. I guess she saw that I was just standing there at a respectful distance. The boy, following his mother's attention, looked at me. They looked at one another again, but where before they had been locked into feverish combat, now they appeared to be sharing a common disconcertion that they had an audience. "Why are you looking at us?" the mother shot at me. "Well," I replied with simple childlike appreciation, "you are very interesting." I continued in the role of audience. Why shouldn't I? They were enormously good at what they were doing with one another. They were a class act. They exchanged knowing looks, appeared to consent together to a radical shift in the manner in which they were addressing one another, and walked into the shop. I continued on my way for a few steps, turned around, and returned to where I could see them through the glass walls of the shop without their being able to see me. They were ninety percent engrossed in their engagement in the role of companion customers. I say ninety percent engrossed. I noted each stealing glances a couple of times to see if I was anywhere around. After making a purchase, they left the shop, a picture of familial conviviality.

David looked pensively at me as I completed my account. He said to me, "I have always supposed my world of theater to be apart from the real world. I don't see how I could have missed the obvious. All the world *is* a stage. You were both audience and on stage with that mother and son. You dramatically affected their scene. While I thought I have been living in a make-believe world all these years, I have been schooling in theater workshops to know living theater all about us. So long as I have the energy to move about, I will enjoy observing people in the play of the moment, and I will see how as audience and as fellow player I affect the unfolding stories. I am thinking differently about myself now. I had come to feel that I was living a fable existence. Now I see that in absorbing myself in drama and theater I was being true to myself after all, that I have been living fully within my limits. Now I like my own story better, and I see how I can continue in the time that remains."

References:
Baum, L. Frank, *The Wizard of Oz*, Bobbs-Merrill, 1899, pp. 145-148.
Le Guin, Ursula Kroeber, *The Left Hand of Darkness*, Ace Science Fiction Books, NY, 1969, p. 147.
Rako, Susan and Harvey Mazer, (Eds.), *Semrad; The Heart of a Therapist*, Aronson, NY, 1980, p.5.
Zeig, Jeffrey (Ed.), *A Teaching Seminar with Milton Erickson*, Brunner\Mazel, NY, 1980, p. xxv.

PART II

THE THERAPUETIC PROCESS

4

RECOGNITION OF AND ATTENDING TO PERSONAE

My daughter, Judith Helen, is unusually adept at spotting needles in haystacks. Judi is a person who is available to what wants to be found! She advises me not to try so hard to find what I am looking for, rather, through scanning, to let what is before me come to my attention. Spotting personas calls for such an attitude. There is a paradoxical twist to the notion that to see clearly what is right in front of your nose, you do well to farfetch.

Farfetching characterizes my style of attending to the presence and play of personas appearing before my own eyes. And so I will do what I can to capture what I mean by a farfetching frame of mind.

The Psychotherapist as Farfetcher

Colleagues who report to me that they are engaging in personas work with their clients are finding their own ways, responsive to how their minds work and how each of their clients think, to engage in psychotherapy granting the existence of personas as integral to personality. Following are indications of my own mental process.

As appealing as a clearer and more linear account of the structure of Personae Theory and its application might prove, the structure and process are inseparable. I am mindful of Fritz Perls' observations that all thinking is fantasy; even highly precise scientific rational discourse is fantasy and, that some forms of fantasy are identified as more or less delightful nonsense while other forms are dignified as empirically sensible. The thoughts that follow defy linear, empirical presentation.

I am comforted by the first three paragraphs of Jeffrey Zeig's Introduction to his book, *A Teaching Seminar with Milton H. Erikson* (Zeig,1980):

> A friend of mine who is a Swiss physicist told me a story about the famous Danish physicist Neils Bohr. At a lecture, Dr. Bohr was discussing Heisenberg's Uncertainty Principle. This principle of 'complementarity' suggests that when an observer discovers information about the location of a particle, he sacrifices information about the momentum of that particle. Conversely when the observer discovers information about the momentum of a particle, he sacrifices information about location. At the lecture a student asked Bohr, 'What is complementary to clarity?' After a moment of thought Bohr replied, 'Precision.'
>
> Though possibly apocryphal, this anecdote expresses an important understanding. When it comes to truths, in order to be clear, it is necessary to be simplistic, thereby sacrificing precision; in order to be precise, it is necessary to be lengthy, detailed and perhaps confusing, thereby sacrificing clarity.

Following this line of thought, allow me to be precise in setting forth an operational definition of farfetching!

In the process of psychotherapy, I identify with Ursula Kroeber Le Guin's notion of farfetching. I perceive myself as a Farfetcher. Le Guin captures the essential features of farfetching in her book *The Left Hand of Darkness* (Le Guin, 1969). The intuitive perceptiveness she asserts as essential to functioning effectively as an Envoy from one world to a thoroughly alien culture on a far distant planet, I see as an essential capacity required in facilitating recognition of and therapy with personas. Here we have Le Guin's fictitious Envoy thinking about himself as a Farfetcher:

> This kind of rather highflown speculation is an essential part of my job. Without some capacity for it I could not have qualified as (an Envoy), and I received formal training in it (on my world), where they dignify it with the title of Farfetching. What one is after when farfetching might be described as the intuitive perception of (an)…entirety; and thus it tends to find expression not in rational symbols, but in metaphor.

This chapter identifies therapeutic objectives and the character and quality of minding I believe best suits discerning and engaging with personas.

Initial Steps and Process Objectives

People inadvertently introduce their personas. They may offer more than one side to a story or an issue. They may evidence ambivalence. I invite them to explore various contrasting thoughtful and feelingful reactions to whatever is before their attention, and in the course of this exploration ask them to see how their struggle is like two or more people at odds. Typically they themselves will tumble out with the confession that they indeed feel at odds within themselves. Now we are on our way into personas work.

Once in a while the introduction of this theoretical perspective and technique follows a more directed and inquiring course. I may ask my client to suppose that all the world is a stage and that one way each of us can understand what is happening to us is to identify scenes in which we have a part, and to describe what that part is and how we are playing it. I ask them how they were supposed to turn out, how significant persons in their life wanted them to develop. Then I ask them to think of scenes in which they feel happily at home and scenes that are distressing, perhaps dreadful. Now we take a close look at how they present themselves in these pleasant and unpleasant scenes, how they describe themselves as characters in these scenes, as playwrights describe each of the cast of characters at the beginning of published plays. We come out of this process with a list of *dramatis personae*, some of whom are copers, others thrivers, and still others playful.

As we identify scenes in which they cope well enough, perhaps very well, and scenes in which they struggle (or are in an awful struggle), we alert to principal audiences: present or phantom. We typically experience ourselves and behave according to the supposed reaction of audiences we keep in mind. The expression: "If my mother could only see me now" witnesses to the conscious realization of this. Thoughtful exploration reveals phantom, which is to say imagined, audiences that nonconsciously affect our experience of ourselves and our moves. I ask them in addition to identify the mentors and supportive compatriots they carry with them in their imagination.

An attending step in this exploration is to be alert to the salient and peripheral scenarios that compose the story complex of the client's life. This includes scenarios dictated by others and those that each client has invented for himself. In the former case we have been cast by others with errands to run, parts to fulfill. In the latter case we each have something to do with casting ourselves and defining the purpose and style of the part we are to fulfill.

For most clients beginning the process of psychotherapy, much of this material is nonconscious. Few of us are aware that our Self is a composite of discrete personas, selves more or less congenial, one with the other, and each deriving from critical scenes in which we have had a part. Everyday comments such as "I'm all mixed up inside," "I feel guilty about what I almost want to do, " I'm ambivalent," and "I am so different in different scenes" are as close as we often come to recognizing our composite selves.

Over the course of time I have found that clients introduce their personas without prompting. Figuratively speaking, I take snapshots of these personas as they emerge. This is an elaboration of Carl Rogers' mirroring technique. Instead of reflecting in the simplest fashion the key words and feeling posture offered by the client as he or she talks about life situations, I share responsively to what they are saying, the candid snapshots that develop in my mind's eye as I listen to and watch them. I assure them that every snapshot I develop is a projection on my part, and invite them to accept or reject the usefulness of my projections.

In building toward a mutual understanding of my role in the process, I suggest that my "developments" are more like those of a courtroom artist than photographer. About half way through a session with Val, she said how she is never happy. I asked her to think about this picture of herself alongside three others I had of her that same session as she talked about happy moments she'd enjoyed the previous week. This simple intervention moved Val to acknowledge: "Well, I can come from different places. A couple of minutes ago, I was forgetting that anything nice ever happens." From this awareness emerged an increasingly clear identification of and delineations among these "different sides," i.e., her personas.

A colleague's therapeutic style with Vietnam veterans applies as well to work with personas who continue to be stuck in unresolved existential predicaments. "After all the work I have been doing with Vietnam veterans I am now feeling that I am a veteran! I go with the guy to the Vietnam situation that has been haunting him. I do not protect us via the establishment and preservation of clear ego-boundaries. I journey with him. engage as active audience, joining him in his traumatic situation. Then, as he is actually there, he sees me there, an added person in his dream. Through this experience, he can walk out with me into the immediate here and now, the previously tormenting scene reframed. You see, so many vets see themselves still in Vietnam having never been able to extricate themselves from that scene. Now they walk into the event in which they are traumatized, and with supportive company find themselves able to walk away somewhat less tied to that place."

How this therapist works, how she walks with her Vietnam clients into their situation may come clearer with the help of the following awareness exercise that I introduced to a small group of graduate interns and their clinical supervisors. I invited the supervisors to suppose they were blind. Having enjoyed vision previously, they could now see with their mind's eyes. Each intern was instructed to take their supervisor on a "blind walk" through pure fantasy to an important place in the intern's life. The place might represent a pleasant or unpleasant piece of the intern's life experience. The intern was instructed to provide all necessary tactile, sound, sight, smell, and taste information to their "blind" companion so that their companion on the journey could be there as fully as possible. After the exercise was over and the companions compared impressions, time after time the leader reported finding that the one he had led was in the scene with him now. It also occurred that the blind follower experienced truly having been led to a special place and being with his guide.

Once the therapist has alerted to a snapshot exposure of a client's persona, he can invite the client as that persona to take the therapist on such a "blind walk."

Non-verbal gestures and odd voice inflections incongruent with the sense of the verbal message may evidence distinctly different messages from one or several personas. A familiar example occurs when one hears another say how everything is fine between the two of them and yet the speaker's fingers are drumming in a fashion that implies some resentment coming from some quarter, i.e., another place, another persona not being represented by the one speaking.

Noting shifting postures also aids identification of personas. Clients often explain that they struggle with an issue because they can come at it from very different places. If the therapist invites the person to "come at the issue" from a different chair for each "place," the client is very likely to strike markedly contrasting postural attitudes in different chairs. The employment of chairs, while useful, is not necessary. People shift spontaneously as they argue and wrangle with themselves and others. If the therapist is working with a person who is assuming for the moment the existential posture of vincular self alerting to and attempting to manage/direct/ prompt the play of various personas in a given scene, the therapist can foster the person's appreciation for how body postures greatly affect thinking and feeling. A slouched body tends to evoke slouched thinking and feeling. The point here is not to suppress personas through guarding selectively against the assumption of certain body postures. The idea is to foster awareness and exploration.

The process of persona exploration in the psychotherapeutic encounter involves:

—identifying each persona,
—identifying introjected compatriots, antagonists, and
   introjected audiences,

—externalizing each persona through costuming her or him and assigning each a chair in the therapeutic setting,

—facilitating the capacity of the subject to identify behaviors produced by each persona, as important issues and life situations are processed,

—developing appreciation of the assets and liabilities of each persona,

—increasing the capacity of personas to recognize their collusions with one another and the capacity to strive for problem-solving bargains,

—keeping ever alert to the subtle or swift "hit and run" emergence of latent personas,

—inspiring a gradual release of the subject from overly conscious preoccupation with problem-solving through contrived "group sessions" of personas, so that the subject can proceed in living informed and inspired by creatively productive cooperation between conscious and deep (unconscious) minding, and,

—through the introduction of hypnotic story, accessing deep (unconscious) and conscious assessment and reassessment of the story or stories inspiring and/or crippling the unfolding drama of a person's living.

Upon reading an early draft of this piece, my brother commented: "It appears that you use 'story' in a special way, that it means something other than many of us have in mind when we hear the word." My brother's prompting was helpful. Story wihin this context denotes and connotes something other than mere narrative account. It is different in kind than a narrative account *about* a person's or a people's epical experience. Sometimes I place an article such as "a" or "the" before the word "Story." At other times there is no article. "A story" is an artifact; "story" is process. My father told stories in class and before congregations adeptly illustrating instructive points, and since he intended instruction, this frame of mind conveyed itself to his audiences so that those in his audiences were keyed into seeking for his instructive points even as they enjoyed his stories. When, in contrast, I tell story, and as I intend the word "story" to mean within this context, story *is* the point. When I tell story, as I have story in mind in and of itself, my frame of mind conveys itself to audience, and audience is therefore keyed into engaging first and foremost in story, free on their own to derive instructive awareness from story. This process is in keeping with Milton Erickson's "utilization principle," which when applied strategically facilitates productive diss-assoication and re-associa- tion, leading to more life-enhancing life stories. (Gilligan, 1987)

With this framework and these components of personal explo- ration in mind, I invite the reader to check out his or her understanding of persona theory in psychotherapy through consideration of some case examples. Each case illustrates the identification of personas. The first account is rich in farfetching.

The Case of Ross and Florence

Ross and Florence sought psychotherapy to see if they could understand more clearly and come to terms with Ross's need to act on his gay desires. It soon became apparent to me that they loved one another very deeply. Ross is sexually attracted to Florence. He loves her and he likes her. He wants children with her, and looks to a life with her as his very best friend. Ross is also powerfully attracted to certain males. He insists that an emotional bond, a strong sense of mutual compatibility is essential before he can become interested in sexual intimacy with another man. He cannot imagine a male ever approaching the significance Florence has for his life. Ross cannot understand why Florence has to feel threatened by peripheral gay relationships. Florence feels that sexual intimacy is the most special and exclusive sharing a loving couple can have. The thought of Ross making love to another person, male or female, whether or not, but especially if, she knows it is going on frightens and infuriates her. Ross is frustrated that he cannot seem to get across to Florence that intimacy with a man is different in kind and quite aside from his experience with her. They came to therapy assuming that if they could not change one another's minds, they would have to separate.

The picture I've presented so far suggests that these two would probably be grimly unhappy as they met in therapy session. And yet, more times than not, I'd find them cuddled up together and joking in the waiting room. In session their demeanor toward one another has been featured by comraderie and many gestures of gentle, humorous affection punctuated by moments of hard, bitter, distressful difference. It is clear to me that they care very deeply for one another. I altogether believe them when they say they are one another's best friends in the world.

I find myself harkening back to the mid-nineteen sixties when I was employed jointly by the Unitarian Universalist Association of America and by that denomination's legally autonomous, continent-wide high school youth corporation. My principal assignment was to aid the youth and adult populations in overcoming intergenerational conflict, and to cultivate shared values. In consultation with Boston University's Human Relations Center, I designed a human relations protocol designed to facilitate among youth and adults clarification of their shared values. The successful introduction of this protocol in key settings across the United States and Canada confirmed our expectation that conflict in regard to specific differences can be resolved and/or managed most effectively when the parties have become clearly aware of the many areas in life where they share values. They tend to work effectively with one another when specific troubles arise. People who have a lot going for them in their relationship tend to solve problems because there are so many reasons for them to want to overcome difficulties.

There are situations in which difficulties between two parties can be brushed aside or isolated. I know of Sunday afternoon softball teams from neighboring villages who enjoy playing against one another every once in a while. There's a hitch. While the games tend to go very well, and the spirit runs high, not everyone on each team is buddy-buddy. About five players on each team are. Three on each team respect but are casual in their attitude toward members of the other team. One member of each team has a severe personality clash with a member of the other team. Because there's a modest amount of beer drinking, controls can become somewhat tenuous. Each season is marked by at least one nasty fight if the two cross one another. No big deal is made of it. They don't have to live together. Most everyone regrets the incidents. Efforts are made to keep these on a close leash. But this is Sunday afternoon softball and things will sometimes get out of hand. The fight is broken up and the game resumes. People tend to handle the situation by reminding themselves that some people just rub each other the wrong way and that's how it is sometimes.

We can't brush Florence and Ross's difficulty aside that easily. They want to live together. I engaged their attention hypnotically through telling them these stories about working with kids and their parents, and about the softball game incidents.

While Florence and Ross naturally wanted to reach a resolution to their impasse as quickly as possible, they became intrigued with my snapshots of some of each of their personas. I urged them to help one another develop an inventory of their various selves. They wrote letters to me with the results of their research; they spent some time alone and a great deal of time together on this project. Both reported that help from the other had proven of essential importance. Here is what each recorded. First, Ross:

Bobby: I am love and companionship. I will be very loving, tender, soft, and caring of you. I want to hold you, to know your every thought and movement, to touch and explore every inch of your physical and spiritual being. We don't have to say anything to each other; we just know. If something is wrong, I will hold you and comfort you. You can lean on me because I'm there for you. I will do anything for you. There are no restrictions to this relationship. We are so dedicated to one another that we can share anything and it is O.K. I trust you totally, and you trust me. I want to share everything with you. I feel at peace with myself, you, everyone and everything. I want to be in very close proximity to you, always wanting to touch. I am very aware of my sexuality, and am very aware of all sexuality around me. I can smell it, taste it, feel it, and hear it. I can uncover anything and feel safe.

Taurus: I am anger and rage. If you push, you'd better bet I'll push back harder, without regard to the consequence. If you piss me off, watch out. I'll give you so much shit you'll wish you were never born. God Damn it, you are going to pay through the nose for what you've done. You are going to be more than sorry; you will feel like shit. Fuck you, sucker! You stink! The hell I'm going to do what you want. I'm going to teach this whole world a lesson; look out for me. I feel rotten! You *are* going to listen to my every word and are going to do *everything* I tell you to do, you scum. I am going to teach you a lesson. You are wrong! Strength, power, endurance, cunning, and ruthlessness are my qualities. Keep away from me; get out of my way. I am just waiting for the attack. I am a loner; I don't need or want anyone in the way. I will dredge up anything and everything that I can to hold and use against you, and I will cut deep.

Beau: I am cool, really with it. I am cocky, sure of myself. The world is my stage. I am the most desirable, sexy, hunky piece of meat on the face of the earth. People don't know what they are missing here. I am physical! I want bodies, and bodies want me. I reek of sexuality. I'm not tender, but not rough either, just firm and strong. I need to be doing something physical: walking, running, hiking, driving, canoeing, swimming, waterskiing. I want to be in touch with the world, people, plants. I thrive in extreme environments: busy cities or malls, the back woods, hot days, but never cold. Never cold, I am dressed to kill. People turn their heads when I walk by. Feel that beat! Calypso! Very controlled.

Gary: I can't think; I can't cope. I am lost. I am scared and feeling helpless. I feel vulnerable and have no control over my environment. I feel as though I am not capable of thinking or taking care of the smallest, simplest task. I've emptied myself out, pulled down the walls, and am open for any and all shots, which, of course, will come down in torrents. I have no control. I have no control. I am drowning. I am falling, falling, falling, knowing that I will hit the bottom with crushing force, but I don't know when. I don't even know when it will end. Will it end? I am in panic, frozen in my tracks. *I can't do it. HELP!* I am slipping slowly but steadily down. Shit, I'm in for it. This is the end. ant so easily intimidated. Here I am. Walk on my face. You are going to anyway.

Jack: I am frustrated, listless, restless, unsatisfiable, impatient. I am alone, even with people. Nothing is right, nothing is good. Systems to the outside are shut down. I just want to sit and stare, not even thinking. I don't want to be dealt with. I am in a rut—a long, solid, deep rut. I don't want to think about it. I don't want to deal with it. I will put it off and it will get dealt with one way or another. I may even just go away.

Brett: I am the achiever. I go out there and do it! I have lots of motivation and energy. I can do anything. I'm a workaholic, a whirlwind. I just can't stop now. This is great! I knew you had it in you Ross! Do it for yourself. There is nothing I can't do. I just can't go fast enough. I am just looking for the next thing to do, the next challenge, the next project. I am so excited to see what I am doing or what I am getting done. So impressive, Ross! Look at what I am capable of doing. I have got it together, on my own!

(Quinton)* #7: I love the excitement of danger and the unknown. I love the terror involved with the possibility of not making it, wondering what would happen if . . . . My heart rate flies and my adrenalin is jumping. My eyes are wide and my fists are clenched. There is tension in the air. This is life. I am the adventurer. I am ready to take the chance, especially if I have no idea how it will turn out. I am ready for new experiences and adventures. I love feeling my blood ice cold in terror.

Jon: I am carefree, happy go lucky, and easy going. I do things to enjoy them. Going for a stroll arm in arm, or a nice easy horseback ride, or a lazy canoe ride is what I am all about. I'm confident, at ease, mellow, energetic but not bubbly. My head is not cluttered with lots of issues or thoughts. I take things as they come. I am quite relaxed. I am at my best with no limits, no appointments, and no commitments. I am at peace.

Daddy: I am paternal; I'll look out for you. I know what is best. Eat this, drink that, put this on, lie down, you'll be comfortable here. When things fall apart I'll be there to pick up the pieces and pull us through with comforting strength. You can count on me as being one with a useful idea; you will find me calm, cool, and collected. Don't worry, we'll find a way. I make sure everything is set and in order. I want kids to love.

*(Luke) * #10:* I want a man, a real, masculine feeling man. Male companionship is all I need. I long for the feel of a man in my arms. I need to spend my life with men. I don't need or want a woman anyway.

(Gavin) #11:* I want a woman; I need a woman. I love the touch of a woman, to hold her. I want to spend the rest of my life with a woman. I would throw up at the thought of being with a man.

Sebastian: I love music. Music is the most important, most moving, most beautiful thing in this world. I love being so creative when I conduct or sing in a good group.

*[Names assigned to personas in later sessions.]

According to Ross, Bobby gets along with his as yet unnamed numbers 10 and 11 as well as with Sebastian. Beau and number 10 are compatible, as are Taurus and number 7. Gary will follow Taurus. He concludes: "I would like to be Jon more than any of the others." By this, Ross does not mean that he wants to be Jon to the exclusion of all the others. He would like to see Jon provide the prevailing attitude that would foster reconciliation and creative rapport among all the personas.

I confess there is an inclination on my part to over-simplify material I am dealing with, to consolidate some of Ross's personas. I wondered if Bobby and number 11 were the same, if elements of Beau and number 7 belong to the same self, if Gary and Jack are one. I have learned to avoid giving way to this inclination.

Florence's personas are as follows:

Nana: nurtures, does not pamper, is ever patient like a good teacher, is calm, collected, can handle any emergency, can figure out how to do anything, is reassuring, always has an explanation, and will play with children.

Ida: pampers, gives back rubs even when she's sick, is dedicated to caring. Anytime at night she's always on call. No sacrifice is too great. If she is curled up contentedly with a book and the bell rings, she goes right to it putting all thoughts about self aside.

Suzie: Suzie's the kid excited over new places. She loves surprises, any unexpected treat. She'd love to skip through the Mall. Suzie loves trucks and train sets. She loves eating in the car or pizza on the coffee table. And she likes to be tossed around in the pool, tickled in bed. She jumps in puddles, wears long soft flowing skirts, soft knee socks, baggy sweaters. Suzie skips through the leaves and gets high on autumn, collects; stuffed animals, loves Christmas and birthdays. She plans surprises and can't keep secrets. She thinks she's immature but is adventurous. Suzie needs a Daddy.

Katherine [The Hun]: is headstrong, angry at the world. She is cutting. While scared and upset Katherine never shows it. She lashes out, gets the last word, the final cut. No one can match her fierceness. Every step is intentional. She's out to survive at all costs. Katherine doesn't need anyone. As far as she is concerned, everyone's stupid and slow. She has tunnel vision, only sees and hears what she wants to see and hear. She knows she is hurting someone and it hurts to do so, but she must survive. She has no control over herself but controls situations. She doesn't say she's sorry nor admits to missing things. Katherine is conniving.

Julia: likes love-making for highs. She is a career woman who wears skirts and suits. Julia wants an aggressive, self-assured hard man and to be passive with him. She also wears blazers. Julia can handle career, family, socializing.

She loves to make money. She's secure, responsible, orga-nized, a perfectionist, plans menus, keeps shopping lists and organizes parties. She likes to exercise, meets new people easily, is assertive without being too aggressive. She requires being respected as a woman.

Mourner: mourns the loss of lots of things. She cries easily drowning in woes and sorrows. She feels blue while Katherine lashes out. She's inconsolable. Mourner is con-stantly pre-menstrual with low thyroid. In her real insecurity she needs love-making to feel secure,

Butch: is the basketball player, the Jock. She's in a street gang, likes to be tough, to beat up people. Butch is from the city.

Eve: is feminine. She would have been a ballerina. Eve enjoys slow, sensual love-making. She polishes her toe-nails, wears jewelry and puts on eye shadow. Her message is: Treat me like a princess. Eve prefers passive men and passive women. She likes fairy tales.

Muffy: is HORNY. Muffy likes to fuck, suck, get down and roll in it. She wants to grab whatever looks good, wants extremely aggressive men and will be an equal match. She is fascinated by penises, wants to try all sizes and shapes, have them on call. Muffy wants two men.

This effort to identify personas proved costly. While excited by what was now open and clear to each of them about themselves and the other, they were exhausted. Florence's food intake controls collapsed and she experienced dramatic mood transformations. Ross became very ill with intestinal disturbance, bronchial conges-tion, and fever sores. It was transparently clear to him that with this naming, pandemonium had broken loose within, that his personas were feverishly congested and disturbed. As for Florence, she was very unhappy with her own conclusion that virtually all her attack upon Ross was concentrated through Katherine.

Ross and Florence were frightened by these ramifications and also sufficiently intrigued by the conscious discovery of their personas to set a moratorium on their direct campaigning against one another in regard to the business of Ross's acting on his gay desires. While both remained adamant as to their positions, each was discovering that his/her reasoning was not as uncomplicated as he/she supposed when they entered into therapy. Ross's feeling and understanding of his commitment to Florence and his responsiveness to her sensibilities were greatly deepened with his grasp of his own personas. As for Florence, bringing Muffy out into the open compromised the unambiguous and unambivalent line we were getting from her Katherine. As valuable as it seemed for Florence to recognize Katherine's protecting strength and directness as her manageable measure, Florence found herself frankly averse to the idea of Katherine acting out unbridled. Florence now saw clearly that granting Katherine free rein would involve an unrelenting striking out at Ross, an unfaltering commitment to triumph over Ross's gay agenda. What if victory included divorce! Thanks to Katherine! This prospect gave Florence pause.

Having agreed to a truce, we turned to other issues. The two most critical areas of concern for both Florence and Ross were their current overloaded day-to-day schedules and the matter of furthering each of their careers: Ross in the arts and Florence as a business entrepreneur.

Wrestling with male and female role orientations concerning domestic activities proceeded with inch-by-inch success. Resentment deriving from confusion and clumsiness in this area exacerbated the more central issue.

Each of their work and activity schedules was so crowded that they had only a few hours a week free to be together. They were hard pressed to find further time for each other as their outside work activities were essential to maintaining their hopes of career survival. Short one year of study for his graduate degree in music, and given the generally poor economic picture, Ross had to settle for a job long on hours and short on pay. A part-time position in music also paid little for the satisfaction it produced. He and Florence figured at least two years would be necessary to meet outstanding debts before Ross could continue his studies. Florence's career advancement would have to wait longer than that. All in all, their situation fostered frustration and a sense of being blocked short of productive satisfaction in their careers. I share Abraham Maslow's conviction that persons very strongly identified with the arts become ill when their exposure to and participation in the arts is severely limited. I have found it tempting to assume that Ross's career frustration has deeply affected his sense of existential well being beyond obvious and conventional security, affiliation, and self-esteem needs.

Mindful of the impressive spirit of comraderie and obvious devotion Ross displays toward Florence, I could not understand how his gay persona managed to outweigh the influence of most of his other personas. Because his gay inclinations trace back before his relationship with Florence, we found it obvious to assume that his gay persona was never invested in this relationship, indeed never included himself in the marriage ritual. When he is being his gay self, when he is addressing himself to Florence from the heart and desires of his gay self, warmth and playfulness with Florence are totally absent. At such times he is unmoved by gestures from any of her personas. When she appeals to him to set aside his gay agenda in behalf of his love for her, he answers that because she does not experience herself as bisexual, there is no way she can appreciate what she is asking of him.

Her appeal suggested the notion that personas would join in group decision in a democratic fashion in which the outvoted minority would honor the administration and program of the majority. Ross's reaction furthered the notion that his gay self never identified with a heterosexually oriented self government.

While I honor the claim by gays that their needs are compelling, and recognize the plausibility of the notion that part of Ross never consented to the oaths of wedlock, not to mention joining in the spirit of wedlock with Florence, I found myself perplexed over the apparent magnitude of the power Ross's gay self held in relation to his other personas.

In session with Florence and Ross I awakened to a realization and recollection: that Ross's gay persona remains unnamed, and that members of a majority often invest covertly in the power and pursuits of members of a minority. Remaining unnamed sometimes carries certain advantages. Also, if someone in the neighborhood can, with a little help on the side, win in some way, why not slip him a hand; there's vicarious pleasure in victory won somewhere nearby.

I recalled my research of McCarthyism. In 1958 I attended an advanced seminar in sociology at the London School of Economics and Political Science. One of my assignments was to analyze McCarthyism from functional-structural and Marxist sociological theoretical points of view. I was amazed to discover how frequently covert wheeling and dealing occurs among otherwise strange "bedfellows." Senator Joseph McCarthy's Congressional Subcommittee on Un-American Activities sought evidence of Communist infiltration throughout American life. This search was apparently supported by otherwise antagonistic public figures and population elements. This support was frequently covert. Washington D.C. friends have in more recent years impressed upon me that political sides are rarely drawn clearly and with mutual exclusivity. It occurs from time to time that the prim and proper subtly prompt the so-called "black sheep" to act-out. The one who for all intents and purposes appears to be the maverick hold-out is invested in that role by members of the vast majority who, in spite of their protestations, derive some kind of vicarious gratification from the maverick's objectionable behavior. Mutually incompatible American sub-populations proved confederates in overt or covert allegiance through McCarthy against "communist conspiracy." The amorphous words "Communist" and "unamerican" represented variously identified forces threatening the self interests of unlikely confederates. With this perspective in mind, it is possible to explain how one persona can manage to prevail over all the others in the process of important decision making by the collective person.

My thinking continued along a related line. Teachers assigning students to desks according to alphabetical order, can at a glance at the seating chart, identify each student. Then, when they have command of each student by name, they can relax the seating plan. Heaven help the teacher of a rowdy crew if he or she has not the power of naming! While control requires considerably more than command of names, without names control is shaky, to say the least. Mindful that Ross's gay persona deserves full dignity and fair treatment, it remains that integrated decision making by Ross requires constructive control, more likely to emerge if his most critically significant selves are known by name. While we do not have to know one another's names to share *communitas*, that is, pure I-Thou encounter, to live together in community we must each invest a portion of our personal power in common wealth and common governance. For this, we do well to know one another's names.

Recalling how, in so many ways, apparent antagonists covertly support one another, I began to question how one or another of Ross's heterosexually committed personas might conceivably invest in his gay persona's power and program. For beginners: Sebastian came to mind immediately. How long Sebastian must wait to enjoy anything approaching rich gratification. He would surely be susceptible to putting some bucks on a favorite; investing in the gay persona could provide vicarious need satisfaction. It is tempting to see how Taurus would react in support of another whose designs are being thwarted. Macho-man Beau is bi-sexual and so can support pure gay interests. And Jack, so bent on achieving for the sake of achieving, stirred by challenge, is someone to look at, too, for more than a token contribution.

At the time I am writing, I continue my work with Florence and Ross as I puzzle in writing about their case. The immediacy involved in committing my best guesses to paper often times proves anxiety arousing as I know full well that in the next session with them my fantasies in their regard, the story that has been taking shape in my mind serving to offer rhyme and reason to their situation, may be thrown into radical question.

I am writing in mid process with Florence and Ross. I have contracted with them from the outset to pay attention to their stories and to how I experience them each and together working in behalf of their interests, concerns, and problems. I have been observing them carefully and sharing impressions. I take snapshots of them and show them my developments. Out of this have emerged farfetching ideas as to who each of them is and what each of their apparent selves, each of their personas, represents. It becomes very tempting for me to want certain developments to occur. When an individual, a couple, group, community, or people are suffering, we are sorely tempted to imagine a story outcome including the resolution of suffering. Farfetching psychotherapists do well to watch carefully against imposing in crude or subtle form their wishful thinking upon the people with whom they are working. I do not know and I do well to avoid needing too much to know what Florence and Ross will do next.

So far they appear to have recognized themselves in terms of personas. Further, they share with me a sense of the validity of the farfetched notion that several of Ross's non-gay committed personas might very understandably invest covertly in his gay persona's agenda. They are also alert to how Florence's personas are remarkably disparate in their interests and styles. They see how the dynamics among her personas affect the dynamics between the two of them as a couple!

My purpose here, rather than tracing a case throughout its course, has been to acknowledge the play of farfetching intuitive perceptiveness as story invention in the process of psychotherapy.

As addendum, one day Ross volunteered that his gay persona wants to be called Luke. He added that Sebastian has been feeling much encouraged over the possibility of a major new opportunity that could broaden and deepen his work in music.

One day in session I stumbled into referring to him as Quinton, the pseudonym I had chosen for him in my first draft. The name Quinton created a considerable effect upon him. He and Florence looked at one another in astonishment. The name Quinton had great significance for both of them. "Why that's my persona number seven's obvious name. Quinton! I am Quinton! I love the excitement of danger and the unknown. Quinton is not a farfetched name at all. Thank you for picking up on who I am. Use Ross as my pseudonym."

Now the matter of his persona number eleven, his unambiguously heterosexual persona interested him. "He's not as prominent as Luke; he doesn't have the strong longing Luke has. He's foggy, difficult to get to know. He seems to be fading; he is not as strong now as how I initially knew him. He is what and how I used to think I was supposed to be. Now that I feel Luke is O.K. this adamantly heterosexual, non public persona is fading. And Gavin fits as the name for this persona, number eleven. Gavin's my middle name, my legal name, the name that was given to me by my parents for my legitimacy."

Florence and Ross have suspended psychotherapy sessions for the time being. When we began working, each of them required swift resolution to their struggle. with so much more to each of them than Luke and Katherine, they are apparently more tolerant of stress and uncertainty, even less threatened by separation. They have their smooth and rough spells. How their story will resolve remains to be seen.

To Whom It May Concern: Cleaning Up the Act in Progress

Vincular or meta self-consciousness includes being alert to which persona at any given moment is playing lead role in the dramatic situation of the moment, and how that persona is being received by the other personas and external audiences. In this capacity, the vincular self is functioning in much the same manner as the theater director in rehearsal. She or he brings to the attention of the player and cast observations and questions that are intended to increase the effectiveness of the performance.

If you have very clearly in mind to whom you are addressing yourself, this is to say that you have done your homework carefully and know your audience, then the chances are pretty good that you will make and keep a connection with them. Some years ago I observed Viennese psychiatrist, Viktor Frankl modeling this discipline. I served as his day-to-day companion while he addressed a number of groups in the Boston and Cambridge neighborhoods. It was important for him that we use the time available between engagements to review with me how he had done with each group. While he was sensitive to whether he appeared in a good light, more important to him was whether I thought he had been in touch with his audience, whether I thought he had been experienced by each group as having related to them as persons and to their interests. After reviewing how he had just done, we then turned our attention to orienting him in preparation for a contactful encounter with the next group he was to address.

Another incident comes to mind that illustrates becoming contactfully alert. I had prepared long and hard before leading a Gestalt workshop at a conference on the Isles of Shoals one summer week in 1974. The assigned focus was "A Gestalt Approach to Profound Loss and Personal Transformation." Having just completed the first draft of an essay on the subject and having just come from a semester conducting an academic seminar featuring this theme, I had a carefully preconceived map in hand that was to guide our morning hours together. At the close of the first morning session a gentleman in his late sixties approached me and said: "Well, Peter, it looks to me as if you are going to have a very good week. You have prepared carefully; everyone should value their time with you. By the way, I'll not be coming back tomorrow morning; I think I will do some water color painting by the side of the sea." What he said and his manner nudged me off balance. I asked him: "If you think this is going to be a valuable workshop, why aren't you returning?" He didn't respond to me directly. "I have a suggestion for you, Peter. Take your manuscript from which you have been drawing from time to time, and take your outline map indicating the step by step plans you have for the group, and place them in the bottom of your suitcase. Don't look at any of your materials before you file them away. You have prepared carefully. Trust the preparation and join the group. All your careful thinking and writing will serve you well during the week in ways you might not anticipate at this point." I followed his advice though it was hard for me to wrench myself away from my cherished writing and plans. His advice served me and the group well. All my wits were not located on paper! As he anticipated, I participated both as facilitator and person, open to the needs and responses of my "audience."

Writing letters of reference can be a chore. Not so when it comes to prized graduate students! I told Frankie Henry that I was glad to compose a letter for her files. My persona Tom likes to keep my desk tidy and paperwork up to date. Unbridled, he runs my life as an obsessive compulsive. Responding to Frankie's request right away, I composed a letter. But something about the manner of the letter moved me to set it aside overnight. When I looked at it the next morning I saw very clearly what I didn't like about it. My persona Alan's influence upon the style proved too prominent. I have named that persona Alan after a distinguished clergyman who visited my childhood home when he came to Phillips Andover to preach before the student body at Sunday Chapel. As important a man as he certainly was considered to be in the eyes of his prestigious church and in the estimate of many people because of his leadership in behalf of social justice in our land, he proved to those of us who knew him reasonably well to be rather too pleased with his remarkable command of form. I will never forget the Sunday dinner when my mother asked him to say grace. He invited us to join him in thanks. He then performed a remarkable recitation in Latin. His manner prompted my mischievous, non-conforming Emily (alias Rascal, Lad, and Pan) to refrain from keeping my head bowed. Hence, I saw the little smile of self congratulation on his face as he performed. Despite my impatience with Alan when he runs unbridled, I have been well schooled in proper form and am grateful for how well I am versed in social and organizational protocol. Here is Alan's version of my letter recommending Frankie:

> To Whom it May Concern:
> Ms. Frankie Henry has asked me to write a letter of recommendation based on my experience of her in classes at Antioch New England Graduate School. She pursued three courses of study in Professional psychology under my instruction. I have more than ample basis for commenting on her scholarly and personal manner.
> It is my style as an instructor to prompt students in class, through weekly and major semester papers, to integrate personal experience, theoretical reflection, and clinical application in connection with course issues.
> I have now been instructing on the graduate level at Tufts University, the University of Chicago, and currently at Antioch New England for seventeen years. A few students stand out as exceptional in their capacity to command a high level of scholarly excellence, to apply theoretical concepts to experiential data aptly, and to demonstrate exceptional knowledge of themselves as persons. Frankie Henry numbers among these few. She presents and applies concepts with unusual dramatic creativity.
> Further, Frankie is a person who is not shy about engaging with colleagues in frank exploration of matters affecting human dignities and group morale. That her Antioch classmates have identified her as their principal class leader speaks to this point.

I am pleased to commend her to you.

Respectfully,
Peter A. Baldwin, Ph.D.

After I had finished this letter, I wrote Frankie a personal note I intended to enclose with the formal letter. In my personal note to her I asked her to let me know if what I had written was okay. I guess I must have been wondering if it was okay. That slight uneasiness nudged me into wondering about the style, to sleep over it before posting it. I imagined Frankie reading it, and, in thinking about her reading it I got in touch with her personally, and hence with myself more fully. Now more of my personas must have raised questions! The upshot was that I found myself sure that Frankie upon reading what I had written about her would question whether the letter had been written by the same Peter Baldwin she knew in class. All this was enough to move me to rewrite her letter of reference. Here is the second draft:

To Whom It May Concern:
    Ms. Frankie Henry has asked me to write a letter of recommendation based on my experience of her in classes at Antioch New England Graduate School. She was in three courses that I offered. I know her work well.
    I ask students in class discussion, through weekly and major semester papers to do the best they can to integrate personal experience, theory, and clinical data in connection with course issues.
    Frankie stands along with my best students over many years teaching at three universities. She writes exceptionally well; she speaks clearly and to the issue. She is very creative.
    Further, Frankie is direct in her dealing with group and community issues. That her classmates recognized her as one of their principal leaders bears this out.
    I am pleased to recommend her to you.

Respectfully,
Peter A. Baldwin, Ph.D.

The audiences before whom we perform communicate by their verbal and nonverbal responses whether we are in touch with one another. If it looks like we are losing an audience, we check out with ourselves where we are coming from, and can check out with the audience whether our losing them is because of the subject matter or because of our personal manner. If it is our personal manner, we can attend to our own personas dynamics, that is to say, get our act together! In the case of my first draft letter for Frankie it became clear to me that one of my personas while representing himself clearly was not "speaking" in behalf of the me that Frankie was seeking. This account demonstrates how we can interact with a phantom (imagined) audience in much the same fashion that we make and sustain interaction with a physically present audience.

One Persona May Not Speak for the Others

Some people are characteristically quicker than others to voice an opinion. The same can happen among personas. Competent discussion leaders take care to aid participants prone to mulling issues over in their minds to get their chance to speak. Without such aid some group members can remain silent so that not all parties are heard. Sometimes the result is a building up of resentment on the part of those who feel they are not getting their fair chance.

Bitter arguments among people spring from their becoming confused over how others contradict themselves, shift positions, and deny what they have previously said. Sometimes the first thing one person says at the outset of an argument represents the position of a persona who by style is "quick to draw." Then, as the exchange becomes more heated, other personas join in and confusion mounts. When two people sorting out a tough issue can perceive the exchange in terms of two groups in encounter, they prove much more open to the play of ambivalence, ambiguity, and contradiction in the interaction.

An example may make this clearer. Clients in couples therapy, Donald and Alice, arrived for their session directly following an Akido class. Alice had gone to Akido for the first time with and at the urging of Donald. He was disappointed and angry because he assumed from her demeanor throughout Akido that she hadn't liked any part of it. When Donald reacted to Alice's sour demeanor, he got more sourness and concluded that was the long and short of her opinion of Akido. Alice then appealed to Donald not to believe that she was unhappy with her experience, that on the contrary, she found Akido a good experience well worth returning to. When Donald realized Alice's nonverbal demeanor did not represent her overall view of Akido and that what appeared to him as sourness was, in fact, a defensive characteristic of Alice's agoraphobic persona, he calmed and welcomed comments from Alice's other personas.

Personae Manifestly Present and Accountable, Others Latently Present Though Discernable

Some scenes engage only one or a portion of the cast. This occurs in legitimate theater and in everyday life. Wherever one observes ambivalence in another person, one can infer that antagonism is occurring among two or more personas behind the scenes. It is commonplace to witness another's internal debate. When one hears another punctuate a sentence with the word "but" or move into a new attitudinal posture with an "on the other hand," there are two or more personas engaged in discussion. Not every persona is necessarily present and engaged! Some may be temporarily out of the picture...... beyond seeing and hearing. Some may have stepped aside to facilitate an encounter between others.

Joseph complained with considerable anger over his lover's refusing to tell him why she was weeping. "I asked her how come she was crying. She said she didn't know why. I didn't believe her. I believe she was withholding from me. How can a person weep and not know how come? She lied to me." I suggested to Joe that while I could not know whether or not she was deliberately withholding from him, it was possible that she did not in fact know where the crying was coming from, that we are all of us only conscious of a very small portion of what is happening within us.

My business of the moment with Joseph was to open to him awareness of an alternative to his judgment that his friend was lying. I suggested to him that she herself might not know what was transpiring on her inner stage; that the "players" with whom he was currently engaged were not consciously aware of what was happening "behind the scenes."

One of the purposes of insight oriented psychotherapy is to render conscious some of what is transpiring within our inner theater in order to engage in referee intervention, values clarification, conflict resolution, coaching, and script re-writing work. Once this intervention activity is completed one can suspend one's effort at conscious attention. Conscious thinking while useful in deliberate problem solving tends to inhibit creative spontaneity.

Most everyone upon occasion has met with the consternation of others when he asks what he supposes to be an innocent request to know what the others have decided about something. The others respond with something like, "What on earth! You have been right here while we have talked it all out and come to a decision! Where have you been?" Of course the answer is that one may have been *behaving* attentively yet all the time "wool gathering." This is to say one may have vacated his or her mind, suspended inner dialogue, or have been imagining themselves in another scene. If a person cannot account for where he or she has been, then it may be that the person has experienced a mini fugue state. (This is to say a short "spell" of amnesia.) That the person was not present and accounted for can be put in another way: "I must have been off stage while all that was taking place; I must have been back stage or out to lunch."

For some months in therapy, Jack had been focusing upon week-to-week situations in terms of the several personas we had thus far uncovered. An initial period of enthusiasm over his selves-discovery and his newly developed success in solving problems was now intruded upon by an acute depression. He returned to therapy each week for several weeks despondent over how gloomy everything felt to him. Finally, and as a surprise to himself, he suddenly blurted anger toward me: "You simply do not understand. You don't understand anything. Nobody understands and nobody cares." I was struck over his demeanor. His appearance was that of a six year old and his voice seemed very young. We had available snapshot and formal photographs of him taken throughout his life. (When photos are not in fact available I ask clients to retrieve old snaps in their mind's eye. Most people manage this task with ease.) I asked Jack which snap he felt closest to right then. Picking through photographs spread out on the floor, he leaped at the sight of one taken of him at his birthday party at age six. He then proceeded to gain conscious access to a persona that had evaded our search thus far. As he permitted himself to become absorbed in this old character, as he gave this persona space and support to come forward, and as I talked with this six year old in a grown man's body, it became apparent that while this six year old persona knew something about what had transpired in therapy over the months before his emergence, absent from the knowing was a sense of immediate participation. And so, in Jack's personas group work, other personas shared with the six year old what had been going on. And he gradually developed the willingness and sense of security to discharge his grief and anger. Our group sessions came to assume the character of a no-nonsense encounter group as Jack's personas forged understandings and agreements.

When an Elder is Chronologically Younger

Many years ago I worked with a client who reported that as long as she could remember she felt that her younger sister was her big sister. She couldn't shake the sense that this chronologically younger sister was older than she. She finally pieced together an explanation that made sense to her. She acted on her insight with both sister and parents. The result was that longstanding issues became resolved among them all, and she was able to accept her sister's desire for her to own being the elder of the two. She was born when her father was overseas in the second world war. The stresses between mother and father were pronounced enough upon his return that they separated for a year. Her chronologically younger sister was conceived and born when the parents had come together again in a renewed and deeper attitude of love and care. My client associated her sister with the true beginning of love between the parents. She supposed that in a sense she had died with the death of her parent's initial relationship. Now that there was a family again and a child born out of that love, she could now rejoin the family as a new sibling. The loving atmosphere being contingent upon the birth of a child, my client looked to her sister, that child, as the one who came before her.

A similar impression can occur in an individual's perception of her personas. Thirty-year-old Nancy recalls having been asked by her grandmother as a small child if she was being hurt at home. She cannot, in fact, recall abuse episodes. When, however, time-regression is induced in therapy, she experiences herself as about four years old and enters into a nearly mute and traumatized condition. Within herself she hears a small child's imploring cries for help. Here we have her experiencing herself as her very small, very young, frightened, mute, and crying-for-help-four-year-old persona. Nancy has come to recognize how as a grown women, under certain circumstances, she is taken over by this child self. In dramaturgical language, the once-upon-a-time child of three, four and five in "real" life years ago is now a persona who occasionally commands the stage as the principle actress of the moment. Nancy's story about how life was for her when she was about ten years old has a remarkably different character about it. She recalls having been very happy functioning as big sister and babysitter for about eight other children including her elder brother, younger sister, some cousins and a couple of foster siblings. Her ten year old self, now established as a persona, disclaims having been abused; this self talks confidently of not having been around when the awful things occurred to Nancy at three, four, and five. This persona, while the elder phenomenologically, is actually younger in seniority within the chronology of Nancy's personal history.

Identifying Another's Personae as Part of Coming to Terms with Them

My client Betty said that while she had been divorced for more than two years, she still felt married. She had great difficulty in resolving her attachment to her husband even while she felt cruelly abandoned by him. Her account of her relationship with her father suggested she would have a great difficulty separating emotionally from her ex-husband until she resolved issues relating to her father. Considerably into therapy, Betty was able to face the fact that she was not divorced, that she had filed for a divorce but had not authorized her attorney to submit final papers to the court. Betty looked closer and closer at her relationship with her father each time with greater depth and specificity. Two years into therapy and two weeks before her father's sudden death, Betty faced the facts f his sexual abuse of her as a child and an incident in more recent years when her father attempted to impose upon her an explicitly romantic kiss.

With her anger toward him focused and sharp, she attempted to simulate a confrontation with him in therapy. She began by trying to imagine his presence in a spare chair. I asked her if she could see how he was dressed. She saw immediately, began to detail what her father had on, and then it occurred to her that there was a second, and then a third, way in which she saw him dressed. This led to her seeing him in three separate chairs dressed appropriately as three sides of his personality, each different from the others. Each "side" she saw as a separate persona, each embodying and recalling for Betty different experiences and associations. The three personas Betty discerned in the chairs were: (1) the unhesitatingly "Let's do it" sexual imposition initiator; (2) a sleazy "Who me? I don't know what you are talking about" escape artist; and (3) an intellectually rational and removed "I wasn't present" and "Anyway, you are older now and don't need to be afraid" personage, who by character separates himself from the nitty gritty. This one dwells at a high level of facts, is a Justice judging others and washing his hands.

At her next session, one week before her father's sudden death, Betty reviewed the previous week's experience of her father as three personas and her beginning work with each around issues of molestation and abandonment. She introduced the information that on the occasion of his heart attack some years before she was not notified of his condition for ten days. She added that she had not been informed of her younger brother's death until after his cremation several years ago. The rest of this session was devoted to issues concerning intimacy and abandonment. Her father died the day after this session. His interment took place the next week on the day we customarily met.

When I saw Betty two weeks after her father's death she expressed great relief over having broken through and into the fundamental facts of her relationship with her father. She felt as if, through the simulated encounter with her father in therapy, she had come to sufficient terms with him so that she was released from silence just in time. The abandonment that is so often suffered whenever a parent dies was eased for her having cleared the compound wound of being previously abandoned.

In this session she re-engaged in her simulated encounter with her father. She visualized the three she had identified previously. Suddenly and deeply moved by powerful feelings of tenderness toward him, she found herself unable to assign these feelings to any of the three. Now she envisioned a fourth persona sitting considerably apart from the first three. To this one, whose dress and deportment and demeanor were so in contrast with any of the others, she poured out her tender love. In relation to this one she associated a whole body of memories which she shared with him. Betty, recognizing and re-membering her father, bought for herself the first stuffed rabbit she has had since early childhood. She wept.

At her next therapy session, Betty continued her work in connection with her father and discerned from her experience of him two further personas: (1) his hypochondriacal self, whose clothing featured a pink shirt, the pink capturing his little boy "poor me" attitude; and (2) his melancholy "Life isn't supposed to be fun or happy" side. This persona she dressed in a green shirt capturing a ready envy toward anyone who appears happy. These two do not lend to being reduced to one personality though they do reinforce one another. Now Betty had before her in her mind's eye six images of her father that served to aid her in sorting out the ambiguities, incongruences, and ambivalences defining her previously felt snarl and confusion around him. Whereas before, she had a confusing mess of snapshots of her father, which defied being sorted out in any kind of rhyme or reason save chronologically (which sometimes makes no sense at all!), now she could assign them to separate albums as many of us arrange albums for each child in a family.

In this last session in therapy, Betty concluded, "I am feeling a lot more centered, secure, like sitting on somebody's good lap."

This story of some of Betty's work illustrates one person doing another person's work, not for the other person, but rather, for one's self, separating out another person's pieces in order to make peace with them and to recognize and acknowledge the positive assets characteristic of one's other personas.

Betty sees how, after finally realizing a clear enough sense of her own personal story and realizing sufficient separation and individuation from her parents, she is beginning to live in a grown-up way. Previously, she had lived for the most part letting things happen, re-enacting with one person after another the dependency and counter-dependency characterizing her childhood relationship with her parents. Now she is facing the truth of her sexual seduction by her father, as well as her mother's consistently turning her attention away from what was happening. Part of Betty's resistance to seeing her father's actions for what they were was because these sexual abuses were so hard for her to believe, so out of character with how she experienced her father when he was with her as his loving, respecting, tender, trustworthy non-abusing persona self. In seeing him as multi-dimensional, she is able to deal with the incongruities and contradictions.

Reference:
Gilligan, Stephen, *Therapeutic Trances; The Cooperation Principle in Ericksonian Hypnotherapy*, Bruner\Mazel, 1987, pp. 211-220

5

OBSERVING INTER-PERSONAL DYNAMICS

T he following cameo presentations illustrate a number of ways in which personas interact with one another. These cases depict a facilitation of conflict resolution among personas resulting in the person as a whole functioning more effectively in solving problems and in engaging productively in the existential moment.

One Persona Up-staging All the Others

I sing folk songs and accompany myself on the guitar. At best, all my personas are absorbed together in harmonious cooperation: Allen, who is a master of good public form takes charge of my appearance and manner. Tom, who must get everything right has all the words and music down pat. Petee, who is my little child, lends simple spirit. Bagweed, who is poignantly aware of pain and sorrow, and failure, adds humility. Harry, who in a manner of speaking packs a side gun and takes shit from nobody, contributes a hardness and ruthlessness where called for. Jacquie adds soul. Lad, alias Rascal and Emily, provide panesque mischief. David, who out of love of the out of doors would have had me become a forest ranger, inspires earthy texture. Pete, who never thought about anything more than just enjoying things with others and being part of the gang, offers charm and enthusiasm. George, who sprang like Athena out of dyslexic struggling into being creative minding, lends healing and enabling thoughtfulness; and so forth. There are four-teen of me at present count. Susan is my singer! While I see now how she was being fostered throughout my childhood, she came out into the open when I was eighteen. She got the name of celebrated concert folksinger Susan Reid, to whose Celebrity Series concert my parents took me one evening. The following day marks the beginning of Susan's enormous outlay of delighted energy in gaining command of scores upon scores of folk songs as well as a story involving one guitar after another. Susan keeps a mental scrapbook of all her concerts and Folk World friends.

Some years ago I attended a concert by Tom Rush. Following the concert I had a chance to meet and speak with Tom. The pity of it is that face to face with him, Susan was upstaged by Pete who goofed around in an anxious adolescent way trying too hard to be recognized and liked by Tom Rush. If I had gotten myself together as Peter, my integrated Self, all of my personas would have had a part in meeting Tom Rush. Moreover, I would have surely intro-duced my wife, Carolyn, who was standing right beside me, to Tom. As Pete, out-of-hand into adolescent nervousness, I was oblivious to Carolyn's presence and, hence, neglected meeting Tom Rush with her. Actually, neither of us met Tom Rush. That's the pity!

Personas Distract, Dissemble and Distort

"I cannot understand how I could have misunderstood you so peculiarly." I suppose the answer to this is that when someone is talking to me I may be all ears, or only hearing with the ears of the persona playing skeleton crew while the rest of the crew is off duty. I'm learning that when I get into trouble with someone for how I took what they said, I better ask them to tell me again what they wanted me to hear in order to be sure I really get a chance to hear with reasonable accuracy. When I'm distracted by other business or the person talking to me is a threat in some manner or another, the accuracy of my attending to what I hear diminishes. Confusion in registering what comes my way can be likened to group attentiveness. If the group is very together and unthreatened, the tendency is for all ears to hear and construe what they hear with reasonable similarity. If, on the other hand, the stress level is high and there's distress among the members, each is likely to hear with varying forms of selective attention and inattention. What's more, each will construe what they attend to differently. Hence, the one who, in the example, is disconcerted with how she so peculiarly misunderstood the other was probably not attentive, and "got the word" through another persona who was threatened or distracted and therefore distorted what was said.

When this sort of thing comes up in session I invite clients to check out each of their personas to determine what is at stake for each in relation to the story being told. The findings are illuminating and instructive. I encourage clients to accustom themselves to checking out which personas are most actively engaged in each situation we are considering.

The Composer Who Does Not Compose

In some cases, one persona will "steal" the name or image or credit from another. Perhaps this persona envies the other's talent or facility in social situations. Or perhaps this persona longs for the spotlight but fears his ability to merit "applause," and, thus takes on the identity of another.

I asked client Terry the name of the persona who was most singularly prominent in his composing of music. "Not Composer," responded Terry. "Composer is preoccupied with wondering if others are thinking of him as a composer. Composer flatters himself that others think well of him for his musical compositions. But Composer is never at all helpful in the composing. He is forever in the way worrying what people will think. I haven't a name yet for the one through whom the music comes."

Sculpting

Family therapists sometimes engage families in constructing family sculptures. This amounts to inviting one family member after another to envision and then arrange family members in a tableau that captures part of the story or one of the stories of the family interaction. I am struck with how aptly my eldest daughter accurately captured a principal difficulty troubling our family. She observed that while some families deserve family therapy because family members are so scattered that they need to be helped to secure some closeness and shared involvement, our family suffers from being too intimately crowded one upon the other. When our family therapist invited one of the younger children to sculpt the family, she placed us all together at the dining table that extended from our A-frame roof. There we all were: too crowded around a table too small for us. Our therapist prescribed that everyone in the family help build the table bigger. We did, and the result was aesthetically pleasing and interpersonally liberating. Now we had elbow room and private space. Inspired by this paradigm, we payed attention to other ways in which we could allow for increased Personal space.

My client Liz identified six personas constituting her working personality. During one session she grieved over how she had managed herself at her attorney's office some weeks previously when she broached with him the prospect of filing for divorce. She was scheduled to see him again this week and did not want to because she feared she would repeat what she described as her folding and slobbering act. She began the rehearsal for this next appointment by claiming a minute or two to gather her thoughts. This was a good line as it would surely be respected as normal and reasonable. Then, during this minute or two she situated her six personas about the attorney's office so that her most vulnerable personas would be "under the wing" of stronger personas with whom she had direct eye contact. With the quick-to-rage Cathy attending to no-more-smiles to-please, and-I'm-on-a-sitdown-strike Denise, with undaunted Bella Abzug-like Jane keeping an eye on sensible and practical Eve; with free spirit and life-is-into-love-and-fun Lilyth cradling hurting and terrified Julie; and, with quick-to-take-leave-of-absences Abbie placed where she could not slip away; Liz sat before the attorney as "meta-selves" vincular Self rehearsed at conducting business with the law. When she went to her lawyer's office later in the week she acted on what she had rehearsed in the therapy session and felt good about how she fared. Through personas sculpture she discovered a means by which she could manage with her personas in dynamic and creative integration. Her personas were integrated into a well functioning team. During her appointment with the attorney she felt all her personas at play in a common effort.

Each persona reflects an aspect of one's true self. Each functions to protect and enhance the well being and potentials of the elemental humanness of each individual. Each in his or her own fashion alerts to peril and opportunity. Unintegrated with the others and acting out willy nilly, the individual is scattered and impulsive, reactive rather than responsive to every circumstance. When unbridled, when playing loner, personas tend to overplay their errand. In the case of Liz, Cathy will throw a tantrum, Denise will go mute and moribund, Jane will campaign without cause, Eve will play witless servant, Lilyth will frolic carelessly, Julie will panic and accept comfort at any cost, and Abby will block out everything. The body in which they reside named Liz will consequently run crazy, will be imperialized by whichever persona steals the scene. In contrast, when integrated together, the personas act like a team composed of different sorts of players so that they enjoy one another's special natures and work well on the field. When this is the case for Liz, she has Cathy's fierce spirit, Denise's nose for crap, Jane's assertive clarity, Eve's pragmatic and sensible practicality, Lilyth's mischief, Abby's watchfulness against overload, and Julie's sensitivity to pain and peril. Every strength is an essential.

Discerning Personas in Projections and Working With Them

The attribution of virtue or evil to supernatural entities as well as to living or historic persons involves, at least in part, a projection by the attributor of some of his or her own potential for virtue and evil. In other words, if a person is, for whatever reason, unwilling

to attribute to himself the capacity for certain behaviors, he may
locate the source of these in an external agency. Expressions such
as "Don't thank me; thank God or Christ in me," and "The Devil
made me do it," or, "The Devil did it" illustrate projection.

Projective attribution frequently takes place when the thought
occurring to a person is judged by the person as inconsistent with his
or her image of self. The disturbing thought may have been
generated by a persona the subject has either not yet recognized or
has forgotten.

Had I kept a list of Liz's personas immediately at hand, I
probably would have, in time, aided her in establishing for herself
a greater working attention to the play of her persona Katie. Katie
was recognized months before the attorney's office scene. As it
was, both Liz and I forgot about Katie as we rehearsed for that scene.
Not only had Katie escaped Liz's attention when she rehearsed for
and then visited her attorney, I had also forgotten about Katie when
I wrote about this event. I can only suppose that when Liz (operating
as vincular Self in the attorney's office) had coached all the other
personas (with their consent) into an integrating posture in relationship to one another, Katie fell into harmony as well and contributed
to the realization of Liz's interests in a productive fashion.

Liz came to therapy at a later date distressed and furious with
me over something I had said to her the previous week. I asked her
what I had said. She told me that I had said to her that she could only
enjoy herself when she was being hateful. It was evident to me that
she must have distorted what I had said to her that previous week,
must have missed the context, and listened with selective inattention.

Tempted as I was to react defensively, to "set the record
straight" and exonerate myself, I asked Liz which among her
personas were shocked and angered? I also asked her if any of her
personas were prone to shaming her? She did a doubletake on the
second question and said: "Katie! I forgot about Katie. You were a
stand-in for Katie. She shames me. You, Peter, are off the hook!"

We recalled Katie's features. She is the persona that can be the
harsh judge. When running wild she sees herself and others in their
worst light. Then she is like a monkey on Liz's shoulder whispering
awful things about what is going on or what has happened. Here is
a seamy way of doing to one's self what others would do to you if

you didn't do it to yourself first. Gestaltists call this retroflection. For some readers the concept of "bad introjects" will come to mind. Katie is Liz's intrapersonal trustee of proprieties, morals, and ideals. When running out of control, unchecked and out of harmony with her other personas, Katie is at one and the same time harsh judge and vile sinner. When Katie is balanced by the others, i.e., when Liz is in integrated state, Katie offers ethical and moral concern.

Having forgotten Katie and her Katie propensities, yet becoming alert consciously to "thoughts," that is to say what Katie whispered into her conscious mind's ear from the unconscious, Liz had to find someone to blame for the awful thoughts. Her therapist offered an inviting target. She supposed he had put these thoughts in her mind.

Paying attention to incongruous attributions, attentive to the ubiquitous play of projection, we recalled a persona of which the client was not currently conscious. And now that we discerned the presence of Katie in revolting against my alleged careless remark, sharpened awareness of her presence and role within Liz, plus my appropriate gestures of respect prompted resolution of our crisis of the moment.

The "Cyrano" Syndrome" and the Evolution of Second Generation Personas

From a persona of one of my clients, I have coined what I refer to as the Cyrano syndrome. This syndrome conjures up a whole association of features characterizing the group facilitator who, with great skill, fosters a powerful, healing, loving, growth inspiring group culture into which he does not permit himself entry. When group members express gratitude for his gifts to the group, he deflects the loving gesture, admonishing members to take responsibility for their own gifting of one another, explaining his part as that of a trained catalyst. In other words, he cuts himself out of the play. Reflected in his behaviors are great love and personal shame.

Such was the story of playwright Edmond Rostland's *Cyrano De Bergerac* who ghost-wrote love letters for another man to a woman he in truth loved deeply, yet could not approach in love because he supposed his gigantic nose an object of revulsion.

My client's thus far identified personas were:

—*Daddy* after his own father, insatiable in his need for approval and an obsessed scientist committed to the highest level of excellence;

—*Johnnie*, child self intimidated by the Daddy part of him: impotent, shy, timorous, apologizing;

—*Bill*, after a kind and thoroughly self reliant woodsman and guide: wise, patient, generous, unflappable and gently humorous;

—*Tom*, after Tom Sawyer: youthful, adventuresome, curious, and undaunted.

One day months into therapy, John brought to the session and shared with me a letter he had written and posted to the parents of one of his college students. He explained how college parents get little enough word about their children; this student's manner and contribution in workshop moved him to let her parents in on his positive view of their daughter. I asked what he hoped would come of this letter. The answer was greater appreciation and love from parent to child. The letter John read to me was as exquisite a love letter as I have been exposed to. It recalled the love letters between Abelard and Heloise, between Francis Bernardoni and Clara. Here was a display of John I had not spied before. I invited John to imagine his student reading this letter. He flushed. I invited him further to imagine revising the letter in such a way as to be a letter from him directly to her. This nearly undid him. He retreated behind thoughts in regard to their difference in age and role appropriate behavior. I invited him to place these important considerations slightly aside. He owned his feelings toward the young woman. Left were his misgivings as to what she would see in him. We recalled together the last scene from Cyrano De Bergerac. It fit for him.

With his mind's eye he assembled a small album, a selection of memory snapshots of himself as a Cyrano lover full of unrequited love, unrequited because of his tendency to seek cover in roles and proprieties, all smoke screens hiding his misgivings about himself.

Was Cyrano a persona of the first order? It struck us that the Cyrano about and in him was an invention by all the first order personas, a sleight-of-hand solution. Cyrano has: Tom's adventure;

Johnnies child-like sensitiveness and timidity; Bill's rich earthiness, generosity and wondrousness; and Daddy's attention to good form, hidden shame, and obsessiveness with excellence. His Cyrano was a figure composed through collusion by all the primary personas as a way of being wonderfully and safely enough a member of a loving community.

Personas Running Errands For the Family

Before Jeremy's father placed the pistol at his head and shot himself to death, he put everything in order. He left detailed instructions for the care and feeding of his fish, arranged essential documents where they would be seen right away, and noted which key of several had to do with the desk, cabinets, and deposit box. He took meticulous care in providing against confusion. Then, late in the evening, he went out on the front lawn, wrapped his head in a pillow case, and shot himself.

Jeremy's father never wanted to join the business that was owned and managed across several generations by his family. But hard times induced him to comply with his father's wishes. What benefited him in wealth cost him dearly in personal happiness. Jeremy saw his father as trapped and demoralized.

Jeremy did not join the family business. In his thirties, he is in one of the traditional professions. The manner with which he conducts himself in his practice and with friends is not confusing to him; what transpires from situation to situation makes sense when he thinks about his principle personas, given each of their personalities and adaptive styles. What puzzles him and has generated feelings of depression in him is what he is going to do now that he has painstakingly extricated himself from virtually every professional responsibility. What is he going to do now?

What Jeremy has been systematically carrying out is so clear to us now that it is difficult for us to understand how it has taken us so long to see. We have been very close for some time to the fuller truth. The everyday expression that "a miss is a mile" applies.

That his father's compulsive drinking and miserable frame of mind derived from his voluntary entrapment has seemed obvious. Furthermore, that Jeremy's pattern of avoiding entrapment all the way through his school years, in relationships, and now in his profession struck us both as a function of determined counter-dependency. Every indication to me from Jeremy about his relationship with his father featured hostility toward one another. Throughout the last six months of his father's life, Jeremy remained icily cold and deliberately silent when with his father. Jeremy's last letter to his father, which did not arrive before his father's suicide, was formal and distant. It pertained to an unavoidable piece of family finance. To repeat, his pattern of avoiding long term personal, professional, and institutional commitments seemed counter-phobic. He sought avoidance of entrapment. Jeremy did not want to make the horrible mistake his father had made. He did not want to be like or do like his father.

Many of us who have participated in bargaining and negotiating teams know that when the two parties in confrontation are at a stalemate, it is sometimes the informal contact between two members of opposing groups that not only plays a part in continuing negotiation, but also provides the basis for an eventual breakthrough. There can sometimes be a virtue in the right hand not knowing what the left hand is doing. I am alluding to a transaction far more subtle than the deliberately acknowledged, unofficial contact. The contacting I refer to is unpremeditated; neither party appreciates at the time the significance of the exchange in relation to the bargaining drama. What applies here in relation to group interaction applies as well in regard to persons. One persona from among a person's several personas may, virtually be unbeknownst to the other personas, be in subtle relationship with one persona of another person. This appears to apply to Jeremy and his father.

Unconvinced that Jeremy's pattern of extricating himself from any commitment that sniffed of entrapment was exclusively counter-phobic behavior, led me to review with him his personal history in extricating himself from autonomy compromising situations. I ventured the following: "Jeremy, I wonder if you have been doing your father's work for him! All these years! Out of loving kindness to him! The fierceness between the two of you reflects deep intimacy and care. We have missed the fuller truth in simply featuring your long history of acting contrary to your father's nightmare of family entrapment. Of course the avoidance is part of

the story, but only one part. Children frequently sacrifice themselves out of love for their parents. Let me tell you a story."

"Years ago," I related, "when I was Executive Director of a
continental youth organization, I received a phone call from the
parents of one of the organization's leaders. They asked if they
could drive to New Hampshire, where I was vacationing, to talk
with me about their daughter, Celeste. I agreed to the visit. We
would have only a little over an hour. There would be no time to
waste. They reported how Celeste was a diabetic and was misusing
herself nutritionally. They spoke of her sadness all the time. They
were upset that she assumed more and more responsibility and
failed to meet these responsibilities. I looked at Celeste's father. He
struck me as not a very happy person. "Do you like your work?" I
asked him. He seemed thunderstruck by my question.

They hadn't driven so far to talk about themselves; they were
with me to consult about their daughter. I asked him my question
again. "No! I do not like my work. I am in my mid-fifties. Do you
think I am going to leave my position? What could I find now? What
would happen to my pension? I go to work early and stay late." I
asked him if he ever talked with Celeste about his feelings toward
his work. Never. I asked him if he sometimes felt like simply neither
calling in nor going, just taking off for a day. Many times. And he
never acted upon his inclination. I turned to Celeste's mother. She
looked to me as if she had suffered in life. "Mother, you look stoved
in; you know suffering, probably from before you and this man were
married." She looked at me aghast. "How can you tell?" I answered
her that I thought I saw suffering in her face, more than the worry
of a mother over a teenage daughter's irresponsibilities. She responded: "Why cry over spilt milk!!" I asked her if she shared with
her daughter any of her personal story. I should have known better.
Her initial response: Why cry over spilt milk was answer enough.
"Your daughter," I said to the mother and father," out of her loving
kindness to you both, is doing your work for you. Father, she knows
very well that you are shouldering extra responsibilities because
you are frightened for your security. She knows you would like to
dump them from time to time. She is putting your nose in your own
story by assuming responsibilities beyond what is fair to her, and
then dropping them. Mother, the sadness and grief she senses

around you she is mirroring so clearly that you cannot get away from it. Mother and Father, Celeste does not feel that you are taking good care of yourselves. She is giving back to you what she is getting from you. Of course, all of this is my best guess. You can test the validity of my guess by talking with her about these things and taking better care of yourselves!" A few weeks later they phoned me to say that apparently my guess had proven valid. They shared all this with Celeste. Though she was not conscious of what she was doing, it all made sense to her.

I turned to Jeremy. "Does any of this have a meaning for you?" He responded with a story out of character with all previous reports about his father. "A few years ago I bought a van and outfitted it so I could travel and live in it comfortably. When father looked at it and had finished assessing its quality as merchandise, he dropped an aside: 'Jeremy, I really like it. Oh to be free to go where you like. Have a good time with it.' I really appreciated his saying this; I have forgotten this until now." This recollection pried loose other similar memories with his father where it seemed his father and he came up beside one another and exchanged an appreciation. Now Jeremy was appearing in a very special manner, one with which I was familiar. As he retrieved these happier moments with his father he sounded and looked like he has from time to time when affection between the two of us has been acknowledged, like he did one session months earlier when he burst out with acknowledgement that he had love as well as anger and resentment toward his father, and, like he always appears when talking about an older man in his profession for whom he has respect and affection. I said:

"You are introducing me once again, Jeremy, to one of your personas, one who is fiercely loyal as a son to his father whatever the difficulties between you. One who all these years, like Celeste, has been doing his father's work for him. Feverishly avoiding entrapment is only half of the story; it is incidental to realizing the important objective, being one's own person free to be with others, being one's self, and free to work at what a person wants to work at. This persona, Jeremy, is probably still trying to do for your father, what he sees so painfully, your Father isn't able to do for himself. This persona, Jeremy, has his eyes glued to the rearview mirror. His father is not gone. If dead, not gone. He continues to do his phantom father's work for him. Jeremy, it may be out of love and kindness, but nobody can effectively do another's work for them. One more thing. There is a woman who you love and with whom you live. This persona you have introduced may well be working in such a way as to protect you from letting yourself go with her. In spite of his loving intentions you may lose her." Jeremy responded:

"I don't want to let that happen. It may be I have been running a family errand for my father. Okay. I must be free now to run my own errand. We'll have to look some more at this."

On the Prompting of Personas From Within and Without

Among my fourteen clearly discerned personas, Pete was how I was addressed and the most prominent persona during the calendar years from about 1939, when I repeated the first grade, to 1956, when I assumed my first professional position. Now I no longer wished to be called Pete. I asked to be called Peter. While other personas emerged and assumed increasingly clear form and activity within my psyche during these years, Pete was the principle player. My salient interests during these years and Pete's uppermost concern even to this day have to do with being included in the group whether the group is family, a pick-up ball game, the neighborhood gang, those graduating on to the next grade level, and, more recently, my extended family, professional clubs and associations.

Now, if I get lost in the shuffle or everything looks like I am being left to the last in picking sides for a game, I, as Pete, am sometimes up-staged by Bagweed, my self who was given this name in the summer of 1945. Bagweed is myself discouraged with dyslectic learning difficulties who felt helpless, who drifted off into daydreaming in the schoolroom grade after grade until he was sent to a private pre-preparatory school in order to get special academic help. When I visited my childhood grammar school ten years after receiving my Ph.D., my old Principal recognized my name and greeted me with: "Ah, Peter Baldwin, our dreamer! You completed HighSchool? I think that is just wonderful!" I was so affected by these words that I became too tongue-tied to say I'd gone to college. We parted. If I get lost in the shuffle or something goes wrong, Bagweed figures that "it's" happened again: that once again he has been singled out, left out, left behind and unable to meet expectations. If overlooked or left out, Pete gets angry, but can't deliver his anger cleanly if Bagweed interferes, because Bagweed doesn't even consider himself a good fighter. Then I become confused and the result is a storm-cloud demeanor. It is apparent to others that I am silently unhappy. Bagweed tends to over-react. He misconstrues what is happening in a situation and troubles Pete into thinking "we" are being left out of something when in fact there may be little factual foundation for this apprehension. Part of what can happen is that, given his ever active memory for how he suffered, Bagweed whispers in Pete's ear that whatever is happening in the present moment is just like a long ago scene.

In 1963 my parents, my brother, myself, and our wives were gathered together in my childhood summer home having cocktails before dinner. While I had every reason to be relaxed and happy— all sorts of fine things were developing very well in my life—I found myself being a storm cloud sitting there in the living room. The same spell befell me the next late afternoon and the day thereafter! After dinner on this third day when my wife and I were alone in our own rooms she asked what was happening to me? I responded that I simply did not know! I acknowledged that I felt terribly distressed and knew I must be showing it, that I was surely proving a wet blanket, but could not figure out what was happening. Then it came to me. I was filled with astonishment at the thought that occurred to me. I said to her, "I see what is happening! Look at the tableau my family has arranged. My father, my mother, my brother and I are sitting in precisely the chairs each of us has either claimed or been relegated to since I first joined "the adults" when I was thirteen. And you and our sister-in-law are sitting on 'extra' chairs just out of the circle! This is a re-enactment of the scene that I knew so well and so unhappily when I was fourteen. I have been into my fourteen-year self these past three nights. Don't you see? At sixteen, my brother is into being in the adult world and knows far better than I, at fourteen, how to do it. I'm fourteen, no longer a child and not yet an adult, and feeling extraneous. What have I to add to the adult conversation or to my brother's stories! I try to get into it and whatever I say doesn't count or doesn't take hold. Here I am at thirty-one. I have all but completed my dissertation. I know I'll have my Ph.D. in a few months, I have a fine professional position. We have a wonderful little child. Everyone is here to help us build our summer cottage! And, in spite of all these good things, I am feeling like I did at fourteen. The house we are in, the living room where we gather, the arrangement and assignment of chairs has prompted me to experience myself and others and to behave as if in another time and circumstance."

I now see that this was, dramaturgically and existentially, precisely what occurred. Pete didn't know how to play a member of this group now that he was between being a child and being a peer adult. He was, as it were, sitting out a lot of the game on the bench. And that might have been O.K. had it not been that Bagweed was upset and couldn't sit still.

It is interesting to me as I write that I am dwelling on the time that I was, in fact, fourteen, instead of continuing with an assessment of what was actually occurring when I was thirty-one. The actual situation, being reminiscent of an earlier life scene, prompted me to regress in time to that prior situation. Given the insight that came to me in that private exchange with my wife, I deliberately re-assessed the current situation among us all, and directed myself to up-date my act on the strength of my current life situation. The following day, and through subsequent days I prompted myself to assume a demeanor and to act in ways that presented myself to the others as a peer adult among adults. Consequently, I assured myself that my Bagweed misgivings were currently without foundation. Happier days followed.

Anita engaged in psychotherapy in order to seek relief from her profound spells of depression. The depressed moods that befell her derived from unresolved grief and rage over the long years she suffered in coping with her deceased husband's alcoholism. She reported that the only way she found relief from her depressed spells were either when a child or grandchild prompted her into activities with them that were, in fact, productively satisfying and/or simply fun, or, when she took herself off to some favorite woodland or stream-side place. At the outset of our work together she disre-garded the authenticity of her happiness when engaged with others or at one of her favorite private places, as she supposed these were only distractions, only the joy of others or the grace of a place from which she benefited "no thanks to herself!" She and I explored the notion of promptings from without and within.

The function of a prompter is to remind an actor of the lines and moves she or he already has command of and has forgotten for the moment. The one line offered by the prompter alerts the actor to the idea, the line, and the behavior the actor commands. Anita came to see that she was giving too much credit to her children and grandchildren for their part in drawing her away from her depression. She began to appreciate how their initiatives were answered by authentic readiness within her to be and act as their invitations prompted. She saw that she was leaning on their promptings unnecessarily. She acknowledged that she knew her lines in the scenes she enjoyed very well, and that there was no reason she couldn't assume far more responsibility for prompting herself from within herself rather than looking so much to others to prompt her. It became apparent that she had lost sight of a lot of her selves, that her grievous and enraged self was not all there was. Now she was in a better place to work with her grief and rage as a part of her life rather than as the only reality.

Pertinent to all of this are two adages that come to us from both moderate and radical Behavior Theory. Behaviors, which I refer to as the dramatic presentations of one's various selves, reinforce themselves. And, if one changes one's behaviors, one feels differently.

On Will Power and Being Willing, the Matter of Resolving Ambivalence

Experiencing one's self as feeling positively willing to do as one is doing without enervating hesitation reflects a high degree of inner integration, integration among one's personas. This is similar to a team proceeding together without rankle because they have realized singleness of purpose. To reach a difficult objective despite marked hesitation, as in conquering an undesirable habit, reflects willpower. Overcoming a personal weakness, doing without something one continues to want, getting some place when one was tempted not to go at all, keeping one's self strictly in line, keeping up a brave front are all behaviors we typically attribute to the play of willpower. Willpower so defined reflects an inner struggle among our various selves. Sometimes the struggle is clear and decent and enhancing of all parties, as happens when a team that has been losing and suffering discouragement is inspired by fellow members to overcome past losses through constructive self-criticism, hard work, and continued practice. Sometimes the struggle is characterized by a dreadful play of wheeling and dealing, shaming and ganging up one part against the other. The forces that come into play among fellow citizens, workers, church members, and family members are also at play within each one of us among our personas.

Collette Dowling, drawing toward the conclusion of her book, *The Cinderella Complex* (Dowling 1981), writes of the long process she underwent before she felt positively willing to assume management of her own life, including the writing of her book. She states she could not have written her book on the strength of willpower. Writing a book is work, at best, playful work. When I sit down with pad and pen, I have to take time at the outset to deal with those personas who do not write, who never signed up for a period of time at desk and wordprocessor. When I disregard them, I am easily distracted by inclinations to sleep, take a walk, daydream, or tend to cordwood. There are spells when my writing seems to flow effortlessly. I presume that at these times all of my personas are invested. There are times, on the other hand, when I have to sense out what is happening within, sort out disagreements, commit myself to the care and feeding of all my inner folk before I feel free to proceed. Ms. Dowling's disparagement of willpower is, I believe, an over-statement in the service of making an important appeal to getting one's self clear of inner dissonance so that one can move in freedom and strength. I quote:

> I should tell you that the moment when the inner self said "Move!" had nothing at all to do with will power. It's not possible to "pick yourself up by the bootstraps," do or die, and take action in the face of overwhelming conflict. If willpower were the answer, I would never have written this book. That forward leap of the inner self came as the result of a long and meaningful *process*, the process of identifying the contradictions within me and then working them through. Will can't be commanded to perform. When you are clear and unconflicted, your will operates quite automatically.

On the other hand, when you're swamped by feelings and attitudes that are mutually opposed, your will shuts down. What that means is that you aren't able to choose what you do in life you act only because you're *driven* to act."

I read these two paragraphs from Collette Dowling to a colleague familiar with her own personas. She said: "Ambivalence is the word therapists typically use to account for indecision. What a weak and dehumanizing term! And people generally suppose that to be ambivalent is a weakness." When we encounter indecision in group work we welcome opportunity to foster openness and sharing among group members such that willingness to move along reflects input from all parties. We worry when decisions come too easily. Discord, confusion, contradictions, and divergence carry promise of novelty and creative invention. The same holds true in individual work. Indecision stimulates and is evidence of lively dissonance among one's personas. Something important is at stake. Each persona is trustee of a piece of one's true self, a champion of survival at least and well being at best. Being "willing" means the most as it flows out of creative turbulence.

Reference:
Dowling, Collete, *The Cinderella Complex: Women's Hidden Fear of Independence,* Pocket
    Books of Simon and Schuster, NY, 1981, p. 228

6

ENGAGING IN PERSONAE WORK HYPNOTICALLY

This chapter, and the longer chapter that follows are designed to draw the reader into the process by which I facilitate personas work. There are no A, B, C rules and procedures guiding personas work comparable to Root's *A,B,C, —X,Y,Z* on the keeping of bees. It is my hope that what follows in these final three chapters will foster within the thinking of the reader a receptivity to the play of personas and a heightened imaginativeness relative to how the psychotherapist can effectively join with the client in fostering increased management of their selves.

In meeting my clients I am affected by them. An understanding is established at the outset that I will share with them what it is like to be with them, the impact they have upon me, the associations that occur to me as I pay attention to them, as I think and feel in response to them. As the session is primarily for them, rather than a matter of engaging them to work with or for me, I reflect upon what I experience in their presence in a way that fosters an atmosphere of trust and introduces and develops strategies designed to facilitate their therapeutic work. In this process I attend to the impact upon my personae of the client as person and of the person's situation. I endorse Freud's observation that at the heart of the psychotherapeutic process is work with transferential and countertransferential material emerging in encounter. Meeting another person constitutes a crisis.

Counter-transference as Personas in Crisis

Frieda Fromm-Reichmann urges psychotherapists to join with clients in the substance and process of their work by offering effective dynamic interpretations in the form of statements, questions, and metaphorical interventions that prompt deep self confrontation, stimulate the cognitive reframing of troublesome situations, and increase awareness of heretofore unconsidered problem solving options. In fulfilling this function, the psychotherapist attends to the impact the client and the client's situation have upon the therapist and the aroused states prompted in the therapist by this impact. If and when the client as person or the client's situation affects the therapist so that he or she becomes inordinately engrossed with or profoundly distracted away from the client and the client's work, here we have a clear indication of a counter-transferential state affecting the therapist and the therapist's work dysfunctionally. This development calls for the therapist to work with the counter-transferential material, bring it to consciousness, attend to the issues appropriately, and reframe his or her work with the client as guided by the information now available.

Not every incident of counter-transference needs to be worked with so deliberately. Many spontaneous interventions non-consciously informed by counter-transferential reaction work well. Much of our therapeutic work occurs spontaneously and nonconsciously. Promptings to explore the counter-transferential bases for our interventions occur out of curiosity or when counterproductive difficulties develop during the course of, or as a result of, interventions. As valuable as introspective reflection can be, obsession with each and every one of our moves hinders creative spontaneity.

Clinical apprentices in internship situations or in graduate practicums frequently wonder how their mentors see so clearly, as if around corners, into the subject's heart and mind. They wonder over the apparent miraculousness of the mentor's interventions. The senior colleague may wonder herself! Or she or he may reconstruct the situation in process, explaining how their clinical interventions were based on cues offered by the subject, cues which the less perceptive failed to observe. The interventions, therefore, were based substantially upon material offered by the client to which the clinician was consciously and deliberately responsive. Or, upon reflection, the senior clinician may become alert, now or after the fact, to his or her own counter-transferential material and share his or her best guess as to how this material lent, through intrapersonal, introspectional processing, to intervention appropriate to the subject.

Gaining access to nonconscious material is no more a mysterious accomplishment than Sherlock Holmes solving a mysterious crime. To Dr. Watson's exclamations of bewonderment, Sherlock Holmes invariably responds: "Elementary, my dear Watson; the clues were all before us." Magicians, masters of illusion, tend to prefer the adult audience as adults are inclined to stare at what is happening, trying too hard to discern the secret of the trick. Adults trying too hard not to be distracted are all the more distractable. Children, in contrast, hanging out, joining in the fun, engage in an attitude of receptivity in which they hardly ever miss a trick. Forever scanning, they pick up on cues and clues. The attitude one does well to assume if one is to gain access to initially nonconscious material is to use the colloquial expression, "hanging out."

Antioch University sponsored a colloquium in Los Angeles in the Fall of 1984 at which selected university professors presented their work to university colleagues from the nine university centers across the country. I was invited to present a paper on Personae Theory. My Antioch New England colleague, Bill Feinstein, attended my session and afterwards asked me to visit his Spring semester course on Transference and Counter-Transference; he asked me to consider how dynamic interactions among personas prompted by encounter with the client and client situation informed productive clinical interventions. We understood together that counter-transferential activity can be understood in terms of lively impact upon personas and their inclined reaction to the client and the client's situation. I accepted Bill's invitation. Six months passed. I awakened very early the morning I was to present in Bill's class aghast that I had not prepared. Panic struck. I dressed and went to a local diner for breakfast. Then I went to my office with a little over an hour to gather my thoughts. I recall vividly my mental state as I sat in my office with pad and pen. My earlier fit of anxiety had passed. I was now, "hanging out", with myself, relaxed and open, happily trusting that my own personas were fundamentally invested in my work and in the worth of this task. I was not disappointed. Solid support and rich material became available.

This commonplace, popular expression "hanging out" occurs to me as an apt way of capturing the attitude necessary to create creative, productive receptivity and responsiveness to self and others. I secur myself at the edge of trance state, on the threshold of conscious and nonconscious process. The Buddhist master speaks of engaging in excitement without indulging in it, that is to say becoming excited by, excitement. Gestaltists speak of being receptive to intero, extero, and proprioceptive awareness, Each in balance with the others. When I am hanging out, I am sustaining an attitude receptive to conscious, unconscious and environmental occurrences.

By hanging out I mean being accessibly present, accounted for, and effectively on the job. This calls for being relaxed. Here are some illustrations of hanging out:

—Sitting in with a group of adolescents absorbed with planning a non-traditional worship service, I was appalled at ninety minutes of babel, everyone talking at once. I ached for order, rhyme and reason. Specified planning time swiftly running out (only about ten minutes left), the Chair astounded me with her announcement that she understood what the group envisioned. In five minutes she laid out the format for the service. She was clear; what she said made sense. Everyone present seemed pleased they had been heard. Trying too hard to follow every line of thought, I missed virtually everything. They had been hanging out with one another. I had been hanging in, holding on too tightly.

—In my third year of clinical internship at Massachusetts Mental Health Center, now serving as an Assistant Clinical Supervisor, I met a seventeen year old boy in the lobby whom I did not recognize. To my inquiry he responded, "I've lived in this neighborhood all my life and never been in here. I thought I'd look around." I invited him to hang out with me. That was fine with him." When a little while later I saw how naturally he was getting along with the adolescent court case patients playing pool, I drew the attention of some novice interns and bid them watch this young man's manner with the patients. My supervisees were stunned. "He's engaged them at a deeper level than anyone on the staff has begun to approach! What's he doing?" I responded: "He's being natural. Staff try too hard. And being normal interferes. His ease is not to be explained by his being close to their ages or at home at a pool table. He is free from believing he has to accomplish something, and so, paradoxically, in doing nothing, everything is possible. He is a natural rather than a normal. Little kids are naturals until they are conditioned and socialized to be normal. Normality emerges as we comply with, identify with, and/or internalize instructions to attend selectively and deliberately to what is happening within and outside of us. You have to have become normal by the first grade when you only pay attention to what you are supposed to pay attention to. This kid is normal enough to respond appropriately enough to environmental promptings, natural enough to have access to internal and external under- and over-tone messages.

—At eight o'clock in the morning on the occasion of the first session in my section of General Psychology at a woman's college, I began with the question: "Is everyone here?" I received the response I was hoping for: "Everyone is here who is here, Professor Baldwin." I approached the speaker and asked: "Are you sure? Are you altogether here?" She did a doubletake, then responded: "No. I'm still in bed . . . . And! I am also waiting in line to see if a letter has come for me this morning; standing in line, it has to be ten O'clock, after this class is over. "And you are also here," I added. "You are in at least three places at the same time. You are here, and there, and in another place. Probably in some other places too! So your presence here is as skeleton crew, with other crew members on shore about different activities and errands. That's fine; that's natural. And if you need everyone on board for a while, you blow your ship's horn." I addressed myself now to the whole class: "Don' t try to be here. Arrange to have your body here with at least one member of your crew on duty. I'll make strong signals relative to essential points. If you relax you will hear what you need to hear in order to do as well as you intend to do, and you will hear and become altogether present as we talk about issues in psychology that are of interest to you personally." Later in the semester students observed that my having granted the inevitable, they found themselves more altogether present in class session more of the time than they had anticipated.

—At eight forty-five in the morning I sat waiting for the opening of a three day workshop in Ericksonian hypnotherapy. I became aware that I was physically restless and agitated, not at all properly set and centered, nowhere close to being present and available to workshop opportunities. I asked myself: "Where do I want to be right now if not here?" One scene after another presented itself to me in which one or another of my personas were featured: I experienced myself as my persona Lad saddling my Morgan horse Shamrock; that I was saddling him meant that I was joining a scene at least twenty minutes in progress since it takes time to lead the horse out of the meadow and groom him before saddling up. The scene shifted and I experienced myself

as Dave walking with chainsaw in hand to the westerly
edge of the upper meadow to where my wife and I have
been clearing brush back to the stonewall; here I am
twenty minutes into this activity since filing the teeth of
the chain saw is always a preliminary. The scene changes
again and now I am in my truck heading down the
mountain to town to run errands, a list of items in my shirt
pocket. Petey is in the passenger seat; he likes to go
trucking; Tom's driving, and Tom has sat over coffee
making up a list before departing. Again the scene shifts
to the living room where I as Susan am playing my guitar
and learning a new song. Here we have my personas Lad,
Dave, Tom, Petey, and Susan absorbed in what they
really want to be doing. Now how am I as I sit in the
Exeter Room of the Hotel Lenox in Boston awaiting the
beginning of the workshop in Ericksonian methods?
Fine! Relaxed, very present, hanging out. And knowing
full well that as things begin to happen in workshop, all
of who I am will be available, present, and engaged as
what occurs affects their interests and needs.

I am defining counter-transference as the clinician's initially
unidentified and therefore nonconscious pronounced distraction
away from, or inordinate engrossment with, the client as person or
the client's situation. Something has developed in the course of their
work together that has gripped the clinician personally and engaged
him or her in ways not immediately discerned. The clinician has
become subject to strong subliminal reaction. Viewing this occurrence from the perspective of Personae Theory, one or more of the
clinician's own personas have become aroused, have been prompted
by client behavior or the client's situation into absorption with their
own issues. The client as person or the client's situation has become
part of the clinician's psychological business.

If and as the clinician becomes alert to his own counter
transferential reaction, and if she or he is inclined to figure it out
from nonconscious process, access into conscious awareness is
available by engaging one's own personas in group session, and
conducting that session with attention to the strong reaction as the
principal agendum. I mean quite literally the engagement of perso-

nas in group session: either in the Gestalt tradition of moving from chair to chair, or in medium trance state envisioning, hearing, and observing interactions among personas relative to what has been provoked in the clinician counter-transferentially. As a client can be trained to engage in inter-personas group process relative to compelling issues either with Gestalt chairs-work, or in trance group encounter, or in trance psychodrama, so the clinician can render into conscious awareness what is transpiring within him or herself by these means. In this work it is critically essential to attain the mental and emotional attitude I have characterized as "hanging out" with one's self in order to allow for flowing activity and receptive attentiveness.

I will return now to reporting on my presentation in Bill Feinstein's class and my discussion with graduate students of how attention to interaction among personas can lead to clinical interventions informed by counter-transferential experience. I began by presenting five clinical cameo snapshots:

—*Christopher* has attended every class session in a small experientially oriented college seminar. While his written work has reflected conscientious study, he has only been present in body. It bothers me that he is not interacting with the rest of us. My restlessness over Christopher is distracting me. I sense there is much more to my restlessness than the instructor's commonplace irritation over the inactive student.

—My client *Fred*, the owner-proprietor of an old business firm, leaves a message on my recording device informing me that his assistant manager, Tim, wishes to talk with me about Fred as he has a perspective on Fred that he feels will help with Fred's psychotherapy. This message bothers me; I feel anger.

—I am in the fourth session working with seventeen year old *Shelly* and her family. Her outrageous conduct has prompted her highschool counselor into securing the family's consent to engage me in family therapy. In session I retrieve a fleeting reference. I am intrigued and

can't for the life of me discern how come I am so
engrossed with something that has affected me by
someone's passing reference to an Aunt Libby. I can't
recall the context, the connection, and now I am not
hearing what people are talking about.

—I am joined at breakfast at the diner by *Geoffrey*. He is
acquainted with Personae Theory. He says: "Here's a
mystery for you to solve, Peter. I always carry a check in
my shirt pocket when I go to see my therapist. I reached
for my check at the beginning of session yesterday. I
know I put it there when I was dressing. It wasn't there
when I reached for it. Back home last night I found it
made out in the checkbook I keep on top of my bureau.
But I saw myself tear it out of the book and place it in my
pocket! I remember! I saw the whole thing. How can I
understand this!" I saw a plausible solution to the mystery right away. My solution appealed to my friend. How
did the solution come to me, and so swiftly?

—My client *Ethel* opens the session. "Janis, always the
sweet and gentle Janis suddenly has a Big Mouth, Peter.
And Janis' mouth has suddenly come in like a summer
thunderstorm." Janis is fourteen. I read her mother as
intent upon dealing with Janis. I feel frightened, defensive on behalf of Janis. What is happening to me?

Hindsight informs me that in each of these five cases I provided
an intervention that proved useful to the person involved and that
released me from over engagement with the impact the client or the
client's situation was having upon me:

—In my discomfort with *Christopher* I recognized my
dyslexic persona Bagweed's discomfort in the classroom
throughout my early years in school, and his propensity
for daydreaming as a welcomed escape. Prompted by
Bagweed's identification with Christopher, and my task-
oriented persona Tom's sense of urgency that Bagweed
and Bagweed-like people should be awakened from

daydreaming and engaged in the real world, an intervention occurred to me reflecting input from Bagweed and
Tom. Honoring both being-aware and being-present I
asked Christopher where he really wished to be right then
if only he could be where he wanted to be. This question
prompted a wonderfully growing smiling as he drew all
of us, increasingly entranced, to his favorite Cape Cod
scene. In due course Christopher recognized that his
happy Cape Cod place was within him. And in finding
within him what he had supposed was only available to
him if he literally went to that external Cape Cod setting,
he joined us in class sessions for the rest of the semester
more actively, his inner Cape Cod place now being
available to us all.

—My persona Chum, the good boy of painful conscience
who has had it impressed upon him from very early that
others have a wiser slant on what is good for him and how
he should conduct himself in the future, identified with
Fred in receptively accommodating to Tim's initiative to
advise me concerning Fred. But my persona Harry, my
persona bodyguard, my paladin, my law-unto-himself
gun carrier, moved in quickly with the word: "That
fellow's got the draw on Fred." Alan, properly reared,
properly tutored, properly civilized and instructed, properly "finished" at Eaglebrook and Andover, properly
impressed by his Lord and Taylor socialization, peculiar
accomplice to Harry recalls Robert Langs' injunctions
against complicating and corrupting the therapeutic situation, and supports Harry's caution by urging against
accepting the proffered consultation. My intervention
with Fred, informed by the dynamic interplay among my
personas, especially featured by the interaction among
Chum, Harry, and Alan, consisted in asking Fred to
characterize Tim's performance. I asked Fred: "If there
were a play written in which Tim's role, whether billed
as principal, supporting, or bit part, cast him as central to
the unfolding drama, how would you characterize Tim's
role?" Fred's response came promptly. "The Master

Puppeteer." And in seeing this, recognizing at play within himself his persona-counterpart to my Chum, appreciating Tim's genuinely positive intentions, recalling how he himself had asked Tim to share with him what Tim wanted to share with me, Fred reinforced my disinclination to accept Tim's request to consult with me relative to Fred. Fred resolved to take up the issue with Tim in a firm and positive fashion. My intervention facilitated resolution of both Fred's and my inner crises.

—The case of *Shelly* and her Aunt Libby was introduced in Chapter II. Recall my intervention. I drew the family's attention to my interest in Aunt Libby. My interest was met with moderate resistance. I nonetheless asked each member of the family to relate in turn their image of Aunt Libby. The composite image came as revelation to Shelly and to no one else. The Aunt Libby turned out to be, in the parents' generation, an "outrageous character." Shelly was stunned that she appeared to have been cast as the younger generations' spitting image of Aunt Libby. While in fact she found the picture of Aunt Libby attractive, she wanted to be sure she was her own self rather than a stand-in for a transgenerational family personage. Recall that I all but missed the passing, low profile, reference to Aunt Libby. It was experiencing myself as intrigued, overly engrossed with this fragment reference, that prompted me to pause to study my reaction and discover it to be a strong positive counter-transferential response. My impish Emily, later to be renamed Lad and Rascal by my mother and father respectively, picked up on a mischievous inflection in reference to Aunt Libby. And Jacquie, black and outrageous, sniffed outrageousness. Rascal and Jacquie, two of a kind, male and female tricksters smelled out a compatriot in Aunt Libby. What these two had sensed and identified with in Shelly was scrambled in the airways before reaching my full conscious attention as I believe that my mental attitude in session was being dominated by promptings from Alan to attend to facilitating family therapy with earnest propriety. By attending to my own counter-transferential reaction, by engaging my personas in group meeting, clarification emerged.

—Now the case of *Geoffry's* missing check. My plausible explanation of the mystery came swiftly from my persona George, who "sees" more than meets the eye. My breakfast companion reported conviction that two things were true and contradictory: He was sure he had brought a check in his pocket to therapy session, and he was certain that he found the check secured within his checkbook at home. My friend's riddle generated "back of my mind" reflection among my own personas. My inter-personal psychodramatic session yielded questions of my friend with which he could identify. As a result we were both the wiser. I guessed that one of his personas was intent upon preparing and pocketing a check. Knowing we perceive our moves at least one half step ahead of our actual actions, I guessed that another persona distracted the check-writing persona between the writing and pocketing behaviors such that the pocketing behavior was never enacted.

To these questions Geoffrey responded: "Yes, I do have one persona for whom my therapy session is the most important hour of the week, and I have a persona who is supportive of therapy but who is concerned over the time and money therapy is costing, and another persona who thinks therapists are charlatans and therapy is quackery. And now that I think of it, yes, there was something odd about what I was wearing; I tucked a handkerchief in the breast pocket of my jacket, something I never do! Huh! So! My skeptical persona interrupted the sequence of acting upon seeing by having me open the top left drawer of my dresser, reach for a handkerchief, and tuck the handkerchief into the breast pocket of my suit jacket rather than the check into my shirt pocket! Sleight of hand?

—*Janis'* mother Ethel declares how Big Mouth has come in like a sudden summer thunderstorm, and I become frightened. I sense mother intends to gird herself during session to shut up Janis' big mouth. My experiencing myself as frightened evidences development of counter-transferential reaction. How Janis' mother actually conducted herself later that day when Janis came on "mouthy," reflects what transpired in our session together. To Janis' display of mouth, mother responded: "Fantastic spirit, Janis! The trouble is, your form is terrible! You thought I might want to shut you up? No way! You are fourteen. I play a big part in how you are when I deliver you into the community when you come of age. We don't need another "shut up woman" out there. I'll tell you what I'm going to do. Not break your spirit...even if I could. I am going to coach you the best I know how until you have fantastic form as well as fantastic spirit." Janis loved it! And as the days and weeks passed, mother and daughter became closer than ever.

Where was I coming from to have prompted mother to assume this frame of mind toward Janis' big mouth? My persona Pete who above everything else all my life has wanted to be included in friendships and groups rather than shut up and out. My beloved Christian Gentleman father acting upon and through Chum inhibited Pete from unseemly displays of freshness and revolt. Rational discussion and attractive considerateness were preferred. There was no leave for the play of big mouth or coaching into fine form initially crude spirit. Then in college, I strayed into theater following along after my good friends E.B. Baker and David Bridges. There, in one play after another, Directors Jim VanWort and Erie Volkert coached Pete on and off stage into how to object, speak back, push headlong according to conviction and feeling. Janis' mother became for me in session a stand-in for my parents and I became frightened. In counter-transferential reaction, Pete retreated or advanced (I'm not sure which it was, maybe both) , to Jim VanWort and Erie Volkert. Psychotherapist Peter Baldwin role-played coaching-mother to mother-as-janis. The strategy worked. Janis' mother liked the scene. Janis bought in. Mother and daughter became closer. Pete wasn't frightened any more.

The occurrence of counter-transference is inevitable in the course of intensive psychotherapy. To the degree that the therapist is able to hang out, and join with the client, he or she is alert and receptive to the most important disclosures, especially the unintended and undeliberated disclosures, by the client. As the therapist is able to hang out with him or herself, to that degree he or she has access to inner psychodramatic reactions and interplay among personas. And essential to the finest quality in hanging out with self is profound confidence that nonconscious activity is fundamentally trustworthy and self enhancing.

Psychotherapeutic engagement involves encounter by the personas of the client with the personas of the therapist. In this, therapists attend to the impact the client as person and the client's situation have upon their own personas. Clinical interventions occur as the product of effective or flawed internal group-work by the therapist.

The Importance of Being Where You Are Not, and Knowing That Quite Clearly

This peculiar statement offers an allusion to a manner of working with people involving and attending with the client to the implicit, engaging the client in trance state such that the client secures access to the epistemological ground from which their problems figure in sharp detail.

Social structures and process assume a rhyme and reason for me as I think of human interactions as living theater. All the world is a stage; everyone of us is engaged in common and idiosyncratic theater; there are plays within plays, personal plays woven within the fabric of public, conventional plays. Irving Goffman has written in detail in this regard in *The Presentation of Self in Everyday Life*. He directs our attention to the various forms of space in which we perform explicitly and implicitly. While physically back stage, we may be actively engaged implicitly on stage. While down stage, a person may effectively up-stage another character. Clearly on stage, a character may experience themselves and convey to audience that they are "away," otherwise engaged. All of these modes may figure within external or internal space. The following case fragments may illustrate this orientation and the therapeutic process informed by this epistemological way of "mapping" or "punctuating" experience. The case illustrations I have chosen happen not to include reference to personas.

When my client *Heather's* friends asked her how come her brother committed suicide, she was used to answering: "Because he lived twenty-two years with our father." Her father never threw anything away; he kept receipts for years. He hoards his money and kept Heather on a very tight lead. He mocked her, twitted her, forever baited her with his obscenely racist and sexist remarks about what occurred in the household, the community, and on the television screen. Virtually everything she has lived and believed derives from acting and thinking contrary to her father, as in opposition to her father. That she learned to support herself and earned her own away through college are valuable, but costly, benefits of this struggle.

One day in session Heather carried on about her ten years younger sister's plans to marry a childhood sweetheart. Her father had, by and large, left her little sister alone, and she was following the conventional route in repeating her mother's patterns. Now her sister was five months pregnant and the reported reason for getting married was to give the child a name. Her sister's young man worked when work came his way. No great love figured between him and Heather's sister. They were used to each other. He supposed he ought to do his duty in marrying Heather's sister. I say Heather carried on. I sensed well founded distress *and* I sniffed an over-reaction. I found myself thinking of a television "soap" series and the loyal viewer's remarkable depth of commitment and identification with the sagas. General Hospital, Dynasty, Dallas, and other "shows" are compellingly real for many viewers. As Heather talked, I felt that she was mostly a thousand miles away in her home-town engaged in a family drama. She told me that her New England friends who saw her distress urged her to let well enough alone, to turn her attention to her own life away from her family and home-town, to walk away from the old and abiding grief. She was struck by their indifference, their boredom with the developments. I experienced myself touched by her anguish and trusting that some very important issue was at stake.

I said to her: "Heather, your story has always featured your need to get away from your father and your childhood home." Heather nodded in assent. I continued: "The need to be away from a certain place requires that you really *know* where-you-are-away-from, and that you can see from where-you-are-away-from that *to be there*, without getting lost *in being there*, you have to get away from there; you have to get some distance from there so you can see *where-you-are* there."

Heather responded: "But I don't want to be back there." I asked: "Where do you want to be?" Heather: "Here." Baldwin: "Where besides being in New England is here?" Heather: "Not there! Away from there! Better my sister than me....I see what this is about. What is happening back home is very immediate for me; I am absorbed with what is happening there. I'm there in many ways..., in order to be here. As I think what is happening there I am glad I have some distance from it. And I see more clearly now how a lot of who I am is decidedly other than who my father and mother and sister are. And more!" Baldwin: "Yes. A lot more! To be very much other-than-what-you-are-not means paying a lot of attention to being other-than-what-you-are-not,...and to see all this with increasing clearness."

Walker has been divorced for two years. His ex-wife's daughters from a previous marriage continue to be very important for him. He refers to them as his daughters. It was natural to have been invited to a party on the occasion of the high school graduation of one of the girls. Going to what used to be home for him was a confusing and distressing experience. On the one hand, he felt very touched by the greeting he received from his ex-father-in-law. As Walker entered the house by the back door he was greeted warmly by his ex-father-in-law who said: "Walker, let me put a beer in your hand." The house was very much the same as ever. He and his ex-father-in-law exchanged chuckling teasings about some plumbing Walker had gotten scrambled in an interesting sort of way that now was set aright by his father-in-law. So the business with the older man was fine. On the other hand, the brief appearance of his ex-wife's current male companion set Walker's teeth on edge. He felt kicked in the stomach and he felt jealous. Walker shared with me how this reaction made him worry that nothing had really changed for him. He wondered if he had gained any personal growth over the past two years.

"You didn't like running into your understudy. Walker, think about this in terms of theater. What does the understudy of one of the star actors do when the star is about?" Walker replied: "He or she stays well out of the way." Baldwin: "What's the point of having an understudy?" Walker: "To take over if the star is ill. That's one reason." Baldwin: "And if the star has had to miss a show and the understudy fills in, how does the understudy conduct him or herself upon the return of the principal?" Walker: "If the understudy wishes to accommodate to the feelings of the star, he or she will pretend it never happened and stay out of the way."

Then I asked Walker if he had ever seen characters change or develop during the course of a play. Of course he had. I asked him if he could imagine his life in terms of acts and scenes. Again he saw this to be the case. He began to punctuate his personal history in terms of acts and major scenes, though in some cases it was difficult to determine whether certain scenes fell at the end of one act or at the beginning of another. Then I asked him how he thought it possible for an actor who had played in a show night after night to portray a part in the second scene of Act One when he was so aware of how he experienced himself in a late scene of the final act? Walker's response was that the stage setting, the business among players, the substance of the story, plus prompting lines and gestures explained all that. I asked Walker to see if he could apply the same reasoning to explain his feelings and thoughts while "at home" at his daughter's party. He appreciated the appropriateness of the metaphor and was able to make the personal connections. I paraphrase his conclusion:

"The feelings and reactions I am having now do not mean I am in my present scene as I am thinking and feeling and acting! Though most of my time now is way into a later act, I can be right now experiencing myself as prompted to being in an old scene. If I find myself feeling right now like I did almost all of the time when I was mostly mid-way through my life's second act, that doesn't mean I have not gone beyond that scene. I see now that I can conjure up any scene right now; I can think of the setting, where the story is in progress, the interactions among the characters, the typical prompting lines, and really get into it. Whew! In a way I wish I could just be where I am now with interesting scenes ahead."

Baldwin: "Then how would you know where you are right now?" Walker: "From where I have come from and where I want to go. Oh! I have to know where I am not most of the time; I guess it is important to be able to feel my way into an earlier scene and from there see where I am now."

I began working with *Abel*'s wife. Then Abel met with me from week to week separately. When they were each ready, all three of us worked until the two of them were comfortable enough with one another to move along without therapeutic support. I held separate sessions with each of them before the three of us met together for one last session. During Abel's individual session with me, after confirming that he was happy with progress in his relationship with his wife, he announced that he finally felt ready to work in earnest on the business of his mother's death. At our last session all three of us agreed that I would continue with Abel in regard to his mother's death. Of central importance was a failure in his childhood family to express feelings toward one another and talk about stressful situations. His mother's dying stretched on for many weeks. Abel could not recall either his or his father ever talking with her about her dying, about her or their feelings. He knows he couldn't just sit with her for periods of time and is confident his father never did. The thought of holding her hand made him very uneasy. One thing was clear. At this point, following a gratifying experience in individual and couples therapy, Abel was open to exploring his feelings. This would have been too frightening for him at the time of his mother's dying.

Abel proved responsive to the induction of trance during which he was able to locate himself with his mother, by her bed, and move from trance episode to episode becoming ever more comfortable holding hands with her and talking with her about his feelings, her feelings, and their love for one another. This process culminated in his letting her go into her death.

Having reached this point, Abel was now open to dealing with deeply felt grief over the prospect of his mother's not being alive to share in the birth of Abel's first child. His wife was expecting and the baby was due in a few months. The thought of his mother not being alive to be a grandmother, especially in the first days after the baby's birth, moved Abel to feel deep grief over how he and his mother had never even shared his getting married in any depth. That his mother held out through his wedding before her collapse, struck Abel as all the more touching. It was clear to him that she had lived for his wedding, thoroughly enjoyed it, and then yielded to physical exhaustion and the final few months of failing. They had never talked of this.

I walked with Abel toward and through the hard, matter of fact facing of his loss over missed opportunities and the fact that his mother was dead and could not be brought back to be with him and her grandchild. Hopeful acceptance emerged and with it the sense that her love was with him and a part of his being.

Now we engaged in the final chapter of our work together. Having gained so much value through trance in revisiting his mother as she died, in trance he visited with his mother before his wedding. With general suggestions from me, Abel reconstructed and reframed actual events just before his wedding when his mother and father were staying at a motel. He contrived to have his father pursuing an errand. Along with his mother he initiated talk with her about her physical condition. They talked about this with openness and love. He said how much it meant to him that she could share with him the joy of his wedding. He experienced her expressing her joys and care. They embraced. He departed. This episode came to his consciousness with flowing ease from his unconscious deep minding. The actual, so-called fact of the matter was that while Abel had, before his wedding, stopped by to say hello to his parents at the motel, no exchanges of consequence had occurred. When Abel looked at the disparity between what emerged in trance and what, practically speaking, appeared to have occurred in fact, he concluded that everything that figured in his trance-induced daydream was implicit in the exchange of glances they exchanged in the motel. The potential for what he daydreamed was altogether actual. What was implicit in their shared glances was rendered explicit in trance.

In later sessions, Abel re-entered trance state, engaged in time progression and permitted himself to imagine step-by-step every important detail of the birthing night. When his child was born he experienced himself phoning his mother to announce the birth and share the labor and birthing story. In this trance he experienced his mother expressing her joy and readiness to be with the two of them and the baby. Abel was deeply touched by this exchange and it seemed real to him. Now, what to do? Abel went home after this session and shared the experience with his wife. She was appreciative and understanding. They decided together what they would do. They agreed that upon the birth of their child, they would focus together on their reframed experience of Abel's mother and go through the steps of imagining themselves phoning her with the news. Then Abel was to phone his father and share the news of the baby's birth. Assuming that his father and step-mother would volunteer to come right away, Abel was to thank them explaining that he and his wife wanted a few days alone with their baby. Protecting these few days would provide for a ritual act by which the loving presence of Abel's mother would be savored.

As Abel and I concluded our work, he confessed that it was extremely difficult for him to think of his trance-induced encounters with his mother as any less real than what had supposedly occurred.

I will address myself now to the procedure with which I worked with these people.

Heather appeared confused initially by my manner of speaking. She asked me to repeat what I had said before pausing and then responding as she did. I could have said simply that in order to solve a problem it is sometimes helpful to step some distance away from the problem in your mind in order to gain perspective, that dwelling with such absorption on what was happening in her home town with her sister made all the more clear *where she was now*, far away from there, here in New England pursuing her own life's journey. She would have understood this but where would that have led her? To simply concurring. I hoped for more than that. I hoped to provoke a de-potentiation of her deliberate conscious reasoning in order to foster a richer play of thought from her unconscious that might lead to her being in New England with a functionally autonomous rather than counter-dependently reactive frame of mind. Heather's recognition of her being other-than-what-she-is-not, her being "More" than other-than-what-she-is-not emerged as a fresh self validation.

Walker came away from his daughter's graduation party stirred by the encounter with his ex-wife. Now he worried that the progress he had thought he had made in therapy over the past two years was all an illusion. It was very tempting for him to despair, explaining sensed improvement as no more than an "out of sight out of mind" relief. Many share Walker's experience. Meeting old acquaintances is sometimes disturbing. When people who have not seen one another for years meet, they catch one another up on developments;

they establish with one another where they are in life, that they are not where they used to be. Each coaches the other to see as audience the current scene in which each figures. Only then do they seem relaxed enough to reminisce in a more or less pleasant way.

Here is an example.

Driving home to New Hampshire from Boston on a summer afternoon in July 1983 I recognized the driver of a car I was passing. I had not seen him in ten years. He and I were colleagues in Chicago. He was my senior administrator there. A lot of stress figured between us. Driving along, it occurred to me to fall back, hail him, invite him by gesture to pull over, park our cars and catch up. I ran through the projected scene in my mind. I saw myself filling him in, drawing his attention from me as a character in an old scene in which he played principal to my somewhat less than loyal opposition, to a scene in which I am currently thriving and generally respected. I envisioned very clearly how I was bent upon having him see me in a positive light. When I realized I was only interested in affecting his perception of me as not where he and I used to be, when I saw I was not at all interested in asking him for his personal news, I awakened to the heart of my intentions. As a major character in an early scene in the third act of my life I wanted him to see how my character part has developed in more recent scenes. I was seeking his recognition of my current performance, a matter of securing within my own mind confidence that I am more how I am today than I was when I was with him in a previous scene? I believe so. When I saw him on the road I believe I was prompted back into a scene in an earlier act of my life. I believe this is the case since the thoughts and feelings that featured how I was within myself on the road driving just ahead of him for some miles were typically the thoughts and feelings that featured my experience of myself in relation to him years ago when we worked together. Recognizing to what end I wished to brief him, I let it go and drove on home. Knowing where I am today, I do not need him to confirm that I am as I am and am becoming what I am becoming. Thinking about changes that have occurred is not as deeply an affecting experience as experientially delivering one's self into a trance experience of the unfolding play of one's life.

Note *Abel*'s double negative in his concluding statement: "I am not sure I can feel what I envisioned as less real than what I practically speaking know did not occur." One might react to this with "Huh?" Why did he not simply say: I feel what I envisioned (in trance) to be as real as what I practically speaking know did occur. Double negatives are interesting. They suggest to me an end-run play by the nonconscious around rational, conscious common sense. Most important is Abel's personal story concerning himself and his mother, the picture he carries in his mind about her meaning for him in his life. I believe it is often the case that people deliberately attending to "getting to know one another" is a follow up response to their having liked the impression produced in their initial encounter; what happens is that people want to build a good case for how come they liked the other immediately. Or, if the initial impression was negative and they know circumstances dictate that they must get along, they work deliberately, at developing a rationalization for pretending together that they are more compatible than first feelings intimated. I infer that Abel and his mother enjoyed a far deeper bond than they typically acted on or articulated. How often we share regrets with a friend that while we knew we could have done so much more with one another than we have, we never did "get it together," never did act on what we sensed was there between us. I infer that the messages between Abel and his mother were ever implicit in their hearts; the trance state that I invited Abel to engage in and which he experienced so fully for himself brought out what he knew in his heart of hearts, i.e., what he knew unconsciously. People look at a picture and tell a story from what is obviously apparent. With another more careful look, they see the less obvious and then reframe their original story. This is what I believe happened to Abel.

Addressing One Persona Through Another

This is the first of four case accounts illustrating the manner in which I join the client in working with their personas.

One way of circumventing defensive resistance triggered by too frontal an intervention directed toward one among several personas, is to address the persona one wishes to communicate with through another persona whom one experiences as willing to collaborate.

Another way of putting this is that personas vary in their collaborative and trusting responsiveness to the therapist's ideas. Hence, one does well to engage the persona or personas least uneasy in regard to a particular issue in the process of supporting and aiding other less comfortable personas in looking at some piece of business.

Commonplace in group work is the device of discussing some business with one member of the group that does not put that person on the spot so much as it does another. The other is then less on the spot and therefore freer to pick up on or demure from joining in on the development of the given line of exploration. The same device can be employed in working with individuals who have become used to working on issues in terms of personas theory.

In my work it is not unusual for a client to identify various extra chairs and locations in the room where each of their personas are "sitting." The chair where the client is accustomed to sitting is the location of the vinculum or meta-self whenever we are actively involved in personas work. Sometimes, then, I will offer an aside to one of his or her personas assigned to a place in the room other than where the client as vinculum is sitting. Once a client is used to this kind of play, it is done with a minimum of dramatic awkwardness. The client has become used to the behavior and joins naturally in the move.

That this is an obvious and naturally appropriate move may be made more clear by a story.

I am thinking of a family in which the father was killed when his tractor tipped over and killed him. The elder of the two boys was sufficiently overwhelmed by the loss of his father that he remained painfully shy of interacting with visitors to his home for an extended period of time. He would retire to his room when non-family visited. There he remained with his door closed through the visit. After a while his mother noted that he began to leave his bedroom door open though he remained out of sight. She fashioned a periscope sufficiently extendable to permit him to see what was going on without personally being seen. He was observed using it with increasing frequency. His mother's next move was to punctuate her exchanges with visitors with asides that her son could, if he wished, construe as intended to include him. She did this with sufficient naturalness that visitors were not aware of her pointing, as it were, to her son. He volunteered some time later that he recognized what she was doing and appreciated her manner and gesture. In time he began to leave his room and pass through the room in which his mother was visiting with others. When he did this, his mother fit into her exchange, as often as wit permitted her, things said that recognized his physical presence without calling undue attention to him. Finally, he moved toward increased interest in joining and participating with others. In much the same fashion the therapist can provide for the threatened persona devices by which she or he can "see" what is happening without threatening the persona in question with too frontal a bid to "come up front."

Another illustration may clarify further the business of communicating indirectly with a persona who resists direct encounter.

My family lived for some years in a predominantly black Chicago neighborhood. Among the families on our block were two of the Black Muslim church. The Black Muslim point of view instructs its members neither to interact with non-Muslim blacks nor with whites. I worried about how this was affecting my children in their play until my eldest explained to me how it was perfectly simple. They all talked to the leaves. This she meant literally! They negotiated all together in rather complex sidewalk games all the time taking great care to avoid eye contact or addressing one another directly. They had become adept at saying what needed to be said to the leaves above their heads. Of course everyone knew perfectly well who the comment was intended for. They all had great times. I tried it out one day with a Muslim father who was trying futilely to drag a heavy piece of furniture from a trailer into his house. I sauntered by him, made some casual comment to one of the branches over head how a fellow could sometimes use another set of hands. The other fellow, after a dramatic pause, allowed that was how it was sometimes. We managed to do the job easily even with my moving in and out of his house "without notice."

Resistance in psychotherapy can be treated with much the same strategy. That is to say, the cooperating personas can play the part of the leaves to a persona whose resistance is fear or anger based. Another less resistant persona can serve as a communication conduit.

The Association of Personas With Different Body Parts

In our first session Felicity introduced her central problem as having to do with decision making. "The way in which I process decisions is convoluted. Let me tell you about a dream I had."

"I am in a kitchen and looking out into an elevated back yard. A firewood truck careens across the yard and garden, crashing through a stack of cord wood. Then it stops. I am terrified that the driver will get me."

I invited Felicity to be the wood truck.

Felicity: "I am out of control. I don't come from anywhere. I just happen. I see the garden and the house and the woodpile. I am going really fast. No one is driving me. Not much happens. oh! I crash into the wood pile. The wood flies everywhere. I am not harmed. I am an old truck. I just sit there. I am aware there is someone in the house. It's dark inside; it's not particularly dark outside. I can't see the person as it's so dark in there. I know they are afraid and I don't care.

I'm laughing. I think it's funny because, as a wood truck stopped there is no way I can hurt anybody."

Felicity, having completed her fantasy, said: "I thought it would be scary to be a truck. The wood truck is dumb, not dumb as stupid, rather dumb as having no intent. I'm surprised there was no driver. As the wood truck I can carry a lot of wood. I can't be hurt because I am already beat up. I am simple so that I can get fixed easily. I don't have a lot of needs. I'm happy doing what I do. I laugh at things that scare others because I am in touch with the seasons. I know about the forest cycle. I am a philosopher. It appears that I am O.K. by myself. I'm not out of control as I am not trying to control where I go. I'm really tough skinned. I seem to be able to stay in the here and now. The truck says to the insider who feels heavy with all this: Don't try at everything so hard."

Felicity now thinks about the difference between an authentic versus a performing wood truck. "I have performed being wood truck so long that I can't simply be wood truck. I feel a lot of tears welling up around this truth."

She spaces away the tears. "The Maid in me, my persona Maid, sweeps away tears as agent of my mother. Mother is distant and aristocratic. I guess Maid doesn't like wood truck. My father was my mother's maid."

"Right now I am thinking of wood truck as my sexuality. I wonder if I have ever been sexually warm. When I think of me being sexual, it's me with new, strange, intriguing romances. My father held me when I was a very small girl. Mother never held me. I am remembering a time when mother complained how he was better liked by me. So, he withdrew his attentions."

In another session I invited Felicity to enter into a fantasy of herself as a two-year-old. She followed my guidance into a wake-state trance and then produced the following vision.

"I am in an immaculate living room, everything in its place. I am standing still, afraid to move. I see myself as the child: tight and pouting, a resigned face for a two-year-old. Mother is cleaning. The child waits and wants and nothing happens. The child is holding a little rag doll which is very limp. She is holding the doll by the arm. She and the doll are all there are in the world. My head is hurting as I see this. My hurting is me. The hurting is going away now. The room is very bare, more bare than I would have thought. It is austere. I am seeing a big chair, overstuffed, sitting all by itself by the wall. Chair says, 'I am empty. I am empty but I am stuffed. I am stuffed with paper.' Paper is old newspapers, yellow and crumbling. I see on the newsprint scream and rage. Doll is saying, 'Don't you leave me too!' It cries softly. Girl says back, 'You can't trust me.' Doll cries resigned. Both are resigned."

I invite Felicity to see the scene now as she would have it be if all her wishes came to be.

Felicity: "The little girl is laughing and skipping around. Mother is working and laughing with the child. She is on and off mother's lap, playing around. The room has a lighter feeling. But it is wonderfully cluttered. I see a little scotty dog playing with the girl, and there is no doll. In this scene I am aware of the outside: the sun and the warm. I see people dressed like in the old time movies. The little girl's face changes from mischievous laughter into mock seriousness, then spontaneous laughter. Daddy is there too and he is very accepting; anything the child does is fine."

Felicity suddenly assumes a radically altered demeanor and invades her own spell with derision. I ask Felicity to be derision.

Felicity: "I am twelve years old and I am laying sideways across the bed in my own room. I see this girl having a grown up pouting, dour face, mouth turned down at the corners in defiance. She feels that nothing is fair but she does not act on her defiance. She is into herself, drawing circles on the rug with her hand. Hand is saying, 'Boring, boring, boring; take me out of this.'...Something in me is saying, 'I don't care. Fuck 'em; I don't really care.' This is coming from stomach. Chest says, 'They never ever did anything for me.' Cheek is actually crying. 'Not my eyes!' Cheek is crying! Right now left hand is holding cheek and saying: 'There, there! You'll be ok. I'll make it all right..' Cheek responds with more tears. That's O.K. with left hand. Left hand is willing to wait." I asked Felicity whether she thought she had a real or perfect mother. She responded: "A real mother trying to be perfect. That's me, too. I was never permitted to express anger...It is hard for me to be with them without regressing to my eleven-year-old self. At eleven I was awkward and shy and didn't know what to do with my body. I read a lot and stayed out of my parents' way. I felt like I was walking on egg shells for fear of my mother's anger. I had some good times with my father at the breakfast table, mother in the background making derisive comments about our banter.

"I didn't know how to hold my body. Like the pieces didn't fit, especially my hands. I still feel more comfortable with my hands in pockets. Otherwise, they would want to be hitting mother. I have an old memory of a sheet-rag under my bed that I'd tear up."

At the beginning of a subsequent session, Felicity removed an acclusive from her mouth, a device installed to correct for her tempo-mandibular joint (TMJ) syndrome. "It is just too difficult talking with this thing in my mouth. It helps me with my hip. Mother had three spinal fusions and a hip reset. It's all a congenital situation. Since I've had the acclusive, my hip has not hurt. This relates to my neck, too. People observe how my neck posture is such that I stick out my head . It's my little girl posture: looking up at people. Therapist: "A little like a guillotine pose? Some question in regard to your own sense of authority? Talk to your neck."

Head:	"Neck, straighten up. Push weight away. You just can't be trying."
Neck:	"It *is* heavy. You don't understand. I'm doing well to keep from totally caving in. And besides, you don't give me any help. You try to act like I'm not here. You try to connect to body without going through me.
	You are part of the reason my job is so difficult."
Head:	"I try to work through you, but we don't fit. I can't get my balance on you. When I try, you resist me and I'm afraid I'll fall off. So I try to get my own place that's safe. Besides, you stick yourself out in the wrong way. And I always have to cover up for you."
Neck:	"Upper back, you're not helping and you are in the way. You're putting me forward, and are part of the weight, and never let go."
Head:	"Arms, you could help, but you don't know how. You could help me sit right on neck. You just hang down and pull me forward. And chin, you feel safer nearby neck. And this is when

	neck and I are in most conflict."
Neck:	"Ass, I think you can help, or maybe you are helping and I'm not using the help."
Head:	"Feet! Pay attention You are maverick. The rest of us tolerate you because you are out there doing your thing. You believe you can be different! That's why I keep looking at you."
Feet:	"But head, your looking at me gets in the way of my freedom!"
Neck:	"Feet, while some feet are necessary, and old pair, *you* act like you are something special. There's nothing special about your job. In fact, I do most of it. If *I* stood up straight, God knows what you would do. You might run away and do whatever you damn well pleased, even dance! You are not to be trusted. Just look at those socks you are wearing! Maverick feet! Gypsy feet!"
Head:	"I have to keep an eye on you. Hey Neck, you do help me keep feet in line…of course, I am fond of you because you do what I wish I could do!"
Felicity:	"My neck part of me is my 'I'll just have to do it myself.' My head is reaching for my feet like the snake with her tail in its mouth."

Felicity proceeded from this line of exploration in her next therapy session:

> "If my feet are my true self, this doesn't integrate with being a mother and keeping house, carrying a lot of responsibility. My husband sees me as a consumer of the house, rather than as caring for the household. I wait till the wood bin is empty or the dishes are all used up. Once I do get into gathering wood or into washing the dishes I get into it. My husband feels I don't see what needs doing. That's not right. I do see. So this week I played being

good girl. That was my hands speaking! I keep
my hands in my lap or in my pockets if there's
any danger that they'll be used to do bad
things. And, as a result of playing good girl it
is true that I have more energy. I wish I could
get all of my parts to work together."

Feet: "I don't want more ease and energy and feeling
              better because Good Girl is doing her thing
              because it involves me. I should feel good for
              having the rest of our body allowing me to do
              what I want to do and not feel guilty about it.
              Cleaning up home is only a short term compli-
              ance. The real issue is: How committed is this
              body to maintaining house and family rather
              than having some adventures in the world. I
              feel I have to give up too much for the sake of
              the house and family!"

At this point, Felicity looks at specific parts of her body and
supposes what they are each centers for. She associated her lower
stomach with her emotions and her insights. With her breasts she
associated nourishing; with her mouth she associated being nour-
ished. Then in a burst of frustration: "Integrating all of my parts?
No! I am too big a task! I feel angry and cheated; someone ought to
have helped me with this starting when I was very little."

Two weeks later Felicity talked of her difficulty getting to and
completing course papers. "I think there is a connection between my
difficulty with school papers and my fear of telling what I know. I
feel I can't write what I know." I asked: "Do you mean that you
mustn't tell what you know?" Felicity: "A secret, huh? If I did write
what I know, people'd be angry with me."

Therapist: "Right now, see how your left hand is keeping
              your mouth nearly shut." Felicity: "If I didn't
              have to see so much crap around, I'd be freer
              to be. This reminds me of how my feet said
              something about wanting to be free. And my
              head wished it could do what my feet like to
              do!"

Two sessions later, Felicity announced that she was pregnant, that she felt pleased and surprised. I noted how radiant she appeared. "It's my Earth-Mother part of me. Ha! The Earth-Mother who validates my being barefoot and pregnant! My Competent-Grownup would have someone else care for the child. I had a fantasy during my first pregnancy of being peaceful and tranquil. But my first pregnancy was full of emotion and upheaval. This time I do feel the tranquility. It is nice having an event making a lot of decisions for me. Of course I could have a miscarriage."

I asked her how Feet are feeling about the pregnancy.

Feet:	"We are feeling a little weighted down...but nicely. We are enclosed and needing to be wrapped up. We are actually feeling kind of secret. We are wanting to wear things, be warmer and insular rather than running around bare."
Therapist:	"Neck?"
Neck:	"Looser than usual despite a lot of pain lately. I feel less strained to hold head up . . . because head is spacy. Spacy excuse by Head. It makes things easier. Less pressure from Head."
Therapist:	"Head?"
Head:	"Yes?" (Laughter both from P.B. and Felicity) "Things are out of control. I might as well give up. There's a force larger than me. It will happen. I can take a vacation.
Therapist:	"Hands?"
Hands:	I'm feeling responsible. I may have to take care of myself. I may be the only part left. The rest of our body has given itself over to a primitive urge."

Felicity began to reflect on related happenings. "When my period was overdue I supposed pregnancy. My sexual libido went way up. I have had two dreams very recently of making love with my husband. Despite my pregnancy I have been using a diaphragm. There's been a dread associated with intercourse with a diaphragm. If only we would just fuck. Damn the arrangements. I got pregnant because of avoiding the use of the diaphragm." Felicity suddenly began talking from her hands.

Hands:	"I only found out today that I am pregnant. One should not wantonly fuck and get pregnant.
Felicity:	"That was my mother talking, my mother, talking through my hands, saying 'One should not have any accidents. 'One,' according to her, 'should remain properly clean, not be impulsive, always plan.' I am feeling that my hands have just now been taking over the roles of my neck and head. It may just be that they will have to give in to what is happening. My hands have been looking frail. I can't seem to keep them clean. I hear my head thinking it's funny how hands have grease ingrained in them,...can't get it off." "Earth-Mother's hands...in big contrast to mother's!" "I had horrible childhood eczema difficulties. It went away when I left mother. There's been a little between two fingers recently." "It's my eyes that do the monitoring of my *proper* hands."
Therapist:	"Are your mother's eyes easy to visit with?"
Felicity:	"No! They are darting. And they are afraid to be seen by me! They veil."
Therapist:	"Do you suppose she let her eyes visit with her on her husband's genitals?"
Felicity:	"No...She's complained over my immodesty. She's said to me she can't stand my immodesty."

I talk with Felicity about how eyes change in character and appearance as they are in the service of different parts of the body.

Felicity responded: "In every one of the photographs of my mother her eyes look bad. There are circles around them. They are cast down."

The next week, as she was working on a difficult issue between her and her husband, I noticed that her eyes seemed to me to be resigned. When I invited her to place her eyes in the service of her feet and repeat presenting her position on the issue, she reported feeling much stronger. I shared with her that her eyes appeared to me much more grounded and fiercer.

The issue had to do with her husband's questioning the wisdom of her accepting a particular professional leadership role given her pregnancy. She felt that losing out on this kind of opportunity interfered with her need to keep up her high sense of performance. Felicity thereupon did a harsh number on herself for having to be a performer. I invited her to repeat several times over: "I am a performer," each time placing her hands on a different vital area of her body. There was a dramatic change in the power and vibrancy of her statement as she placed hands on her breast and then placed them on her genitals. This exercise provoked her into observing that her stomach during pregnancy feels badly when she forgets she has other parts of her body.

In subsequent sessions, Felicity became increasingly aware of how an integration of her different self perceptions into a sense of personal wholeness required her to attend to the various parts of her body. She came to appreciate that her most centered decisions in relation to day-today issues required attending to messages "broadcast" from every physical part.

The Death of a Persona

Case Study One:

While this case and the case that follows have many features in common, the principle figure in Case Two, Keith, has been diagnosed and is recovering from Dissociative Identity Disorder, (formerly Multiple Personality Disorder), and the person referred to as Margaret in Case One has not warrented this diagnosis. While Margaret's experience of her Self most of the time is characterized by the sense that she is one person, Keith is aware on a daily basis of his inner voices and of shifting among his personas for dominance in his Self presentation to others. These cases provide interesting illustration of Personae Theoretical comments on the mental health continuum between disturbed and disturbing Self fragmentation and disturbed and disturbing single mindedness. In these two cases Margaret and Keith are engaged in productive, health enhancing inter-personal work.

A weekend workshop on Death, Grief, and Personal Transformation included asking all participants to imagine the occurrence of their own death, to date the time of their death, and to compose a letter they imagine a friend might write to a third party reporting the loss and sharing feelings and thoughts about the life and dying of the deceased. Each workshop participant shared this letter in session.

Ernest's letter was dated two weeks following the workshop weekend. He imagined his demise to have been caused by an automobile accident, his death instantaneous, and without drawn out agony. This letter written from one of his friends to another featured his fine qualities, and how, despite his efforts to manage a good job and family with balance of attention and energy, the family had been short changed.

He read his letter to fellow workshop participants in a manner that invited simple acknowledgement. Something about his entire presentation proved disarming. We were simply touched and respectful. We moved on to another letter.

His manner moved me to ask him a little later: Hadn't he a sadness about being snuffed out? "I wished for a wife and child. I have realized that dream. I wished for a vocation of value. I found a vocation and have made a contribution." I looked at him. Young. Mid thirties. I found myself uneasy. Something struck me as awry in his matter-of-fact demeanor.

I was moved to share with him the story of a woman about his age who was suffering acute grief because everything she had wished for over many years had come true except for one thing that spoiled the pudding. Ernest's reception of the story produced the appearance about him of a boat slowly lurching over and irretrievably capsizing. Now he disclosed the story he had assured himself he would not share this weekend: "I love my wife; she is such a fine companion. And I have a beloved child. Our home is a joy. And, I have a lover! I love her! I love each one of them. What can I do? What a mess!"

As Ernest talked, Margaret, another group member, wept. He turned from his own work to comfort Margaret. I drew his attention to how his turning to her was all very considerate, and to how it was also providing him with the chance to get away from his own problem. He returned to his own story. While not a person really inclined to commit suicide, he confessed that a fateful accident would bring relief! He could not see any way clear before him. He could not imagine any way by which he could resolve the stress he felt over his two powerful loves. He was sure that were his wife to find out that he loved another woman, there was no way she would hear him say he loved and cared for her as well. He realized now, clearly, that he would have to make a choice, and that a necessary loss would have to be suffered. Turning to others in the group could take place now.

We turned our attention to Margaret. Margaret was nick-named Maggie until a few years ago when she narrowly survived a serious bout with cancer. She told how her break-away from morbid resignation had occurred at a summer conference, how powerful the singing of "Morning Has Broken" as the breakfast grace in the conference center dining room had affected her. Now, years later, she found her attention once again on the part of herself she used to be as Maggie.

Margaret identified with Ernest's wishing to die, and yet she found it had to do only with a part of all she was. "Maggie's life came to an end that summer morning years ago." Margaret pleaded with us to help her let Maggie go. I asked her if she were ready to see Maggie dying. She sobbed that she was. I asked her if she wished to have any of us say words to Maggie. "Tell her she is important." I asked Margaret to see Maggie lying within the circle our gathering formed. She saw Maggie, her facial expression, her clothes. I spoke to Maggie. I said to her how she came to life to do just as she had done, to live out her life for Margaret, that she had helped in every possible way open to her to bring fullness to Margaret's life, and that if she was tired, was she ready, to know our love and our blessing, and to let go of Margaret's body and go in peace. Others added words of appreciation and blessing and love. I sang "Morning Has Broken." She recognized my voice.

Margaret was now radiant, lighter, released. She said how she'd experienced spells from time to time in which her mind was full of funeral sayings and music. And while it didn't make sense to her, she felt she must have, while she lived, a funeral. It was not clear to her that Maggie was the part of her that called for a funeral. "Do you know what it has been like for me? It has been as if I'd been carrying Maggie dead weight. No! I know! It is that I have been dragging her casket behind me wherever I go. It is gone now. That was a beautiful funeral. It is finished. She is free. I am free. And her spirit is a part of my wholeness. Up until this hour I have resented her, winced when old acquaintances who haven't known any better have greeted me as Maggie. I no longer resent her or her name. I am Margaret and Maggie is with me closer than ever, and released as I am released."

Case Study Two:

"My name is Keith R. I was diagnosed with Multiple Personality Disorder and Post Traumatic Stress Disorder a year ago. I guess I have known this for a long time, but waited to get help until the last minute. Now I wish I had secured help sooner.

"In my mind there are several clear and very distinct personalities, each with his and her own character and special qualities, even their own set of moral rules. This makes for conflict among them sometimes, and in a few of them there are what could only be called 'gifts.' I am writing now about one of my gift-personas. His name is Joe Campbell.

"Joe Campbell is an old man, a farmer with a vast knowledge of agriculture and animal husbandry. He usually gets two of my other personas, Brian and Rickie, to carry out the physical labor he wants done. Rickie is a young girl of thirteen. Brian is a young boy of eight. Yet I'm not a farmer! I'm a journeyman in an industrial trade, which makes all this farm knowledge so unusual!

"For the past few months I have been mentally back tracking to try to find out where and at what point in my life I developed my personas who are so real to me. I've had surprisingly good luck doing this. Joe, however, was not so easy to explain. It wasn't until I told my mother recently about Joe and my other personas. I thought she would be a skeptical.

"When I told her about my troop of personas, and that one of me is Joe Campbell, she became very quiet, and then she opened up to me first by saying she believed me, and this was truly a revelation. It finally made sense to her why I had been the way I was when I was younger. And now, given this explanation of having a troop of personas, she understood me.

"My mother said she knew who Joe Campbell was and that *he* was *me*. As a small boy I lived on my grandfather's farm. He was my step grandfather, and my grandmother was weird about our having different last names. I called my grandmother Aunt Olive and my grandfather Uncle Arnold. To make this less confusing, 'Uncle' Arnold told me my name was Joe Campbell, and that I was to say I was Joe Campbell to anyone who asked me who I was, and that I was Arnold Campbell's boy. I grew up forgetting all of this until very recently.

"Now my persona Joe Campbell has died. I was confused by this thought, but it is true. I knew two weeks ahead of time because I became depressed for no reason. Then, finally, at meeting time among my personas, [They hold a meeting every day in the early evening when I talk with them], my persona Brian whispered to me that Joe was dying. My neck hairs stood up. He said low, like Joe was nearby and did not want me to know he was dying. When I asked Joe to explain, all I got was, 'I am a very old man now, and its's past my time to go.' I have seen Joe dead in my mind in the position of someone who has passed on. I feel a very real loss, and am truly grieving for him.

"Looking back now I can see that he was a key player in my life. His death follows the real death of my Uncle David, a real farmer and my grandfather's partner. I now feel that the death of Uncle David provided the suggestion that brought about the passing of my Joe.

"I am wishing now very strongly that I had addressed the voices in my head a long time ago, for now I have real fun in my mind both consciously and sub-consciously. Now when I see events where people have acted out according to a voice in their heads I believe them, and feel for them because I would never have believed either if it had never happened to me. Now I know we all have voices in our heads, but to say that too casually to a person with big time MPD is like telling a liver cancer patient that we all get cramps. It hurts and only confirms how little a lot of people really understand a condition like this. I understand my condition. I am not always happy with it, but I am not shy at all about saying I am having it. I don't need to make anyone a believer, and I don't even try. My wish is that others who have this condition and don't know they have, will get help, and find out how good it feels to know yourself totally. I take my personas seriously, and do listen to them. They help me more and more as my life is getting more normal.

"I have written a special letter for Joe to say farewell, and would like to share it. It goes like this:

> "Dear Joe,
>
> This is a letter to you from all your friends. We want to say how much we have learned from you but never gave you the proper recognition. You are without a doubt the drive that kept us all moving forward, and always have been constructive. More than once I've gone to bed totally drained and not knowing how I got so much done. Now I know!
>
> It's hard to say 'Goodby' because the past is still fresh in my mind, from the days on the farm to now. All your trees and stonewalls and driveways are going to last forever. We planted a weeping crab tree in your honor so we will always be reminded of you and what a big part of us you really have been.
>
> Die in peace, our friend, and know we will never forget Joe Campbell.
>
> Truly,
> Rickie, Dick, Snerd,
> Brian, Turk, Duke,
> Harry, Richard, Neil,
> and the Cat
>
> p.s. We will carry on right where you left off just as you would have done."

A Phantom Persona

For nearly two years, Arlene and I supposed that six personas sufficiently accounted for the ways in which she experienced herself and was experienced by people close to her.

One day we accounted for a seventh, and wondered how it had been possible for us to have overlooked the obvious for such a long time. We guessed we had nonconsciously prompted one another to disregard what was there to be seen.

Arlene named this overlooked persona Betty after Betty Crocker, for her the epitome of super-mom devotion. Here's what happened. Arlene began by saying that for her to meet her parenting responsibilities the next day she'd have to be in at least three places at the same time. In addition, she had signed up for a continuing education graduate course and the first class was scheduled for the next day. "How can I attend class? I can't be there. I'm going to be busy at home." I asked her how she would be missed if she were not at home. This anguished her. She observed she'd been screaming a lot at her family concerning how much they need her though they don't say they do. A notion came to my mind which I shared with her. "You require a child to need you to teach her how to tie her shoe laces. When they learn, you are mad at them because they don't need you anymore." She responded: "How can I get passed needing so much to be needed?"

It was clear to us both that none of her thus far identified personas fit the job description of super-mom. She reminded me that some months previously we had talked of a possible persona she might call Hazel after a television series character who played the part of housekeeper. I had not securely registered this identification.

It looks like I may have gone along with her not wanting to pay close attention to a part of herself she was not ready enough to look at closely. Hindsight suggests one potent reason why I might not have wanted to look at this myself! I have been deeply affected by Irving Goffman's discussion of servants as non-persons. I have trained as a professional waiter; I know what it is to be a non-person. They perform an intimate service and are treated and must act as if they are not there. Hazel fits the existential situation. My failure to stay with Arlene's mention of Hazel, my willingness to go along with her inclination to move right away to other thoughts reminds me of the novel *Who's Afraid of Virginia Wolfe*. I remember Richard Burton and Elizabeth Taylor in the movie version reinforcing one another's common flight from reality. But now Arlene was able to see she had developed an illusion of herself as valuable to her family as a critically needed wife and mother. Her agoraphobic spells, her spells of pronounced anxiety when away from home, can be understood now as a reflection of not being where she supposed she ought to be, right at home all the time or doing errands for the family.

I told Arlene about a husband and wife in their early forties, whom I had seen because of the wife's suicidal attempt and continuing inclinations. That they had no children was a source of grief especially for the woman. The husband noted on two or three occasions in a gentle and tolerant fashion that his wife spent virtually every evening picking up and vacuuming their little house, vacuuming, as he put it, for invisible dust. I asked the woman if there were times over the years when she felt a strong sense of wanting a baby right now. She indicated that she understood me, and that this had happened three times. I asked her how old those three children would be now. She responded that one would be a toddler, another five years old, and the third seven. I reviewed the description the husband had offered of her lengthy after supper clean-up rituals first in the kitchen and then through the family room. I shared with them how I could imagine her caring each night for three phantom children. She burst into tears and shared for the first time ever her private fantasies of children upsetting her home and how important it was for her to tidy up the kitchen and family room as gestures of care and love.

I then turned to Arlene and asked her if it were not the case that her early childhood years were featured with learning how little girls grow up to be specially needed by hardworking husbands and dependent children. She responded with acknowledgment that this, of course, was what all story books and lessons were about. We remembered together how it was that several months previously she had come to session reporting a particularly heavy spell of depression over the past week. on that occasion she asked: "Even though I know I want an interesting life for myself beyond home, even while I know I don't want to simply retreat back into being house and children bound, and this in no way means I don't want to share in the care of home and children, can you understand that to do something new is like dying?" At that time we shared clearly together how we *are*, our being alive, our experiencing ourselves *as being*, is typically defined in terms of what we *do*. Therefore, if we cease *doing* what we associate with *being*, we exist no longer. This involves a dying, a death experience. We saw this much more clearly now than months before. Now we were faced with a clearer realization that Arlene's image of herself, her self as needed housewife and mom, was fighting for her life; that for her to have a life of her own aside from husband and wife might be understood as a threat to the life of herself as housewife and mother.

Drawing upon the story of the woman with three phantom children, she came to see more and more clearly how wherever she was in fact—at her part time job, in class, doing volunteer social service—that her phantom supermom was at home or on family errands Therefore, her resistance to acting on her desire to develop a life for herself beyond home and family constituted a loyalty to her Betty Crocker self, and, we can add, to her Hazel self, the two components of her supermom illusion of herself: Betty in the kitchen and Hazel cleaning up and running errands.

Arriving at this insight called forth an association which we explored. I asked her to recall some play or movie that she could remember in reasonable detail. Arlene indicated she was thinking about a scene in a movie. I asked her if all the principal cast were on stage in the scene she was reviewing. They were not. I asked her what those absent from the immediate scene were doing? We agreed that an absorbed audience rarely thinks of actors off stage watching from the wings or chatting in the dressing rooms. To the contrary, if we are engrossed in the development of the plot we assume characters not present are continuing to pursue their part in the play in character in other places. We suppose, for instance, that the butler is busy in the butler's pantry, the inspector following leads, the villain covering his tracks, and so forth. How can the audience remain absorbed in the unfolding drama if they think otherwise? I suggested, therefore, to Arlene, that when engaged in other than housekeeping and parenting activities, she think of her Betty Crocker-Hazel self as operating on her own in her specially designated scenes.

This moved her to exclaim: "I am missing the present scene, whatever that might be, because I am preoccupied with the whereabouts of someone absent from the scene! And, I am failing to remember that important characters do not have to be included in every scene! Just because they are not included in a scene does not mean they have to get lost or die or something. And, during many movies and plays characters change for better or for worse!"

Plays can be revised after they have opened, both in regard to the development of the story line and the features of the characters. As Arlene continues in therapy she can rework her existential life drama. And this can include re-framing in an updated fashion her conception of herself as a valuing and valued partner among partners in the home.

7

Employing Trance in Personae Work

hile engaging clients in talking about troubles may
prove valuable in many ways, inducing clients to be
come immediately involved in scenes of critical importance to them often generates powerful discovery and therapeutic
gain. Hypnotic enactment in the therapeutic session is very different
from acting out in session. An illustration will underscore this
difference.

Twelve year old Jacky came to therapy because his sudden fits
of uncontrolled temper were jeopardizing his welcome in school
and in his foster home placement. To begin with we talked over his
problem and talked about temper episodes. I advised him that while
my manner, the tasks I might introduce, and my observations might
well upset him, I would not allow him to fly into a temper fit with
me, that he could be assured that if necessary I would constrain him.
We talked together about the game Red light/Green light, imagined
together watching a group of kids playing the game out in my
meadow, imagined further how he as a baby sitter watching over
some little kids might signal to the kids his acceptance of their

interactions with one another in terms of calling out to them "Green light" when their playing together was just fine, "Yellow light" when he felt he needed to warn them they were beginning to mess up, and "Red light" when he felt they must stop some difficulty among them immediately. Now we imagined my employing the same technique with him in session.

Anticipating his declaration that the arrangement was useless because his temper tantrums occurred suddenly and without warning, I engaged him as we talked in a game in which we played with children's stone blocks. We built towers with the blocks, the winner being the one whose last block topping the tower left the tower still standing, the loser being the one whose last block caused the tower to collapse. As conscientiously as I attempted to play the game with my utmost skill, Jacky won more often. He could not disregard my observation that his hands were steadier than mine, that he had access to impressive control. He seemed surprised and pleased with this skill.

We personified his temper and this persona he named Sudden Lightning, Lightning for short. Continuing to talk about his temper outbursts, he was surprised to uncover how in every case there was reason for his outburst; he came to appreciate how Lightning appeared and did his thing as a way of solving some problem his other identified personas failed to manage. Convinced that he would, despite protestations to the contrary, display early storm warnings, I advised Jacky that I would employ the color signals with him as his manner prompted. Reversing roles, I produced verbal and non-verbal gestures to which he assigned these signals. Having talked over matters, having set clear in our minds that acting out was out of order, we explored the meaning and experience of enacting difficult scenes.

I explained to Jacky that if I could be with him in a terrible situation, we might see together better solutions than leaving it to Lightning to settle matters in his own way. Jacky chose the school classroom scene in which his enemy Barney sat several seats behind him, and in walking down the aisle past him provoked him in various ways. I successfully engaged Jacky in "seeing" a bad scene develop, and letting me in on what was happening step by step and blow by blow! By prompting Jacky to fill me in on increasingly specific mental and sensational details, Jacky appeared more and more absorbed in the scene as if it were occurring immediately. Calling for a few seconds time out, a signal with which I was confident he would associate with rest, but only for a short spell before re-engagement, I secured his recognition that while he was literally sitting with me in my office, he was vividly experiencing himself elsewhere at the same time. I stretched his attention one step further in requesting that he "take me" to the safest place he enjoyed. This safe place was his bedroom at home. In response to my question as to what relaxes him in his bedroom he offered specific detail. Now I observed he was proving to his own satisfaction that he was quite easily and naturally capable of experiencing himself in three places at the same time: being with me in my office, sitting at his desk in school, and relaxing in his bedroom. Signalling the end of time out, Jacky re-engaged in a crisis scene in which Barny was starting down the aisle. As Barny came closer, Jacky left his persona Scout at his classroom desk busy with his workbook, while the rest of his personas retreated to his bedroom at home. When Scout signalled to the rest that all was clear, he returned all-together to school. At our next week's session, Jacky reported that when he applied this routine the next day at school, he felt like he had done it before and was pleased that it all worked out well again.

Much of the remainder of this chapter draws from a major case study in which psychotherapist Hsuan-i Chiu and I corresponded relative to Hsuan-i's psychotherapy with her client Elizabeth Stacey, the pseudonym the client chose for herself. Elizabeth has been deeply invested in this correspondence and in my consultation with Hsuan-i.

Hsuan-i's letters include progress reports, transcriptions of sessions with Elizabeth, Elizabeth's automatic writing tales depicting personas interactions, and reflections by individual personas upon daily events in Elizabeth's life. My contributions consist of theoretical points, clinical observations, and the introduction of techniques I employ in working with personas.

Elizabeth's work with Hsuan-i and her automatic writing are featured by trance states similar to that induced in Jacky as he and I worked on his classroom crisis.

Trance induction and in-trance work feature virtually all the following examples of work with personas: prompting the blind walk, engaging personas in group sessions in which personas are group members, directing deep and specific engagement with the concerns and intentions of a given persona, coaching the vincular process, consulting with one persona while "forgetting" and "stepping aside from" the other personas for the moment, directly and provocatively leading one or more personas in their individual work, engaging the client into telling fairy tales as a way of disclosing personas and a given persona's psychological features, encouraging automatic writing of tales depicting personas interacting and addressing critical situations, illustrating the use of personas sculpting in the form of dramatic tableaux, and stimulating attention to personas absent from the immediate scene.

As Elizabeth's psychotherapist, Hsuan-i Chiu requested suggestions as to how to guide her client. I used the assignment as an opportunity to set down a number of concepts and clinical strategies informing my own work. Readers familiar with the therapeutic approach associated with Milton Erickson will find that Hsuan-i Chiu consistently offers Elizabeth Stacey assurance that answers lie within, that each of us brings to tough problems past learning and accomplishments that when combined with external resources provide working solutions to these problems. Note how Hsuan-i facilitates Elizabeth's utilization of her own resources. Note how Hsuan-i working with Elizabeth engages in interventions that prompt Elizabeth to keep wondering. Wondering, in contrast to "why-ing", generates attention to conscious and unconscious openness, receptivity, and perceptive playfulness. Child-like wondering opens the mind to novel ways of taking experience apart and reframing experience. In following Elizabeth Stacey's hypnotic journeying, you will see how she finally gets to her deepest stories, and reconsiders her intentions and options. Elizabeth's personas working together succeed in breaking the hold of childhood abuse and mobilizing her personal vitality.

My first letter to Hsuan-i follows.

Facilitating Group Work Among Personas

Dear Hsuan-i,

Your report of Elizabeth's work is very interesting. You want my suggestions.

I am wondering what each of Elizabeth's personas like to wear, both outer and under apparel. Do they do various things with their hair? People have their special places: rooms, outside places. If I were to have the best way of introducing someone to the various "who-I-are", I would take them to various places that are my special haunts as well as to places where I have lived. Hsuan-i, I'd spend a day walking with you around the neighborhood of my childhood. I'd take you to a special place up in the White Mountains, to a neighborhood in the south shore of Chicago, and so forth. If we were not actually to travel there, I'd take you on an imaginary blind walk. I would get us ready by explaining to you that you are blind now though you once had vision. Therefore, you can see with your mind's eye. Hence, I'd be your outside eyes and explain to you what I want you to see, smell, touch, feel, hear. Hsuan-i, when I offer a client an invitation to take me to one of several of their special places, once they get under way, both of us are in trance. During the induction to trance, I suggest that special places may be comfortable or uncomfortable places. While they may go into light, medium or deep trance, it is important for me to retain access to at least the edge of consciousness to insure that I am mostly attending to their work rather than to my work. I may suggest to them that they know which persona is most prominent in leading me where we are going unless we both know the answer to this question from the outset. Now, once the client is clearly absorbed in being in one of these places, I suggest that they know a great deal about this place, especially what works well for them there, and what they have learned they must watch out for. Further, I suggest that many of our special places have much to tell us or remind us in regard to how we are able to solve important problems in our life, that information of this kind may be immediately apparent or may come to us in its own way and in its own time. I suggest to them that the therapy session is not necessarily the most important place in which important developments take place, rather, that we may begin things happening during our sessions that take form in their own way and come to our attention at surprising times. In facilitating their openness to this kind of exploration I suggest to them that they may now be ready for surprising recognitions, and if they are not ready now, that they will be ready soon, and that they will know when they are ready for surprising recognitions as these will be occurring.

I may ask if the place the client has taken me to is special for every one of their personas. If the answer is negative, then I will suggest that each persona may or may not know if they would or would not be welcome here. What I am particularly interested in is the dynamics among personas.

This leads to another technique I have used. I have a number of clients who go into personas' group session from time to time. One man places his various personas in chairs or in cushions about the room in which we are working. His vincular self sits in the group facilitator's chair. On occasion I have fostered this process by sharing with the client that I am aware of the phantom presence of their personas in the room; the client accepted my suggestion and joined me in identifying their various locations. On other occasions I have invited the client to place his personas about the room. It began as a deliberate exercise devoid of any feeling of authenticity. In a short time the feeling of authenticity emerged. I have succeeded in securing clients' confidence that at any time the group can be dismissed in order for them as vincular self to talk *about* what has been going on with me. It is important to know one can be in charge of how close and how far away one wishes to be to or from one's self at the moment.

Andrew teased out of his experience of himself and from impressions about him others have shared over the years, ten principal personas. In session after session he has referred to one or another persona to explain to himself his feelings and reactions in critical situations. And he is now at an impasse relative to central issues in his life. He and I are standing in the kitchen alcove of my office waiting for the coffee to heat up. Our session has begun. I sense his impasse and begin to feel tense and fidgety. I am aware that I am experiencing counter transference. I perform at appearing attentive as he talks. My presence with him is characterized by skeleton crew duty on shipboard. I call my own personas into session in the town hall of ny mind. My vinculum/"I"/group-facilitator-self calls the meeting to order and asks what is happening. Everyone is in agreement; Alan speaks for the others: "How Andrew is right now is like where we have been. Remember those bargaining sessions three years ago when representatives from the Psychological Association and Society of Psychologists met time after time to see if we could resolve our philosophical and by-law differences? Remember the pre-session jitters? How we made small talk, and talked about but didn't get into the business? We were torn between holding off and getting right into business. When we did enter into formal session, that was tough, but not as tough as the delaying." O.K., I had it—I adjourned my own group session and returned to Andrew. Informed by my own internal process, I saw clearly our therapeutic situation. Here were Andrew and I waiting for coffee in the kitchen anti-room. I sensed Andrew's personas seated in the other area. I spoke plainly: "Andrew, your personas are around the corner, seated around the room out there. Go see where they have seated themselves; you will find one vacant chair for your vincular self. Don't sit down there right away. Stand in the middle of the room, see where your personas have chosen to sit. Note there is no accident to where each is sitting in relation to the others. You don't have to figure out the reason in order to see where they are. The story will come clear as you see where they have each chosen to sit. While you are still standing in the middle of the room, and after you have seen where each of them is sitting, sense where you are being drawn. Don't move yet. Pay attention to the quiet ones. The one or ones that do not seem to be drawing you, who may be hiding. Be informed by what you pick up on the situation with each. You can move to and from the vinculum's chair as you are inclined. Be sure to return to the vincular position from time to time in order to assess as objectively as you can what is going on in the room." Andrew, despite obvious ambivalence, was compelled by my suggestions. And he went to work. A lively and powerfully illuminating group session followed as he moved from chair to chair engaged in inter-personal encounter, and when he became stuck, he stepped to the middle of the room where he was available to another persona drawing him.

I am always intent upon facilitating integration among the personas such that they know one another well and come to see how, in proper measure, each is essential to the welfare of the whole person. Blocking or frustrating this process of integration is often the failure of one or more personas to present their stories in full enough detail. Groups can fall into trouble when one or another is not heard in sufficient detail and with decent respect. When we experience others as slighting or being bored with our stories, resentment mounts. We need others to draw us out and to encourage us to move to the very furthest boundaries of our story. We do well to ask one another: What will your life or what will our life be like if you go and we go with you all the way through with your story line?

A Vietnam Veteran kept an evening appointment with me; he just barely kept it. We later concluded that it was one persona who managed to get him to swing by on his way to "wasting" a man who had infuriated him. He had a magnum hand gun; he was in a state of profound excitement. I am morally certain he could have completed his action. He has killed in combat. I risked inviting him to walk through every step of the way to enacting his intention. I engaged him in trance. I kept prompting him to keep slowing down so that he could "see" and feel and attend to specific details; he was constantly wanting to get into high speed. I secured his willingness to attend to details, to feeling the car seat beneath him and the wheel in his hands, the sweat breaking out as he drove toward his destination. Having parked outside of his intended victim's house, he was inclined to racing up the path, breaking in, shooting the bastard, and beating a retreat. While inclined to rush through the final moments of violent action, he responded to my suggestion that he walk up the path, experience himself knocking on the door…Once again he accelerated and whipped through the final move. Once again I commanded his attention and prompted him to move though the shooting slow motion so that he registered every minute detail in squeezing the trigger while seeing the face of his victim and taking in the specific effect of a magnum's bullet upon his victim. At this point, my patient began to shudder and was so nauseous that I wondered if he would vomit. He gathered himself, slumped, and told me that he was not going to act on his original intention. While unusually dramatic, this case illustrates what I mean by prompting each persona in group session with other personas to explore the far reaches and the ramifications of each of their story lines. And, out of this process typically emerges a fuller appreciation among the personas of one another and of how they need to work together in developing a story line for the whole person that all can endorse.

Hsuan-i, Elizabeth describes her marriage as in crisis. Can you envision her personas in group session considering her options? Have you introduced Elizabeth to the notion of the vincular self? It is my impression in reading her own account of her personas that she does in fact have a reasonably developed vincular self, and that it was her vincular self who was largely responsible for introducing her own personas. Note each individual introduction. Each is a mix of description *about* each persona as well as first person one liners uttered by a given persona. I have an image of Elizabeth as vincular self in private session with each persona catching the essential, principal features, the existential substance of each character. Earlier in this letter I alluded to the case in which one of my patients as vincular self conducted group sessions with his personas. I'll add now that my function during these sessions was to serve as coach observing and facilitating his vincular self. From time to time I would signal time out. As in theater we would freeze the action, and then my patient as vincular self would leave the room with me to consult in an adjoining room. There we would talk for a few minutes about what it was like for him in session; we would review his interventions and make room for him to explore his feelings as leader. Time and again we would remind ourselves that while it is appropriate and natural for the vincular self to share with group members what it is like to serve as facilitator, the leader cannot serve effectively if he or she tries to force rapport or hurry conflict resolution.

Intensive Individual Psychotherapy With Selected Personas

It is possible, of course, that one, or every one of Elizabeth's personas are nervous at the thought of talking candidly, in the presence of other personas. In this case you may talk with each one of them alone in regard to important issues including the marriage prospects. If Elizabeth has difficulty imagining how one persona can think or talk without the others hearing every word, you may remind her of things she already knows but may have forgotten, that one of the most wonderful and important things we learn as we grow up is to forget a lot of things. Just think how confusing it would be if we were not able to forget an enormous number of thoughts that come to mind every minute. We shelve a great deal of thought on the heels of its occurring; and we shelve a great deal of our thoughts as they occur for future reference. When we bump into friends we have not seen for many years we amaze ourselves with how much we can remember that we thought we had forgotten. All of us have experiences in which a person catches our attention and asks us where we have been. We say we don't know; we must have been woolgathering and can't even remember what we were woolgathering about. We awaken from sleep knowing we have been dreaming. We see traces of the dream and feel the traces slipping away from us. Now we can't remember our dream at all.

There are two "moments" between you and Elizabeth that I would very much like to see transcribed. The first "moment" features your work with Elizabeth's personas Stephanie and Carolyn, each of them postured on opposite sides of a closet door. The second "moment" comprises your use of the first scene in moving Elizabeth into a more effective/adaptive strategy with her husband, Clay.

Peter

The transcript that follows, sent to me by Hsuan-i and Elizabeth in response to my request, involves or makes reference to four personas. Others are implicated. Personas of which Elizabeth was aware at this time are:

Susie: is a very small child and still very trusting and loving, even though she's been beaten for no particular reason that she can see. Her best time of the day is meals; it doesn't hurt so much when there's something in her tummy. She remembers how much fun she had with the kittens, whom she knows her grandmother drowned.

Stephanie: is really feeling a loss of someone near, but "others" are making no allowance for her feelings or even in guessing how she feels. Mostly she would like to know that people care, but asking is scary and she already knows the answer anyway.

Deidre: is around eighteen years old. She appears sweet and feminine, but has all the social values of a vampire because she enjoys reducing men to impotency.

Miranda: is a newborn—(recently emerged)—sex symbol who has dieted herself insane for twenty pounds. Now she's into parties and men . She is twenty-two years old. However, she has to be perfect all of the time. She feels like a robot in spite of her new found social life.

Morgan: is young and pretty and on her own. Except she's never learned independence, and her money goes for phone calls, home, and perfume. Morgan is currently waiting for Prince Charming. She is not really into liberation, not into trying to find herself.

MaryEllen: after ten years of marriage and two children realizes she's unhappy and bitter. But she has given up too much to throw in the towel, so she eats and is drinking.

Femina: is the all time, all knowing Queen of Space and Time. She knows what is best for everyone and they look to her for loving care and warmth.

Faleen: is an older, mature female cheetah, a little long of fang, but has killed to protect her cubs.

Mona: appears to have it all, but is the original white nigger.

Jenny: is middle-aged. She committed mental suicide sometime ago. She has affirmed her position of never expressing herself or reaching out to others. She has a mean streak and a low regard for life.

Carolyn: has been buried for forty-eight years under Jenny, Stephanie, Mona, and all the others. She was afraid of them because they were overwhelming for a long time. She had a hard time knowing that she was there, but she is emerging for a struggle with them all. She has leadership skills, but has limits to her resourcefulness.

Here follows the transcript. It features Carolyn, Stephanie, and Jenny. Therapist Hsuan-i Chiu begins.

H:	Elizabeth, I see Stephanie so sad, wanting someone to hold her, then getting angry because no one is responding. The way she fights back is to close herself in a closet. She's so afraid of expressing her feelings, anticipating punishment if she expresses her feelings.
E:	I guess I equate expressing feelings as being abandoned, but there is a difference between expressing feelings and being left. Stephanie gets very upset when she tries to tell her feelings to people who don't have any:...Mona and Jenny who sit in silence, expressionless. They are the living dead.
H:	When you are being Stephanie in family therapy session I see Clay very confused.
E:	And frightened.
H:	You have been so enmeshed. You are seeing that you've wanted Clay to give you what you wanted from your mother, your mother who didn't know how to express her love and support.
E:	Clay is always one up on me. By this I mean, I always thought parents should have their children's best interests at heart, and he's never thought me important.
H:	In your wanting security and nurturing, your expectation is that Clay would take care of you?
E:	That's gone. Maybe I haven't known what real nurturing is all about. I keep thinking about grandmother Jenny's destructiveness, her killing my kittens.
H:	Who can provide nurturing for you?
E:	I'll have to provide that for myself because no one else knows how to give me what I want.
H:	Is it that Clay doesn't know what you want?

E: Yes.

H: You've changed and that is confusing. You are sorting through the past and present, and assembling new views. Stephanie is so frightened. How do you see Stephanie reacting if she opens the door?

E: A whole new world. She doesn't know what it will be like, so she's afraid. She creeps way back inside.

H: And doesn't talk?

E: Yes

H: What of Carolyn?

E: She's gone way into herself too. Can you blame her?

H: No, when the scenes become confusing I see Carolyn leaving to get clarity.

E: She fights for her right to leave when she's overwhelmed.

H: Let's put some pieces together. Take your friend Arthur for instance. You are getting the nurturing from him that you want from Clay. Arthur is mothering you. And Clay sees this, becomes threatened and confused and absents himself to his office. He's been replaced. I see Carolyn in a similar situation with Jenny mothering Stephanie. Stephanie is really wanting Carolyn but does not know how to ask for Carolyn's help, so she gives into Jenny who tells her the best way is to be a good girl, and get in the closet. Carolyn gets frustrated with all of this and goes away.

           When you felt Carolyn emerging yesterday, did you talk?

E: No, but I knew she was there. She's angry and doesn't understand. And Stephanie is afraid she's going to be killed.

H: Are you feeling overwhelmed at the moment? (I see Elizabeth's expressionless face ... there is terror in her eyes.)

E: Yes.

H: How can I help you sort through this confusion?

E: I don't know.

H: What do you want?

E: I don't know that either...(long sigh)

H: Do you want to go get Stephanie out of the closet?

E: I think that'd be a good idea. She's been in there a long, long time.

H: Yes, Stephanie is locked behind the door for a few reasons. She's afraid of punishment, that her feelings will be denied. Have Carolyn speak to Stephanie.

E: (As Carolyn:) Stephanie, please come out: I'm out here and I want you to come out.

H: What does Stephanie say?

E: She's very frightened, because she doesn't trust whether Jenny's out there too. If she comes out, Jenny might kill Carolyn too. And then Jenny will get what she's always wanted. To kill is to have absolute control. So Jenny can have Stephanie in her power, ... and can control her by keeping her locked up.

H: Now Elizabeth, Stephanie is listening. Is she saying any thing to herself?

E.   Yes. She's saying: I know Jenny is very depressed and angry. There is something very wrong with her. But Stephanie is not so much afraid of Jenny as a person as she is of her power games.

H: I see something! Mona is like Jenny, passive: passively waiting to be rescued by Clay. They are so frightened! They think no one is going to rescue them but they can't tell anyone or each other their fears so thy entice Stephanie to do their work. Stephanie is the "scapegoat" for Jenny and Mona. They literally use Stephanie to purify themselves. They blame her for everything they think is wrong and put all their sins on Stephanie's head. Instead of sending Stephanie into the wilderness, they keep her locked in the closet. This saves them from searching for a new scapegoat the next time something goes wrong. What about Carolyn, Elizabeth? Is she afraid of Jenny?

E: I don't think she's really afraid. Maybe she's intimidated by her massive size. Jenny's a balloon I can let air out of.

H: How can Carolyn confront Jenny? Tell her she wants to help Stephanie now.

E: She tells Jenny to keep quiet and sit down. She's not going to play games and compete with her. Carolyn says I'm in control now.

H: Be Carolyn and talk to Stephanie again now.

E: Stephanie, please come out. I'm out here and I can help you. Put your hand on the doorknob and open the door. You are not doing yourself any good hiding in there.

H: How does Carolyn console Stephanie who's just opened the door ajar?

E: Carolyn puts her arms around her. Stephanie's never heard anyone talking to her that way before, wanting to give Stephanie support and caring.

H: What does Stephanie say?

E: She feels better but she is still afraid. (Elizabeth weeps being so touched)

H: OK Carolyn, Stephanie is still listening. What does Carolyn say to her?

E: Carolyn tells Stephanie she never has to go in the closet alone anymore. Carolyn is there to talk with Stephanie and to show her this is only a closet. They don't always know where they are going but I know something important is happening.

H: Elizabeth, did Stephanie fear Carolyn was leaving her for good?

E: Yes, but Stephanie knows she has to trust Carolyn because mothers come back to their kids.

H: Stephanie is so afraid of growing up to be Jenny. Is Stephanie afraid to die?

E: Stephanie is afraid of living like Jenny because Jenny doesn't know how to ask or get what she wants.

H: What does Jenny want? That is so impossible?

E: To be a whole person: she's given up. Quit. You know you can die by committing emotional suicide.

H: Yes, you can die by quitting. Our work has been to build a bridge for Stephanie....out of the closet into this new world. I imagined Stephanie wanting to open the door herself although she trusted Carolyn was on the other side, wanting to help her open the door.

E: Yes, I see Stephanie needing to trust Carolyn. She needs to express herself so she can meet new people.

H: Yes, Stephanie is learning to talk to her friends. These friends are your own characters, Elizabeth, that you need to work with before you can get what you want from Clay. Elizabeth, when you place on Clay the demand that he give to you what Stephanie wants from Carolyn and wants to do for herself, you set Clay up. Clay gets confused when he sees you disappearing into the closet. He doesn't know how to respond because you aren't there to tell him your needs.

E: Stephanie disappears into the closet so she can cry. (Elizabeth as Stephanie weeps for the first time in years. She weeps for her mother. Elizabeth sees how Carolyn is the mother she always wanted and she sees how she can mother herself. She as Carolyn is Stephanie's mother. And she sees Jenny as a survivor for the first time.)

H: Elizabeth can you imagine Stephanie being younger than eight or nine? Maybe five or six years old. Such an age! So capable of feeling afraid. Her worst fear is that her mother will leave and never come back. And she is beginning not to feel separate from the rest of the world. This is a fresh new way for her to be. This is frightening and exciting for you. Out of this, then comes the question for you: Who am I? Who are you, Elizabeth, when you are with Clay?

E: I am his original servant. There is nothing else I see other than that.

H: Do you have to be a servant? What can you say to yourself first to change this image.

E: No I don't have to be a servant. I can say to myself, I've had enough of this servant business. Then I can express myself clearly to Clay so he won't talk to me as a servant. I can say to him: Can we sit down and work this out together?

H: And as mother to yourself, can Carolyn talk to Stephanie in a cross way? Can she call Stephanie a brat? Tell Stephanie she needs to go away because she doesn't want to be around Stephanie when she is so bratty. Can mothers tell their children they don't like what they are doing? That this does not mean they don't love their kids.

E: Yes. That happened last session when Stephanie was acting bratty. Stephanie doesn't really want to hurt Carolyn; she gets frustrated like any kid. She does get afraid Carolyn will leave her and not come back.

H: What happened to Stephanie last week?

E: Stephanie found Carolyn away! She asked herself: What did I do? Can't Carolyn stand me?

H: So stephanie stamped her feet?

E: Yes.

H: A little like a mother not willing to go to the store right when the child wants to go to get a new doll. Mother will go in due course but not right now.

E: So Stephanie stamps into the closet, slams the door, and sulks.

E: But I came back.

H: What moved you to come back?

E: I don't know. I guess I knew I had to come back—to give up.

H: And similarly, you slammed the door on Clay this week with a Fuck You. And then Stephanie opened the door and came back. (Now Elizabeth sees how she buys into not explaining her feelings and how this is a kind of death.)

H: When Clay becomes the punishing, critical mother, it is then you say: "I'll show you", and you go slam the door. Who gets hurt?

E: I do.

H: Things get distorted when we expect things from someone when we don't even tell them.

E: Yes.

H: How might you have asked Clay to hold your hand when you were so sad about your mom?

E: Just come out and tell him. Tell him I feel sad and I need his support. I did tell him!

H: How do you want him to support you?

E: I just want him to be here. That's all I want. Honest. That's the way I want. I know he's really bought into that male chauvinist role.

H: He's bought into an affair. The office gives him what you're not giving him. And your sons Gavin and Howard give you what you are not giving Clay.

E: Companionship

H: How can Stephanie ask Carolyn to be companions?

E: They need to talk to each other, get to know each other better. Stephanie barely remembers most of Carolyn's life.

H: What is happening is that you are mourning your mother's death. You are grieving. This makes you a little helpless...Elizabeth, have Stephanie ask Carolyn to be with her.

E: Carolyn, be with me Thursday afternoon to do something

H: What if Carolyn says: I can't. I'm going to be busy.

E: Couldn't you put it off? (answers defensively, thinking Carolyn doesn't want to be with her)

H: What if Carolyn says: I have an important meeting. What about Friday?

E: OK.

H: Hold it right there! You recently asked Clay for time and he said he had an important meeting. Now! You know Clay well enough to know he will not come back with a counter offer. What can Stephanie ask Carolyn to say to Clay about how to fulfill her need?

E: Okay. How about Friday or Saturday? Can we work something out?

H: Did Stephanie ask Carolyn last week to say to Clay that you wanted to be with him?

E: (Elizabeth reacts with a sharp air intake.) Stephanie had a temper tantrum. She didn't tell him how she felt.

H: The most important task is to acknowledge Carolyn's presence. She's only gone into the next room. She hasn't left you, Stephanie. Might you go and find your mother?

E: Yes, I'm already doing it.

H: Yes. You started yesterday. You went to find Carolyn instead of waiting for Carolyn to come find you. But Stephanie plays a good game of hide and seek. You are the only one

who knows where you go. You are aware of
the leavings when you go away.

E: Yes.

H: Elizabeth, if Carolyn were to say: "No, I can't
go with you Thursday," does that make
Stephanie have temper tantrums?

E: Well, it used to, but it's not going to anymore,
because Stephanie thinks she can work something out. Because she knows Carolyn is willing
to work something out.

H: Stephanie is going to open the door and go find
her mother. She's going to find her companion. There's no use waiting for someone to
come looking. You have a lot of power. You
have Carolyn who is the team leader who steps
out for a second sometimes.

E: And then everybody panics.

H: Of all your personas, Stephanie gets so crazy
because she fears her mother will never come
back. And it never crosses her mind she can
open the door and go find Carolyn. Where
does Carolyn go?

E: Maybe to a shop...to have time to herself.

H: Stephanie might not have thought to ask, can I
come with you?

E: Nine out of ten chances she could. Or maybe it
wouldn't be Maybe then, she could just entertain herself for a while.

H: Where is Stephanie right now?

E: She's with Carolyn.

H: Is she out of the closet?

E: Yes

H: How does Stephanie feel?

E: She feels fine.

H: "Fine?" Let's find another word.

E: Okay. Free! Because she knows now she has
someone she can depend on which is what she
always needed.

H: Okay. Before we close let's talk about Clay.

E: He says he has a hard time communicating with people.

H: His way of communicating is to tell people to do parental things. Yeah. He wants everyone to take care of him. He ought to take care of himself. He needs a Carolyn.

H: But Carolyn is not willing to be his Carolyn.

E: Yes. He needs to find his own.

H: So Carolyn was with you last night when you were arguing with Clay. You didn't say no to his demands.

E: I said No to his demands and I said to him: You are always giving me orders and that pisses me off. Can't we work around that? I told him: It's not that I'm unwilling to do things. It's just the goddamned list of orders and I can't stand it. I asked him to rephrase what he wanted.

H: Since you're wanting Clay to rephrase for you and he's not wanting to, how might Carolyn have told him how she wants to be talked with.

E: I did tell him! (Hsuan-i role plays Clay to Elizabeth. Hsuan-i coaches Elizabeth how to re-assign to the other person what he can take care of himself)

E: He doesn't take no for an answer.

H: It's like Carolyn feeling that if she says No to Stephanie, Stephanie might hate her; therefore Carolyn is a bad mother. Carolyn also is afraid Stephanie might not like her because she's not doing what Stephanie wants her to. What can Carolyn say to Stephanie?

E: I'm sorry I can't do it (be with you) today. Can we work out something else? Shall we set up a list and stretch it over a few days?

H: Okay. We are restructuring what happened with Clay last night. (Elizabeth repeats that Clay does not cooperate this way…meaning attending to Elizabeth's needs, listening to her feelings) Hsuan-i coaches Elizabeth toward a shift from combative defensiveness to an attitude of clear firmness. Elizabeth assumes a remarkable change in the tone of her voice. Here we have a clear shift in Elizabeth's response today from Stephanie's sulking to a Carolyn posture and tone.)

H: How do you feel right now?

E: I feel fine....umm...good. I feel good about me.

Looking carefully at this closet scene featuring her personas Carolyn and Stephanie has helped Elizabeth to interact more effectively with Clay and the children. In a subsequent family session, Hsuan-i observed Elizabeth as Stephanie, frustrated and conflicted about coming out from behind her barricade, feeling safer when she didn't, and then getting mad at herself for staying behind closed doors leaving Clay to build up an attack. Elizabeth momentarily left the session in a rage, then came back, announcing to her husband and sons that she didn't have to tolerate their lack of respect or a denial of her feelings. In an individual session with Elizabeth, following the family session, Hsuan-i said to Elizabeth that she felt that Elizabeth's anger had been appropriately directed as she said to Clay: "I don't like how you respond to me. You are not respecting my feelings." Elizabeth appears to be developing new skills in handling difficult scenes. Hsuan-i writes: "Another positive development from our reviewing the tape has been that Elizabeth and I decided that Stephanie needs to work more. Carolyn is working out some limit setting with Stephanie. Stephanie has been manipulating Carolyn to the degree that several times this past week Carolyn has opted to leave Stephanie in the lurch. Stephanie has agreed that when she is behaving bratty, she will leave the room for a while, then she can come back when she is feeling better. Hopefully this will help Stephanie realize Carolyn is not always abandoning her."

Facilitating Automatic Writing
Featuring Inter-personal Psychodrama

A letter from Hsuan-i introduces Elizabeth's clinical situation and a suggestion of the nature of Hsuan-i's work with her. And following this letter are a few fables that Elizabeth wrote in which she engages her personas in therapeutic work. I will comment upon this fable writing in more detail following the letter from Hsuan-i.

Dear Peter:

Has it been three months since I last wrote a letter of substance? Thanks for being so patient. The delay in sending you this package has much to do with my undertaking restoration of an old house in addition to taking careful time to build up my practice in eating disorders. My devotion to anorexia and bulimia involves the same persistent loyalty as I give to continued archaeological hunts for personas—my own and others.

Three weeks ago Elizabeth discontinued her Trilafon that she's been taking for ten or more years. She just decided one day she no longer needed pills. Elizabeth saw her physician last week and as she reports, he was very surprised and concerned she'd stopped them, especially with her history of depression during winter. He advised her to take one now and again whenever necessary.

Now more than ever my responsibility to her rests in concentrating on another way before she pops a pill. This is to say: How she can turn to whoever is angry, whoever is sad, whoever is disappointed, frustrated, and in particular whoever is not talking to whomever. In most instances, we come around to Stephanie and Mona in conflict with Carolyn as mediator. Now Carolyn is more comfortable opting for breathing space from time to time. Elizabeth has been more able in the past few months to identify when Carolyn needs to leave and when Stephanie needs to find her. What I am talking about is that Elizabeth can now say "I need." Elizabeth is so much more cognizant of bodily tensions when Stephanie does battle! She recognizes tension in the form of chronic headaches, back pain, tight jaw, dental pain, insomnia as deriving from defeating episodes of angry silence which she has previously used to punish herself and others.

Introducing Elizabeth to your method of identifying and bringing personas to the foreground for review has allowed her to separate from drugs and alcohol. In short, she weaned herself from drug dependency through Personae Theory.

To continue: Several sessions have been spent discussing Elizabeth's current desire to leave the marriage. My sense is that as she grows stronger she may leave. Hopefully she has the skills to continue placing Stephanie and other personas in perspective during difficult times. I trust she knows now that leaving for the sake of leaving because she finds herself in a place where there is no hope is not the answer. Elizabeth has lived too long in purgatory. I'm not sure the marriage will survive. It has for twenty years because Clay and Elizabeth apparently needed to live in misery together. Now that Elizabeth knows another life besides misery with him, she garners the strength to try life, and living alone.

Continued confinement in a non-nurturing environment keeps her locked in old behaviors. No human being can live in a vacuum, try as he or she might. Our work together has been to show her that she has confused vacuums with safety. I do believe now that Elizabeth knows vacuums are unsafe and stifling for growth. Of course I have never encouraged her to leave the marriage. This would be unethical. She had no other choice than to stay put, to gain a thorough understanding of her *modus operandi* and to see how ineffective and self defeating her previous style has been. Her hard work has been separation and individuation as Elizabeth Carolyn Stacey!

When I saw her last week she looked pale, wan, and tearful. I saw Stephanie, but felt someone else was lurking nearby. I gathered that Elizabeth was angry with me because Stephanie eluded me for twenty minutes. I supposed her evasiveness had to do with my decision to see Clay in individual sessions. There is much competition between them, particularly for the therapist's love and attention. Clay admitted to feeling uncomfortable "spilling his guts" with Elizabeth watching. I clearly saw his urgent need for privacy and a safe enclave. I wanted to work with him on identification of his personas since Elizabeth frequently refers to him as Adolph. He is suspicious of personas theory as he's alluded on occasion to multiple selves as being "very mentally ill."

I will also admit I was setting a trap for Elizabeth because I was tiring of her chronic complaining about Clay not getting into therapy. Now Clay has committed himself to therapy and Elizabeth is furious. I understand her disturbance very well. Though she had welcomed my broadening my role from serving as her individual therapist to serving as family therapist, she held on to me as hers, specially. She resisted recognizing me as a figure in the family system. My motive was to explore and explode Elizabeth's no-win scenes. Though I was aware of triangulation into their neat guerilla warfare, I took the risk in order to expose both of them to their chronic habits of no wins. I approached Stephanie in an individual session last week by remarking how she was able to cry instead of slamming doors and screaming Fuck You. I did not mention Carolyn because Elizabeth is often clever about pretending to be Carolyn to hide her pain.

In this session Elizabeth revealed that she is terrified Clay might grow up and not need her! Their relationship, as you are aware, epitomizes suffocating dependency issues. So I really didn't see Stephanie at the outset of the session! Rather, Mona using Stephanie as an apron in which to hide her feelings. Well, Mona is learning finally how to express sadness! Remember Mona is the original white nigger, angry as all get out. Beware to anyone in her line of fire!

Besides allowing Mona to express her fears about Clay's growth, evident in his refusal to participate in insidious games, I focused on Elizabeth's sadness after a weekend with the boys. She and Clay had travelled some distance for the boy's school events. At first, Elizabeth was too quick to dismiss the occasion, but something in her tone of voice, combined with a face distorted in agony, pushed me to probe even further. Elizabeth said:"No one bothered to talk to me. Clay was into being the great white father by condemning me in front of the boys for leaving the motel sink a mess." Once again we worked on how Elizabeth repeatedly looks for reprimand in Clay's voice, facial expressions, and body language, for her poor performance. This is a painful reminder of all the "You should know better than to do this," reprimands from her mother Vivian. Elizabeth opted to seek consolation in miserable isolation throughout the remainder of the family trip.

I find it interesting that whenever Elizabeth anticipates punishment she is nearly always standing behind Clay. Remember how she visualizes everything? Sculpting and role-playing experiences have revealed how she typically positions herself so that Clay gets the upper hand. This accounts for Elizabeth's continual reference to "what's his face looking down his nose at me." By standing behind Clay, sitting before him, or being in another part of the room, Elizabeth easily slips into the scapegoat role. Elizabeth now sees more clearly how she victimizes herself and then how she conveniently projects her anger onto others. Now she is seeing more clearly how her interpretations of another's behavior tends to develop into no-win schemes, nasty self-fulfilling prophecies.

Elizabeth is tumbling in space; she's frightened. Who wouldn't be! After all, when one has been lonely and been living in crippling isolation, and then advances into a space with company—company being the emerging of here-to-for submerged characters—one can become somewhat overwhelmed. Elizabeth is encouraged by progress in enjoying more integrated moments, this is to say, situations in which her personas are supporting one another. As evidence of this, last Friday, Elizabeth went downstreet to the hot tubs for an afternoon of delight. She treated herself yesterday to another soak. Can you imagine Elizabeth's new found freedom and courage. Can you imagine her doing this by herself previously?

I am proud of Elizabeth and am confident that she will never enter another psychiatric unit again!

I have urged Elizabeth to write down her thoughts following unhappy moments. I have prescribed this as a way for her to see how her expectations about Clay, about herself, do in fact lie in the fantasy world. One of Elizabeth's crucial issues is sexual nonfulfillment. Until recently, she had no idea of her sensuality and her need to be engaged in physical intimacy. She learned that sex is naughty; the implied message from her mother, Vivian, has been that "Nice girls don't do bad things with men; don't give yourself to a man." This has of course, created severe difficulties in the marriage. We have been exploring her anger and sadness about this.

I feel Elizabeth's persistent failure to lose weight no matter how much dieting and exercise is followed, has to do with her inability to receive herself as a woman. That word is receive not perceive! Stephanie, her predominant character, is not yet of age. She is harnessed to a childhood moral code of behavior: "Be a good, perfect little girl! Do not grow up but be an adult." Following this prescription of perfection has blunted psychosexual development. The past month we have focused on Elizabeth's failure to achieve orgasm and Clay's premature ejaculations. Opening up a way for Elizabeth to experience sexual fulfillment has been to let her write down what she needs to say to Clay in order to be aroused. She has been verbalizing what she likes/what she does not like, heretofore described as a wrestling match, so that today she accounted for an orgasm.

I will stop for now and send you what I have.

Hsuan-i

Elizabeth's dramatic sketches are essentially psychodrama. Moreno and subsequent students of psychodrama often invite the subject to choose a fairy tale to dramatize with the help of co-participants. How I, for instance, will recall Jack the Giant Killer and dramatize it will invariably disclose my personal issues and how I am inclined to deal with them.

I remember a psychodrama session I facilitated some years ago in which a young woman first related and then engaged companions in dramatizing the story of Cinderella. Her story concluded with the nasty step sisters and step mother leaving for the ball. Cinderella, exhausted after helping them all get ready, remained, bereft, sitting among the fireplace cinders. I was fortunately able to cue other participants not to communicate to the subject that most of us are familiar with the version of the tale that features the arrival of a Fairy Godmother, various transformations, magical developments, and a Happy Ending. Our subject's version of the story represented a metaphor for understanding her sense of her own existential story. Following her psycho-dramatization, a companion engaged everyone in presenting her version of the classic tale. Now our first Cinderella was profoundly astonished. She couldn't understand how on earth she could possibly have failed to remember "all the important parts of the story." She concluded that while, of course, she had known from childhood how the story goes, it is clear to her that in her life there have never ever been any Fairy Godmother figures. When invited to review her past once more, she startled herself by recalling, if briefly, certain powerfully rich moments with very special older women. She supposed that she had always been so preoccupied with unfairnesses at home she had pocketed, neglected to pay enough attention to, moments when her life had been touched deeply by loving, older persons outside of her family. Now she reworked her first version of Cinderella, departing from the classic story line in ways that followed her own fancy, ways that underscored wondrous moments in her life and contributed to her reframing her story of her personal existence. As I read Elizabeth's sketches I see her engaging in psychodrama and reframing her experience of herself.

Here are several episodes in a running drama written by Elizabeth. Note that the character Hermann is in fact her husband, Clay.

Carolyn, Stephanie and Hermann the Frog Prince

For all intents and purposes Hermann is an ordinary frog. He goes about his froggie business and seems quite content. He's respected by the other frogs

However, Hermann was raised by a "witch-frog" who brainwashed him into being a spoiled little bastard, a true Jewish-American Prince. She bewitched him into believing that he could demand whatever he wanted of people (frogs) and even be destructive and get away with it. Hermann soon grew fangs and was into temper tantrums. Anna, the frog-witch kept Hermann in his own little crystal cage, and when things didn't go the way he wanted them to, he slammed the cover on his cage and stayed there drinking, for days.

One day, Princess Stephanie and Lady Carolyn walked by the pond, and chanced on Hermann. Hermann was not too sober, but in a good mood as Anna had given him a bottle of V.0. and told him to get out of his crystal cage.

Hermann was spontaneous and happy. And Stephanie, having just gotten out of Jenny's clutches, liked him. Lady Carolyn decided this relationship was not for her. But what the hell, Stephanie was of age. So, Carolyn went for a long vacation by the sea.

To make a long story short, one day Stephanie, who by this time felt her closet looked good, discovered that Hermann kept disappearing into his crystal cage. Hermann was a demanding prick most of the time, and she saw him bare his fangs at her, more than once.

Hermann threw a true screaming fit only because Stephanie asked him if something was wrong. He went into his crystal cage and sucked on his left rear foot.

Stephanie got thrown for a loss because of all of Hermann's crazy accusations. She fled quickly to the small house by the sea where Lady Carolyn had been, only to run into Lady Carolyn halfway there.

[A note from Elizabeth's therapist, Hsuan-i, indicates her perception that it was not Carolyn but Mona that Stephanie encountered half way to Lady Carolyn's house by the sea since Mona sometimes mimics Carolyn, and since Mona uses guilt to punish Stephanie]

"Stephanie, she said, You go back there and tell that destructive son-of-a-bitch it is his own fucking fault. You have been kind and supportive to him. And he's to treat you like a human being if he cares for you. If he doesn't want to treat you like a caring person, that's his problem. You don't have to take it. It's abuse! And you're too good and kind a little girl to take that from anyone."

So Stephanie told Hermann, and he sort of thought he should cool down. He is back in his crystal cage thinking about it all.

Stephanie is off for a few days with Carolyn by the sea. [Hsuan-i: I experience Elizabeth feeling anger at Mona's voice and, thus, going to find Carolyn.]

Carolyn told Stephanie it would be nice if Hermann would just break that crystal cage. Carolyn also says he can do this if he wants to.

Stephanie has decided that once you are a frog you can never be a Prince no matter how many kisses and commitments you get from the Beautiful Princess. And Stephanie has also decided, because this way is safer, that once a princess, no matter how many rewards she gets, she'll always be a Princess, never a Queen. And, this is never, never good enough!

So, it is safer indeed to revert to old behavior rather than take the risk and time to try out new ways. A new way is equivalent to independence, being grown up, being a woman.

Stephanie Panics, or Does She?

Hermann came to Stephanie at Carolyn's and asked Stephanie to play golf. Stephanie was not too wild over the idea but it was going to be a long winter. Hermann had seemed to be enjoying himself yesterday and they had had a good time.

Carolyn had gone away for the day, so Stephanie was alone. Boy did she feel alone! Anyway, she had diligently studied her golf book and was ready. Things went along ok for a few holes, not great but ok. But it was hot, and Stephanie's clubs and bag started to weigh one hundred pounds.

Then it all fell apart. No matter what she did, nothing went right, and boy was she trying. By the time they got to the sixth hole, Stephanie told Hermann she wanted to quit. He snarled at her that she couldn't do that. By this time she was really angry at Hermann and at herself. Damn it, she'd had enough! She felt like a kid in math class when she was supposed to be able to do dividing and she couldn't no matter how she tried. The whole class would laugh at her. She was supposed to do this silly shit and she couldn't.

She hated that frustrated, dumb feeling. Anyhow, with her anger directed at herself and Hermann, she blew the next four shots, maybe on purpose; she had really quit by now. By the time that Hermann got to the next hole he announced they were quitting, or rather *He* was quitting. Stephanie, trying to make the best of a lousy situation said: "Why don't you finish without me?" Hermann snarled that he wasn't about to. Stephanie got angry all over again. She wished she could find Carolyn; she needed Carolyn! And let's face it, Hermann is no Carolyn.

So anyhow, she decided to just shut up for awhile and try to clear her head. She had to grow up and handle this one by herself. It seemed pretty overwhelming to her without Carolyn there.

She had a sandwich and cried and wrote. Hermann wasn't speaking to her by now. But she didn't care. She had to think how to handle this herself:

1) She cried a long time because she was so frustrated and humiliated by the whole thing. Here she was again with people expecting her to do something they could do

and she couldn't. [Hsuan-i sees Elizabeth at this point in her story writing metaphorically about old frustrations and humiliations as a child when she just couldn't do things right.]

2) Hermann was no Carolyn! Stephanie certainly realized that! She was pretty tired of trying to make sense of things with Hermann, where all he did was tell her how silly and stupid she was.

3) She was also pretty tired of being angry with Hermann because he was so insensitive to her. Maybe Hermann is an emotional cripple.

4) She decided to take some more time for herself.

So she silently allowed Hermann to go back into his crystal cage, wishing he'd stay with her, but she was so upset she couldn't ask him.

Anyhow, Carolyn finally came home and she and Stephanie talked. She told Stephanie maybe she was trying too hard to please other people. And yes, probably Hermann is insensitive, but she really didn't think Stephanie had bought into it this time. It was OK to be quiet, at least she hadn't had a visible screaming fit and Hermann was just going to have to learn to take care of himself. And she thought Stephanie had done a good job under the circumstances.

Stephanie also noted that Hermann didn't have anything to say to her either. She wondered how much he really cared about her . Damn it, couldn't he *see* how upset she'd been and how frustrated!

Stephanie Reaches Out, or What Happens After You Are Bitten by Bees

Carolyn found Stephanie sitting at the table looking out the window. Carolyn sat down. She was not pleased with Stephanie. She knew Stephanie was deeply bothered by something. Stephanie shot her a look that would kill. Carolyn was getting angry. So was Stephanie. Finally Stephanie growled: "Where the hell have you been!" Carolyn saw red: "Where the hell have YOU been. You've not been here." Stephanie raised her head and looked at Carolyn like a lion sniffing the air for prey. "I was here!" Carolyn was so angry she could spit. "Bullshit you were here. You were creeping around here like a ghost. I could sense you but I couldn't find you. What the hell were you trying to prove? Stephanie's voice became constricted: "I was bothered."

Carolyn:	YOU were bothered!
Stephanie:	I thought you would come and find me.
Carolyn:	Why didn't you come and find me? I was here.
Stephanie:	Jenny and Mona wouldn't let me.
Carolyn:	Huh! What do you mean Jenny and Mona! They're dead, if they ever existed.
Stephanie:	I kept running into them: Mona complaining about how I acted, and Jenny agreeing with her. It was like I was shit.
Carolyn:	You're not. OK. Stephanie, what are you really trying to do?
Stephanie:	Grow up.
Carolyn:	All by yourself?
Stephanie:	Yes. I have to...do it myself.
Carolyn:	Who told you that?
Stephanie:	They did.
Carolyn:	Cute! You were supposed to grow up. When?
Stephanie:	Right away. I guess I was supposed to grow up the way they wanted me to.
Carolyn:	What does that mean?
Stephanie:	I don't know, and I don't think they cared, as long as they felt I fulfilled their crazy ideas.
Carolyn:	What ideas? Don't tell me those two whackoes ever had any ideas about anything.
Stephanie:	I don't know except I was a threat to something, and I was expected to know my place.
Carolyn:	Great. What was your place, Stephanie?
Stephanie:	It was never defined, except I was supposed to be 'good'.
Carolyn:	Lovely! Here they are expecting something of you, and you're not knowing what it was, except when you didn't do anything, or overstepped their boundaries, you knew it.
Stephanie:	I tried. I really tried to be what they wanted, but I never really knew what they expected except

when I tried I got hurt. So I finally really got their message. It took me a long time to figure it out and they kept changing the rules of the game.

Carolyn: What was their message, Stephanie?

Stephanie: Don't be. I can't be whatever they expected, I disappeared. Mentally I mean.

Carolyn: And beat yourself.

Stephanie: It saved them doing it. And I knew they would.

Carolyn: So you just 'faded' away.

Stephanie: Like Jenny. Just like Jenny.

Carolyn: They wanted you to be another Jenny?

Stephanie: Yes. They sure did. They wanted me to be warped and sick. They even said I was crazy...every time I reached out.

Carolyn: Do you know what that is Steph? What it's called?

Stephanie: No.

Carolyn: Child abuse. And they probably would have felt perfectly justified had anyone dared question them.

Stephanie: (giggling) Hear Mona shrieking and yelling now, like some helpless demon: 'What can I do! She's crazy.' And I can see George snarling at me just before he belts me in the head: 'You've got to learn, you bitch!'

Carolyn: That, my dear, is abuse, pure and simple.

Stephanie: And they, all of them, said it was for my own good.

Carolyn: Cute, very cute. Did you believe them?

Stephanie: I believed I was evil, sick and something was wrong with me.

Carolyn: Of course, how could you believe anything else?

Stephanie: They were wrong.

Carolyn: That isn't the word for it. You're being very generous with them, more than they deserve.

Stephanie: It makes me angry and sick.

Carolyn: Of course, but you made it out of the closet and to me!

Stephanie: I don't know what kind of shape I'm in.

Carolyn: I do. You're fine, if you'll just stop disappearing. By the way, why didn't you come and find me, you little shit! Steph, you are NOT incompetent, crazy, or anything else! You've got a lot of courage and just plain old fashioned guts. You're a gutsy lady!

Stephanie: (crying) I always perceived myself through their eyes.

Carolyn: How else could you have seen things when they did everything to deny you...It was a huge conspiracy!

Stephanie: Yes, and I didn't know it.

Carolyn: How could you have known?

Stephanie: I couldn't have known...anything about what they were doing to me. So they could 'live' with me and I could become what they wanted, I mean, needed. They really needed me to be abused and hurt. I was responsible for THEM!

Carolyn: We're back to the scapegoat theory.

Stephanie: Yup. What a mess.

Carolyn: Just remember one thing: You're out. You've been in a terrible, terrible situation, Steph, and YOU made it OUT. You are free!"

In Which Some Ghosts Reappear

[This set of reflections by Elizabeth has been precipitated by a thoroughly nasty encounter with her husband, Clay. He has come home from work, has demanded whether she has written a letter he had expected her to have written, and finding that she has not, tears into her. When she asks him how come he couldn't have written the letter, she reports his having responded: "I have other things to do." Once again, the OFFICE! Ad nauseam! Elizabeth has not yet felt strong enough to share with Clay who her personas are. Therefore he does not know what is occurring among her personas behind presented demeanor and reactions.]

We yelled and screamed at each other for twenty minutes like the Tasmanian Devil and His Bride, dancing around the perimeter of things and not getting to the main issue, which was US!

Stephanie was there scared out of her mind because this was no Jenny who'd put her quietly in the closet. It was a monster who threw her in and slammed the door and locked it, not caring whether he had hurt her or not. Stephanie was bruised when Jenny put her in the closet, but this time she was cut and bleeding and an arm was broken. She was angry, scared, and sick. [Note: this description is to be understood metaphorically.]

Sometime later Stephanie managed to get herself together and out of the closet and into bed. HE was there too, brooding and silent, this monster, that appeared from time to time. Stephanie never knew when he would have his revenge on her. She never knew why he wanted vengeance. Was it because he perceived her as "less than perfect?" She was, after all, still a kid.

HE wanted to talk, but he put Stephanie on the spot of having to beg for him to communicate with her, this old game of "Guess what's bothering me." Anyhow, it all came down to the very ancient issue: "He didn't like the way she kept house!" and "Why wasn't she more organized?!" Stephanie thought: "Help me, Carolyn; this is making me angry and I'm sick of fighting."

Suddenly the monster changed into a little boy, really just asking for her help but not being very direct about it. She could see Mona's ghost rising from the grave: Too busy with THE HOUSE to have time for her and Jenny.

Jenny at three hundred pounds on top of an old stepladder, papering walls. An impossible-appearing task! Jenny always seems to choose August, when it is ninety degrees to heave her bulk up the tottering ladder to do God-knows-what with sticky pieces of paper. It never looked any different when it was done!

Stephanie remembered Mona yelling at her and slapping her because she couldn't make her bed "right." Stephanie had just plain quit because, worst of all, THEY never had time for her.

Stephanie went and found Carolyn and said: "It's an old issue and I want to do it better, but I don't always see things. However, I can try to do better; I just need some organizational skills. I just don't see things like you do. I would like a nice environment too!

Thanks, Carolyn." So they talked, Stephanie and Carolyn, and Stephanie felt better, and the little boy did his crossword puzzle.

I, Elizabeth, don't think what's-his-face realizes who-all I've got "behind" me that I have to deal with first, before I can do things, before I can move with things happening.

When he was after me to help more, I saw MaryEllen, mad as hell, ready to kill. I saw Mona yelling at me because I was not perfect. And, Jenny holding up one of the drowned kittens. He doesn't know about Stephanie who is trying to grow up. And Carolyn who helps her. He ought to know that what Stephanie sees in him sometimes is the terrible monster ready to destroy her because she's LESS THAN PERFECT for Adolf with all his lists. "Goddamn it, Hermann, talk to me! Treat me like a PERSON."

Anyhow, HE said to me later:"They must have really fucked you up when you were a kid."

P.S.: The office is his closet!

Hsuan-i:	Peter, I asked Elizabeth to write another dialogue between Stephanie and Carolyn to see what would evolve. What Elizabeth wrote follows:
Stephanie:	I need to grow up.
Carolyn:	Leave off the 'up.' We all need to grow. It's never too late. No one is ever a 'finished product.'
Stephanie:	Which is what Jenny and Mona wanted in their own crazy way from me. They wanted to point me out to the world and say: 'See how perfect she is? We did that.' Guess what?
Carolyn:	What?
Stephanie:	I wouldn't be there! [Stephanie is giggling.] Their perfect work of art would be a gorilla, a huge, hairy, ugly gorilla, and they'd be proud and all the world would laugh at them. And I would be laughing too. By being ugly I'd have my revenge simply by not being there. I guess it would be better to be a gorilla because then

> everyone could see what their work of art
> really is.

Carolyn: Well, are you a gorilla?
Stephanie: No, of course not. And I am here.
Carolyn: So am I.
Stephanie: We're here together.
Carolyn: Yup, and don't forget it.
Stephanie: I think I've learned something.
Carolyn: Not to disappear?
Stephanie: Nope.
Carolyn: What?
Stephanie: I like gorillas.
Carolyn: I'm going to belt you.
Stephanie: Have a banana, Carolyn!

Hermann Throws a Screaming Fit or
How Stephanie Can't Believe It, or Is He for Real?

It was a lovely autumn afternoon. The sky was blue and the leaves were on fire. It was also sometime after Stephanie had confronted Hermann on the golf course. Anyhow, she was sitting at the edge of the woods behind Lady Carolyn's small house by the sea. She had on her best purple, satin Princess gown. She was drawing with the "colors" on a large sheet of paper that Grandmother Ina had sent to her a few weeks ago. Her drawings were her "talent" as Ina and Carolyn had said.

Her friend, Anthony G. Bear [Elizabeth's younger son] had found her and he was doing bear cub things in a tree. Right now he was hanging upside down. "Hey, look at me, Yerhighness," Anthony called as he started to swing gently by his toes. Anthony always called her "Yerhighness." He didn't have to but he did. "Anthony, be careful," Stephanie asked more for caution's sake than anything else. Anthony G. Bear considered this a bear-cub thing to do. So did she. But, whether Anthony realized it or not, he was getting BIG. Stephanie guessed that Anthony C. Bear didn't realize how much he'd grown 'cause he was into bear-cub stuff still.

Anthony managed to make it back to the top of the branch and then down the tree without killing himself, and was off to explore a large rock nearby. For a few minutes they were absorbed in their "things." Stephanie was drawing a large cat and Anthony was on top of the rock trying to stand on one foot.

Suddenly there was such a shriek from Hermann's pond three miles away that Stephanie dropped her "colors" and Anthony almost fell off of the rock. They looked at each other in shock and said: "Hermann" together. "Yerhighness, Hermann is NOT one of my favorite frogs, but do you think something is wrong?" Anthony asked. Anthony was big and kind. "Probably. "Whatever it is, it must be a disaster. I think we'd better find out what it is, Stephanie said through a sigh of apprehension. So they set out, slowly, toward the pond. Anthony stayed behind Stephanie because he didn't like Hermann too much.

When they got to the edge of the pond there was nothing but silence since the screams had stopped the minute they had started out. Suddenly there was Hermann, his eyes all red and bulging. "Someone stole all my french fried flies!" Hermann screamed. "All of them?" Stephanie asked. "Well, no, not exactly," Hermann gulped. "I counted them this morning and there are six and two-thirds flies missing. It's unreal!!" Hermann was definitely beside himself.

Stephanie couldn't believe it. Not that six and two-thirds french fried flies were missing. Hermann was sure to have more stashed away somewhere. Rather, that Hermann was so out of control. He was hardly his regal self now! "It's your fault!" he yelled. "You did it."

Anthony G. Bear was not pleased by Hermann's perception of things and had advanced to within a large paw plop of Hermann's screaming. Stephanie glanced quickly at the situation and said: "It's OK Anthony. I can handle him." "Hermann," Stephanie looked him straight in his unroyal face, "I haven't been here for two months. I've been with Carolyn." Hermann yelled: "If you'd been here, you could have watched my fly collection and kept count of them for ME!"

Stephanie: "Goddamn it Hermann, you watch it yourself. It's YOUR collection. You spend all of your time with the fly collection and you never have time for me or anything else. There's more to life than FRENCH FRIED FLIES! Besides

that, I HATE french fried flies and honestly, I
don't want to hear about your six and two
thirds missing flies. Knowing you the way I
do, you probably left them somewhere and
forgot about them!."

Hermann rose to his full height of two feet and yelled: "I never forget anything." "Yes you do, Hermann," Stephanie responded, "You forgot ME when I came to live with you. I can't take that. And I'm not going to. You'll have to find your flies yourself!" Hermann yelled: "I'm going back to my crystal cage. So there!" "Go ahead, Hermann, it's your favorite place. I understand," Stephanie said quietly.

With that, Hermann gave Stephanie a terrible look, and climbed into his crystal cage, slamming the cover so hard he almost cracked it.

Anthony G. Bear and Stephanie walked back to Lady Carolyn's house. They were quiet. "We should never have gone," Anthony said. "He made such a noise." "I know, Anthony. We did the right thing. "Hermann doesn't appreciate us," Anthony said sadly. Stephanie put her hand on Anthony's fuzzy head and said: "Hermann doesn't appreciate anything or anyone. It's his big fault. It is sad too."

Anthony realizing Hermann's background ventured: "But he thinks he is perfect doesn't he?" Stephanie nodded: "He does, and I'm afraid he expects too much of himself because Anna the Frog Witch cast a bad spell on him. Well, anyhow, Anthony, let's go see what Lady Carolyn is doing."

As they walked toward Lady Carolyn's small house by the sea Anthony asked: "What does the 'G' in my name stand for?" Stephanie responded: "For Grizzly." "Wow! I didn't realize I was one of THEM. WOW! They're big!" Anthony danced along singing: "I'm a big grizzly, I'm a BIG GRIZZLY." Stephanie listened and thought: Not for awhile, Anthony.

Elizabeth concludes this most recent set of reflections and stories reporting that Stephanie worked for a long time charting her emotional and thoughtful reactions to pressures upon her by Hermann, one of her names for her husband Clay, as well as pressures upon her by her personas Mona and Jenny. Elizabeth writes:

"Stephanie is really pretty pissed off, but:

1.) She's accepting anger. She sees it justified, after being brainwashed into believing that anger is wrong.
2.) She recognizes that she is as valid a person as 'All the others.'
3.) What she wants is to grow and not be alone trying to do it.
4.) Maybe, just maybe she doesn't have to justify herself to others whoever they may be. She can just BE with whatever that is for HER.
5.) She is not about to pay anymore dues to Jenny and Mona's Helplessness Club, nor to Hermann's Ego Trip Organization of which he is President and sole member.
6.) She has been working on this charting exercise for a long time and she is pooped! Writing may be her gift but it tires her out, albeit she feels good afterward and she's never sure it makes sense, but it helps her arrive at valid points!

Peter, when I saw Elizabeth today, she said: "Here is the whole thing for you and Peter. And I have found a new persona! MaryAnne. At first I thought it was MaryEllen, but no, this one is mature. She's Carolyn's twin of sorts. Carolyn is kind of shy about parties. Maybe that's why she wasn't there. And I know I felt abandoned by her. A new development! Read it for yourself."

Hsuan-i

Whoops!
Stephanie was sitting in the dark of Carolyn's kitchen. There was a mental cat-fight going on in her head between old Mona, MaryEllen, Jenny, and good old Hermann. She thought she'd like to climb under the sink and close the door, but she'd had enough of that. Clearly something was Going On!

Carolyn had gone to bed early with a book because she'd said: "Stephanie, I'm sick between the flu and everything else. I've had enough.

Stephanie had understood but it hadn't changed the fact that there was still THAT CAT FIGHT. She'd have to deal with it. As far as she was concerned Old Mona and MaryEllen and Jenny and Hermann could spend infinity screaming. She just wished she could shut them up. So she sat there and cried. She knew what had happened. She'd literally hit a stone wall. Something was OVER. She felt a sense of loss, but she'd live with it. Things were a jumble; that's what was stopping her, holding her suspended. She could of course talk to Carolyn. That helped. Carolyn should at least understand. But there were things she had to deal with herself on her own. And so she sat not thinking, feeling tears rolling down her cheeks. All Stephanie could say, and she's not given to these words lately, was "Damn it!"

And so she sat, feeling physically numb except for a sort of pain inside. She wasn't going to fight it; she let it go on. Last week she had tried to paint and nothing had happened. She's also heard a lot of doors slam. She's felt somewhat guilty because she knew who'd slammed them. It wasn't like her, but she'd done it. Stephanie, with her feeling for people knew what it felt like to throw the tea into Boston Harbor. Stephanie's tears had stopped, and she was contemplating the beginning of a revolution when she saw a soft light [headlights] and heard a car door close shut firmly in the front yard.

My God, thought Stephanie, it's three o'clock in the morning! Then she heard a soft tap at the door. Stephanie was out of her mind with fear. Carolyn was asleep by now. I'm not going to bother her. She got up, wiped the last tear from her cheek, blew her nose, and went to the door. Guess I'd better turn on the light. Idiot! That's not going to help, there's no window. Whoever or whatever is out there, YOU, Stephanie, when you open the door, might get shot. Thanks for that thought, Mona!

Stephanie was shaky, from a lot of things, but her hand went to the lock and she opened the door. Gulp! There in the light was Carolyn, or at least Stephanie thought it was Carolyn. She looked like her. Sort of. Stephanie was getting unfocused. The Voice, so like Carolyn's but a little softer, said: "It's cold out here, Stephanie. I'd like to come in." Whoever it was, stepped in. Whoever it was

looked enough like Carolyn to be her twin. Stephanie quickly noted
that while Carolyn was a classic beauty, Whoever was a knock-out.
Stephanie had to back up so whoever could come in. Stephanie
forgot about Carolyn; she was overwhelmed by Her First Impression of Whoever. The first thing Stephanie noted about Whoever
was her Femininity. The carefully cut hair, the make-up (Wow).
The clothes! Holy Cow, and the wonderful smell of expensive
perfume. Stephanie's mouth was open but things were coming
through, the wheels were turning. Stephanie remembered the great
stores she'd been to. I wonder if her name is Jordan Marsh.
(Stephanie, old girl, you really are off the wall.) Whoever was
quality stuff. (Sexist thought, Stephanie. I don't think she's going
to beat the hell out of me. There's something about her.)

Then Stephanie focused on Whoever's eyes. She'd heard Mona
scream at her that she, Stephanie, had cat's eyes; they were green.
Whoever's eyes were green! And yes! Whoops! Something she'd
seen a long time ago. Oh yes. Gramma Ina's eyes. They were blue,
but they were like Whoever's eyes. There was a sparkle and light
and focus on Stephanie that she'd not known for a long time and
thought was lost! Carolyn's eyes were green too, but they were open
and honest. But Whoever's eyes SHONE. Stephanie figured that
Whoever would accept her. She hoped so!

Whoever: "Hi, Stephanie, I'm MaryAnn, Where's
             Carolyn?"
Stephanie: "Gulp."
Whoever: "Never mind, Steph. I know where she is.
             HOW ARE YOU?"
Stephanie: "Huh?" MaryAnn reached out and placed her
             hand on Stephanie's shoulder. And Stephanie
             knew MaryAnn was Whoever. Stephanie has
             always known. MaryAnn is who Stephanie
             will be. MaryAnn is, a goal. And MaryAnn is
             MaryAnn is Stephanie. MaryAnn. MaryAnn.
             Her name sang through Stephanie's mind like
             a song.

Envisioning Dramatic Tableaux in Trance State in Clarifying Personas Dynamics

Dear Hsuan-i,

I talked with you last evening about my use of another hypnotherapeutic device in working with personas, the envisioning of tableaux to discern where personas stand in relation to one another relative to given issues. A tableaux is a dramatic freeze. Freeze, as I use the term here, is theater language for directing each and every character to hold very still just where they are in the midst of a dramatic statement. Many of us are familiar with the depiction of the nativity presented by one or several tableaux. I recall one presentation many years ago that began with a tableau depicting Mary asleep and an angel standing over her posed in such a fashion as to suggest that the angel was telling Mary through Mary's dreaming that she would give birth to a holy child. The next tableau depicted the shepherds watching their flock at night, pointing to a mysterious star and listening, hands cupping an ear, to the heavenly chorus. Subsequent tableaux presented the three wisemen following the guiding star, the wisemen or kings with Herod, and finally everyone gathered by and around the baby Jesus. The positioning of characters on stage is all important. If Joseph and Mary are sharing "the limelight," that makes for one kind of statement. If Joseph is placed to Mary's left and is clearly up-staged by her and the child, that's making quite a different statement. If the rich gifts from the Kings is featured up stage of the Holy Family, there's another statement. Or, if a young shepherd is featured, offering his crutch to the baby Jesus, here we have yet another emphasis.

I come to a critically important point. As useful as it is to list one's personas and, one by one, capture in a few words their cardinal features, don't necessarily believe each will perform in a manner that is uncompromisingly loyal to the way they characterize themselves! When psychodramatically engaged with one another in critical life situations, each may contribute to a group statement which may be incongruent with the individual ways in which each features him or her self. This is straight Gestalt theory! The whole is more, sometimes other than, the sum or added up particulars of the parts. A fairly elaborate case in point comes to mind.

As one of my clients approached the termination of several years in psychotherapy, I invited him to assess how each of his personas were currently disposed toward the receiving and offering of intimate loving. He polled each in turn and what occurred to him proved terribly disturbing to both of us. What a dismal picture! It seemed that absolutely no progress had been made over several years. I couldn't believe this. Developments in his life argued against the validity of the findings that came of doing this inventory. In that moment it occurred to me to invite him to seek counsel from his unconscious minding through trance induction. He consented. I featured the induction with stories about tableaux. What I have presented to you, Hsuan-i, about the nativity tableaux comes from what I shared with this man. I invited him to recall from his childhood tableaux in which he participated. He displayed in his manner the physical features characteristic to entering into deep trance. When it appeared to me that he was ready and he was indicating to me that he was vividly "seeing" with his mind's eyes, I invited him to request his own personas to arrange themselves on stage, behind a closed curtain, as a tableau presentation of how they, all together, were several years ago disposed in response to the prospect of asking for or being asked for intimate expressions of loving. I suggested to my client that when his personas were ready, a curtain before his mind's conscious eye would open. The curtain opened and a very clear presentation emerged. Withdrawing from deep trance, he reported what he was experiencing. And what he saw made a lot of sense to him. Re-engaging in deep trance, he requested his personas to present a tableau that would make a statement as to where they were currently relative to accepting and offering intimate loving. The curtain opened and the picture was dramatically changed! I am hoping that the briefest suggestion of the characteristic features of each of his personas will suffice for the purpose of this illustration. His personas are:

—JIM, who feels lonesome and unseen; and who needs to just be one of the folks.

—PUPPY, who feels wrong and cringes; and needs petting and walks in the woods and countryside.

—EEYORE, who feels correct yet unappreciated; and needs someone who cares about him, listens to him and ignores his complaining.

—ROBIN, who feels totally living; and needs someone to love blindly.

—TOAD, who feels happy when he's playing, grumpy when he can't, needs play space, play time, and toys.

—SCAMP, who feels mischievous; and needs caringly enforced limits.

—BUD, who feels abandoned, devastated, undeserving; and needs to be reconciled with his loss.

—FAUNTLEROY, who feels fragile, incapable of doing right; and needs to play and get dirty and not to mind scolding for it.

—HARPY, who feels snappish, tenaciously and blindly critical; and needs a spell to bind her to the limb of a tall tree where she can see far, call out, and stay out of trouble.

—DODGE, who feels casual, though it's all an act; and needs to be confident and truly friendly.

—FRANK, who feels relaxed and blissful; and needs a little time now and then to just do nothing at all.

—BERSERKER, who feels blindly enraged; and needs basic training and brilliant leadership.

—TOM, who feels alert, sharpwitted, sometimes melancholy, likes smiling when he's onto something; and needs something worthwhile to accomplish.

—JUMPER, who feels enthusiastic, go-ahead, take-charge; and needs a stage, a cast, an audience.

—JOHNNY, who feels powerful, handsome, and both a little bit vain and lost, and needs to share a mature and exciting love.

—ELECTRO/MAGNO, who feels like a delicate clown; and needs a really good friend who understands his way of playing and likes to join in.

Here follows this man's two tableaux.

Tableau One:
Center stage is a grouping of Harpy, Bud, Jim, Puppy and maybe one or two others. Eeyore dominates the scene from upstage, right of center. He is a silhouette, not lit directly, yet a strong figure. Scamp is sitting on a tricycle downstage right of center. Fauntleroy

is sitting primly upright, hands folded in his lap on a couch nearby. Upstage left is a large grouping entirely in the shadows which includes Jumper, Tom, Johnny. Upstage center the backdrop is lit and appears to be trees and shrubs. Looking closely one can see Electro-Magno peering Puckishly through the greenery. Berserker is standing half in the shadow and half in the light between the Jumper-Tom-Johnny group. Dodge stands in the light, half way between the latter group and the personas in center stage. Robin stands in stopped motion in front of Eeyore apparently torn between the Scamp-Fauntleroy pair and the Harpy-Jim-Puppy-Bud group. Frank is sitting in the deepest shadow behind the upstage left group. He is in the group and yet sitting quietly on its edge. The others are poised attentively towards the center stage group. Toad is nowhere to be found.

Tableau Two:

Jumper, Tom, Johnny, Dodge, Frank and Electro-Magno sit around a table at stage center talking in soft, clear light. Downstage right center Scamp and Fauntleroy are playing actively on the floor. Eeyore and Robin stand watching them, and Robin is alert to the center stage grouping and to others in the scene. Robin has one arm around Eeyore's neck in a most friendly and comforting fashion. Berserker sits a little behind Robin, upstage center, crosslegged on the floor, knitting. Harpy is perched in a tree overhead (perhaps a large domesticated rubber tree, since this is a living room scene). She is simultaneously somnolent and watchful. Bud approaches Scamp and Fauntleroy, one hand on the handlebar of Scamp's nearby tricycle looking as though he wants to join them. Jim stands stage left looking expectantly towards the stage center grouping. He has just come in from the outside and catches Frank's eye in greeting. Puppy lies asleep before the fire. Frank scratches his neck and ears in a way that comforts them both—or is it Jim who is with Puppy: I think so; (it is clear that Frank and Puppy have a strong connection, too). Toad is nowhere to be found. He doesn't come into the living room much.

While, Hsuan-i, you may find it tempting to stay with this fellow's story given the number of questions that may have occurred to you in reading what he has seen, allow me to lure you away and back to Elizabeth. Supposing that each of us is always performing, and that our performing is always before present and imagined audiences. To whom are Carolyn, Stephanie, Jenny, Mona, Mary Anne, and Lee Anna playing? And how are each affected by members of the audience? Back to my original question? Where are Elizabeth's unmentioned personas while her sketches and day to day situations are unfolding? As in movies and stage plays, a cast divides among principal, supporting, and bit players. Pointing this out to Elizabeth may prove helpful. Remind her of something she already knows: bit players, actors who offer few lines as they walk on and off stage, can steal the show behind the backs of the principals, especially if they feel they are being neglected as "not as important, OBVIOUSLY, as the principals OBVIOUSLY feature and flatter themselves!" I am interested in how Elizabeth identifies her personas in terms of principals, supporting, and bit players. And does Elizabeth "see" all her personas arranging themselves in tableau the same now as a few months ago?

I can understand very well how come Carolyn absents herself if she feels that not everyone is helping out to the best of their ability.

Good luck to all of us,
Peter

Summary

In these pages I have introduced a number of techniques by which a client can be induced into immediate involvement in scenes of critical importance. While identification of personas, clarification of each persona's reactions within various circumstances, and reflection upon inter-personas dynamics are valuable in treatment, psycho-dramatizing enactment by each persona and various personas in relation to one another vastly enrich psychotherapeutic process. This chapter has featured the heightening and engagement of imagination in personas work. Trance induction and in-trance work have featured virtually every example of work with personas offered in this chapter:

Jacky learned to handle his Sudden Lightning by engaging a good Scout persona in a high stress scene while other personas led Sudden Lightning to his safe bedroom setting in trance state.

Fantasy, i.e. in-trance, blind walks illustrated how rich information can be secured relative to various personas.

Techniques were introduced demonstrating the engagement of personas in group session and in individual work facilitated by the person's vincular self and psychotherapist. Related to this was the account of disarming a lethal persona by means of engaging that persona in exploring the specific details of his intentions and openly facing the ramifications of his plan in minute detail.

Elizabeth Stacy's fables offer excellent examples of how in-trance automatic writing can enhance inter-personas work on critical issues. In these fables we see how personas in dynamic interrelation can act out of character, this is to say respond for the good of the whole person in ways not featured by them when interviewed "off stage."

And, in corresponding with Hsuan-i Chiu, Elizabeth's therapist, I introduced the technique by which the client can secure increased insight into his or her inter-personas dynamics by in-trance tableaux perception!

8

EPILOGUE

L iken what I have set forth so far to the style of the formal portion of a letter, and the Epilogue as the post script that may follow. In the more formal portion of this essay I have set forth in a deliberate and closely argued, carefully illustrated manner the central theoretical propositions that comprise Personae Theory and Personae Work. Now I am feeling at liberty to invite the reader into my more flowing thinking as I reflect upon the impact upon me that the personas perspective assumes. Personae Theory indicates more than an intellectual mapping of human experience, it offers an articulation of a way of living, including attitudes informing play and work.

In order to launch into the free play of my thoughts, I will review the central points I have set forth and illustrated. Excerpting from the formal content of my essay, I offer a theoretical precise. This exercise features left-brain discipline. And this exercise prompts in turn right-brain free play. Left brain activity is resumed in placing the several right-brain outings into order.

The manner of my writing following the theoretical precis is similar in style to the piece I wrote concluding Chapter One, entitled The Implications of Personae Theory in the Practice of Psychotherapy. The reader may find it interesting after reading the Epilogue to read once again the final portion of Chapter One.

Theoretical Precis

The following paragraphs compress the theoretical line that has been developed throughout this essay.

I. Many of my clients indicate that they experience themselves and are experienced by others as being a number of sub-selves, that is to say, personas. What they have reported to me I find evident in my own personal life. And as I have talked of this with clinical colleagues, and they in turn have talked with their clients, my findings are corroborated.

I propose that personality is invariably composed of multiple ego-states, i.e. personas, each of which represents a full sub-personality. Each persona emerges during the life of the individual as an internally coherent character. My experience indicates that most personas function to protect and enhance the well-being of the whole person. Each one of our selves, each one of our personas, amounts to the personification of a configuration of behavior patterns. Each persona as a pattern of behavior is recognizable and distinguished from other personas in terms of characteristic ways of thinking and performing.

Multiple personalities evidencing grand hysteria, dissociative type, or borderline splitting represent pathological developments in the adaptive histories of some persons. Being multiple is not pathological in and of itself. The view I am introducing is intended to throw into radical question the delineation between so-called "normal" persons and persons appropriately diagnosed as suffering from multiple personality disorder, or, currently, Dissociative Identity Disorder.

II. All behavior is performance. Essential to being socialized is the need to become adept actors and adept audience. From early on we learn to perform before a physically present audience including sub-audiences within the total audience, and we come to perform before imagined audiences. We attend to the actual or imagined response of audiences for prompting and approval. From when we are very young we thus become increasingly aware of how in this Punch and Judy world there are many *dramatis personae*, characters we can imitate to start with and then incorporate within our personal repertoire.

III. The word "I" carries a double significance: "I" is *who* I am, and "I" is *how* I am doing with my selves. *"I" as form* identifies my entity as the, one-who-I-am. "I" in this sense of the word is composed of a number-of-me. "I" speak in one voice variously textured and seasoned by the play in varying measure of each persona.

"I" as process indicates my keeping in touch with, and my capacity to integrate and mobilize my various voices. The "I" that attends to and attempts to manage the various personas with more or less command, comprises vincular activity. The word vinculum derives from the latin word *vincere*, to bind. The vinculum, or vincular self, is the persona that arises as leader among equals, absorbed in the very special task/role of participant/observer: the pathfinder and facilitator of inter-personas group dynamics. Ideally, vincular capacity inspires colorful idiosyncratic initiative and expression on the part of each persona as well as cooperation among personas.

Depending upon its strength, the *"I" as process* integrates the various facets of an individual's personality. Persons featuring weak or diminished vincular capacity are at the mercy of pressures from within and without. Such a person may experience him or her self and/or may be experienced by others as functioning as a group of players lacking teamwork. If a person behaves as a team rigidly bound, such that no member can move out of step with the others, she or he is crippled by vincular over-power; in other words, the meta-self is tyrannical. These contrasting modalities are akin to committees or task forces cursed by leaders who are either excessively permissive or excessively controlling.

Vincular activity is not exclusive to the vincular self; any persona may exercise vincular leadership from time to time, and as this occurs, the vincular meta-self, like any wise and able group facilitator steps back as the group assumes creative and productive ownership of its own process and direction.

IV. The True Self is inherent, pure potential; self actualization occurs as wholeness evolves in process. I proceed from the view that personality is protean, that our personas in active, observable play constitute our phenomenal reality. Further, as operational and

noetic integrity occurs, when all personas are in harmonious cooperation, we are realizing existential reality in Self actualization.
Existential reality becomes evident in process. "True Self" is pure
potential latently inherent in genetic and cultural information which
in active transactional and transformational process may become
evident. I attend to both dramatic and subtle presentation of personas in verbal and non-verbal behavior as well as in interpersonal
interaction in order to assess how a person negotiates with others
and as appearances of the person behind the appearances.

V. In psychotherapeutic inquiry we look with the client at his or
her story to see how "the story" is going well or has gone wrong. The
conscious and/or unconconscious appropriation or fabrication of
story affords each person a working grasp of his or her experience
of instantaneous being-in-the world. Satisfactory story provides
focus and framework within which and through which ontological
angst and ontological guilt play into constructive and sensitive
productivity. Efficiently sufficient story illuminates and directs our
way through our own-world, our world of experience with others,
and the world of our experience in relation to nature as a whole.
Harmony or dysfunctional stress among personas can occur where
congruity or incongruity occurs among their stories.

VI. A person's public persona resembles but is different from
an intimate persona. Both are images suggested by the attitudes
struck by the individual. In the case of the public persona, an
impression is fostered to surround and camouflage the private
identity of the individual. In the case of the intimate persona, the
image projected reveals facets of the individual's personal identity.
Any one of us, as in the case of a celebrity, permits or carefully
cultivates a public persona in order to protect his or her off-stage life
and private time from public scrutiny and invasion, and/or to
capitalize on his or her public performance as a name-brand
property the public will invest in and associate with celebrated
causes or commercial products.

VII. Treating the client as a group rather than as an individual
alters the therapist's assessment of a response to client ambivalence, resistance, self-contradiction, shifting moods, and
transferential inconsistencies. Diagnostic assessment and the design and implementation of a treatment process become an intriguing

exercise as it becomes apparent that within a given person there may figure non-neurotic, variously neurotic, character disordered, and profoundly disturbed personas.

Clients introduce their personas without prompting. Non-verbal gestures and odd voice inflections incongruent with the sense of the verbal message may evidence distinctively different messages from among personas.

Psychotherapeutic objectives include identifying personas clarifying the story-oriented values associated with each persona, and facilitating a productive and creative integration among the personas that will enhance the experience of being a coherent and effective person in the world.

VIII. Personae Theory features the premise that no one of us is of "one mind." Sick or healthy, everyone of our minds is a pie, fully or half baked, nestling a flock of ego states, (or personas, which are natural features of personality development. The way these personas work and play together defines a -10......0.......+10 mental health continuum. Persons evidencing extreme single-mindedness characterize pathology at the -10 end of this continuum. Floridly chaotic splitting among personas characterizes pathology at the +10 end of the continuum. Optimal mental health is therefore characterized by clearly multifaceted persons who experience themselves and are experienced by others as interesting, productive, and fundamentally happy. And all of us experience moments clearly plotted along this continuum.

From discursive review of the central principles of Personae Theory, I now shift into that frame of minding that is conducive to Persona Work. I invite you, now, to join me in playful and venturesome minding.

The Mental Health Continuum

The "I" composing each of us as subject of our own experiencing, as subject existing in the world, is multifaceted. The "I" I am experiencing myself as in the moment is but one facet to all I can be.

Everyone of us is multiple. Everyone of us is a Sybil—the woman celebrated for her multiple selves in Flora Rheta Schreiber's book entitled *Sybil*. Few of us are as dramatically split up as Sybil.

People who know one another at all will look at one another's face, listen to one another's voice, to see and hear where they are coming from in the given moment.

To be selves-possessed is to be able to be aware of where one is coming from, and to be able to direct the act in the moment, to be able to compose and play. I am woodwind and I am percussion. I am brass and I am strings. I am at times like many musicians warming up their instruments, with an ear for my instrument only, before a concert. A cacophony of sounds, of noise, and not disturbing to my ear as I am at home with my sounds. I know the difference between warm-up and performance. And, when the conductor, who I am as well, directs the attention of the players to the piece we are to play as many-in-one, we gather into an integrated body of players.

At a cabaret in San Francisco I attended a production of a play in which two male actors portrayed twelve male and female characters. It was clear that these actors knew what they were doing. My client, Meredith, suffered spells of not being able to keep track of her selves. Meredith would shift abruptly from character to character. She had difficulty keeping track of her selves.

A continuum figures among people in the general population wherein some people experience themselves and are experienced by others as their well known, relatively constant self. Metaphorically speaking, they are the same bread recipe on every occasion. They rely on a tried and true dish for all guests. Others present themselves in the form of a set menu of several set appetizers and several set entrees. A much smaller number within the general population cook up unpredictable concoctions, some of which may prove magnificent, others terrible and undigestible.

A continuum figures whereby some people are mildly various in their appearances and manners and modes of responding to situations that present themselves while others are dramatically various in their faces, their appearances, manners and modes of behavior. And, a smaller number are startlingly variable in the sorts of performances of which they are capable.

All of us have developed a number of personas. In some of us, our personas inter-relate and work smoothly together, like a family coordinating efficiently and attractively in hosting a dinner party. Although idiosyncratic, others among us have personas who entertain with sufficient interconnectedness to carry off the event. The personas coexisting in a few of us are seriously split up, some not at all aware of the existence and performances of the others, or some others. These live relatively chaotic lives.

A mental health continuum figures between subtle, smooth interplay among personas on the one hand, and on the other, gross splitting. Everybody is multiple, and each of us relates to everybody else along this continuum. People suffering dramatically profound split personalities, while ill, are not fundamentally different from those of us who identify ourselves and are identified by others as well. The difference is in measure and form.

Whether we are simply all at odds for the moment, a commonly shared "pickle" everyone of us suffers from time to time, and from which we can pull ourselves together again, or whether we are radically at odds, and unable to retrieve composure, depends in large part upon the effective presence or absence of an internal conductor pulling good music out of the "us" that is ensemble. I have defined this conductor in terms of vincular activity, which is specially associated with the vincular persona self, and shared in various interesting ways with other personas as each plays in bit, supporting, and principal ways from scene to scene.

Minding

When I am not consciously mindful, I am in trance. I am in trance whenever I am not self-conscious. I emerge from trance every time I awaken from sleep, night and day time sleep. I slip away from being self-conscious from time to time during the day. I fancy when I am not watching myself that I am free-wheeling non-consciously. Times like this I'm totally flowing as in this automatic writing.

When I am totally free from being self-conscious I am not monitoring myself. I am being, spontaneously. I may say simply anything that comes to mind. Not "coming to mind" in the sense of "Mind your little sister while I'm in the bathroom or "Pay attention to…" or "Keep your mind occupied with…" or "Don't let your mind wander away from paying strict attention to…" "Mind what you are doing" suggests restricting free play. Rather, by "coming to mind" I mean coming to conscious mind from non-conscious mind. Conscious minding is my thinking about the thinking as it occurs spontaneously. When I poise my pen above paper I am waiting for ideas to occur that I feel like writing down. Much more comes from deep mind to conscious mind than I write down. My conscious minding is audience-minding the play of thinking as it occurs. I register on paper what pleases me, given my present frame of mind.

Coming to mind…I am my feelings about my body. I am the thoughts that occur to me concerning my body. And all the feelings and thoughts that occur do not mix well. Each is a piece that goes with several jigsaw puzzles and yet all the pieces are mixed together on the puzzle table.

Who am I? I am a daydream. I can tease parts apart from my analogue "I." I can comment upon my metaphor "Me". Sitting here wanting to write, my writing hand becomes " tongue-tied." I am waiting for an idea that will set me free, loosen my tongue. Where are my personas when I need them? Is all this personas talk pure madness? I am watching the sun rise over Portland, Oregon. It is early morning. The setting is not conducive to making conversation.

Settings are very powerful prompters to chatter or silence. I am in Portland on the occasion of my son's graduation from college. My family attended the baccalaureate late yesterday afternoon. A potter was speaking. She sat at her wheel in the college chapel chancel throwing pots. The audience was enthralled and moved by her inner quiet. She talked to an audience that was moved to inner quiet.

Inner and external contexts key what occurs on stage within and without.

I as I appear, I in my appearances, am contextual. How am I? I am feeling more the way I do now. I am feeling more the way I do now than I did when I came in. I mind what I am writing if I become afraid that people who are in a position to do something about me mind what I am writing and might very well do something about me or to me that I will really mind. If I gather that the people who are in a position to do something about me or to me don't mind what I am writing or saying, because what I am saying or writing is harmless as far as they are concerned, or fine so far as they are concerned, or I sense that they really do mind what I am saying because they really like what's coming from me, and would feel it a loss if I kept shut up, then I would really mind not minding whether or not I said anything or not.

Then, if I felt supported, even highly encouraged, I would slip out of my mind in un-self-conscious flowing, not minding how or if what I said or wrote flowed freely from my non-conscious thinking through conscious observing one half step behind the happening in progress. I wouldn't pay myself any mind. I'd feel OK about just letting it happen.

The Natural Blend

I am thinking of my emergent family, an extended family composed of some blood kin, mostly found non-kin "comkins." I coin the word comkin to capture how persons feeling they are kin spirits with cares in common can identify their ties with one another. My emerged family is a band, a tribe of folk who have over twenty years wasted much time and tamed one another in the sense of "wasting time taming" offered by Antoine de Saint Exupery in his book, *The Little Prince.* We blend together well. By blend I intend the image of a weaving of complementary colors and threads of varying textures or a marvelously composed stir-fry. These and not these. A dance troop or repertory theater company of contrasting personalities integrally coordinated in aesthetic gestalt. The blending brings ingredients together into synergistic potentiality.

Much of the time I am as "I", a blend of my personas: once composed, difficult to separate out. Whenever I sit down with pen in hand to see what comes to mind in response to what/who/how I am experiencing myself in the moment I feel neither here nor there. I am a quiet blend of all there is within and about me. I am like my extended family gathered together on a wintry, evening, awaiting something to happen that will spark play. One and then another comments about the day. Someone brings forward an anecdote, an entertaining report of some serious or amusing incident. The rest of us are more or less attentive. What one or another brings to the attention of the rest of us may or may not stir up absorbed discussion or playful repartee. We are a blend until someone of us, among us, pleasurably disturbs the blend and prompts colorful interplay, encounter. Given interplay, a visitor observing us will begin to witness the remarkable diversities in wit and manner among us, moving them to see us for the motley crew we are.

"I" am a motley crew! And yet, I do not experience myself as motley when I am waiting, when I am still, when nothing is happening. In between catalytic events, "I" am a blend.

Encounter

I am experiencing shyness at the very thought of encounter. I can feel so shy under certain circumstances, and so outrageously zany under others. By zany I mean at liberty, in free play, any or all of my personas picking up cues and engaged in free play with audience. Theater as space and theater as process occur within and outside of my skin envelop. Theater as space includes the spaces on stage, back stage, off stage, the various audience spaces, out in the lobby, in the streets and everywhere the streets lead to! Don't you know? Actors on stage are at least implicitly "speaking" to those not present. Internally, within my skin envelop, in my head are personas playing actors and audience to one another as well as to introject audiences, introject allies, introject mentors, and introject antagonists. My careful reading of works by Irving Goffman has sharpened my awareness of all this. He is one of my introject mentors!

Imagine a company of street players, a troupe of actors and actresses, each costumed in character playing idiosyncratically to whomever among the audience encircling the troop catches their eye. Imagine players playing off one another from time to time. Imagine members of the audience becoming engaged, and, in engaging, stepping, literally or figuratively speaking, onto stage. It is in just this way that confusion occurs as to who is actor and who is audience. It is in just such a away that in encounter we become confused with one another. The perception that we are separated from one another by the skin envelops packaging our meat and bones collapses in fascination with what is happening in the moment. In captivating encounter we are out of body in dramatic play. This applies as well to the theater of the mind!

Actors on stage carry one another along with verbal and non-verbal cues: in re-presentational theater via cue lines, in presentational, which is to say improvisational theater, with prompting gestures and lines, as in getting one another going, triggering reactions, setting one another up. The drama of everyday life involves both representational and improvisational theater. We know the former is occurring as one person offers the aside, "Oh my, here we go again. It has a life of its own. It will run its course!" And we know we are into presentational theater when we can't believe what is coming out of our mouths for all its novelty, and we keep thinking, "I have never been here before!"

Encounter, being with another person, calls for joining with them in play as audience or "on stage" with them as fellow-players.

I recall how, many years ago, I enjoyed watching a four year old girl "leading" the choir as she stood on a pew somewhere in the middle of the congregation. During the social hour following the church service, I, whom she did not know, spoke to her, telling her how much I had enjoyed watching her leading the choir. She suddenly became self-conscious. I regretted my move. I had intruded unnecessarily. Imagine a grandfather, however well intending, interrupting children at play to say, "I am watching you play. Play some more." Unless the observer is able to join in the play, the observation prompts self-consciousness, and with self-consciousness, play is interrupted.

Riding the Edge of Consciousness and Non-consciousness

My personas are active in affecting my frame of mind as I address myself to the moment. I "listen" for cues from them. I ask myself, "What am I noting? What am I neglecting?" Each persona has his or her own epistemological orientation, its own cognitive habits by which it punctuates and maps, which is by way of saying in more simple terms, assigning rhyme and reason to what is occurring around and to it.

Personas figure out from the unconscious spontaneously. They are not at all self-conscious until they have appeared and are commented upon. Receptivity to the appearance of personas calls for a frame of mind in which one is riding at the edge of conscious/non-conscious attention. Functioning off from the edge in either direction fosters over and under self-conscious debilitation respectively.

I am assisted in understanding what it means to live at the edge by a comment Jeff Zeig wrote to me as he autographed my copy of his book, *A Teaching Seminar with Milton Erickson*, "To Peter: When you are comfortably driving yourself down the road, it doesn't disturb you to look out to orient yourself from side to side, does it? With best regards, Jeff Zeig." Steve Gilligan, Jeff's fellow Milton Erickson protege, said to me when I was training with him, "Peter, stay at the edge of consciousness and non-consciousness. There you will be receptive to what is occurring around you while available to the promptings from your unconscious learnings, all the learnings and wisdom that you have without thinking about it to know you have it."

Woolgathering Material For the Theater of Everyday Life

Woolgathering is entrancing. I have never spun wool, but I have seen people spinning wool at fairs. And if you keep it up for any length of time, I imagine you get into it. After a while you get the hang of it. The trance can't be too deep as I suppose you have to stay at the edge of consciousness/non-consciousness. Conscious thinking involves at least the most minimal element of watching what you are doing without your consciousness getting in the way of doing whatever you are doing fluidly. Letting go of staying minimally attentive to what you are doing might open to dropping the wool and going to sleep or going very deeply into trance activity.

When I spontaneously snap out of woolgathering and someone asks me, "Where were you?" I can't always remember. They say simply, "You must know where you were, what you were thinking." I say, "No, I can't remember anything." I had stepped beyond and out of conscious attention. At the edge of consciousness/ nonconsciousness, I know when I am in fantasy-land and I can follow the imagining featured by very rich, perceptual images running spontaneously along with the daydream.

Human beings are dreamers. My mother talked of yarns, of an excellent story being a good yarn. As writers are word-smiths, we all are yarn-smiths. Yarns come of woolgathering and wool-spinning. We make up stories in our heads a mile-a-minute, and often act on the stories, at least in minimal ways.

People engaged in dramatic encounter, as we all are all of the time, read one another, read between the lines, put words into one another's mouths, and don't tell one another any of this! We make up stories in our heads as to what the other is meaning, act from the stories we have made up in our heads without telling the other person the story we've made up, and then, when they ask where in hell we are coming from, we respond, "You know perfectly well!" Performance is under way, and the scene may prove grim and miserable, witty and illuminating, or marvelously funny.

If all that was actually said were transcribed, most of the story lines would be tucked between the lines. Someone just looks at us in a peculiar way. A fleeting glance will do, and we've made up a story in our heads that explains where they are coming from with us. We are woolgathering and we act on the story we have made up. Most times we don't tell the other person the story we have made up, and, if how we have responded to their glance given the story we have made up explaining their glance, upsets them, then they make up a story in their heads explaining how come we have acted toward them the way we have, and they respond or react to our move, most of the time without telling us the story they have made up in their head. All this happens all of the time. It is a wonder we don't go crazy all of the time. It is a wonder any of us get anything done!

This is woolspinning in our heads. What keeps us on task and out of dramatic stewing all the time is the ritualization of everyday life.

Julian Jaynes writes of "collective cognitive imperatives," fancy words for learning as in learning the school figures of skating according to correct, precisely defined, ritualized behavioral patterns. This includes correct thinking about what we are supposed to be doing in social situations and through phases and stages of life, in the socio-drama and psycho-drama of everyday life.

I am, socio-dramatically speaking, a practicing psychologist. I am the husband of a New Hampshire attorney. I am married and father of three, a tax paying and voting resident of the town of Gilmanton and state of New Hampshire. And I am a tax paying citizen of the United States of America, subject to the privileges and responsibilities of this land. Socio-dramatically speaking, I am expected, and I expect of myself to fulfill the responsibilities of these social roles which includes knowing when and how to conduct myself at one moment as a psychotherapist, as a father, as a son to my mother, as a customer standing in line at the market, as a patient in my physician's office, as a doctor keeping appointments, as a gentleman farmer feeding out my farm animals on schedule.

From a psycho-dramatic perspective, I am Peter Baldwin, host body for some fourteen discernable personas some very invested in the social role identifications by which I am known to others, some very little interested, very little bound by the conventions of my social identity. Psycho-dramatically speaking, how I conduct myself as a resident of Gilmanton or a citizen of the United States, how I conduct myself with my friends, and how I conduct myself as a psychotherapist is profoundly affected by the characterological features of each of my personas and the characterological performances they stage ensemble in one or another situation.

My woolgathering and spinning propensities are kept reasonably in hand by my ritualized attention to all the tasks associated with my social roles within the socio-dramatic theater of my everyday life. As an alarm clock awakens me out of sleep early each morning, so the cultivation of my life in terms of my places in the social world initiates cultivated alarm signals that keep me on task and distract me from free play woolgathering and spinning.

Mid-life crises, sophomore slumps revisited and compounded, occur as alarming realizations that there are untenable disparities between how one's life is proceeding socio-dramatically and psycho-dramatically, and how one's woolgathering suggests life was supposed to have developed thus far.

A woman in her mid-forties consulted with me in profound apprehension that she was surely about to lose hold of her ability to proceed with her work as a public figure to whom many women looked for leadership and counsel. She had supposed her capacity to do as well as she was doing was thanks to the strength and inspiration of her husband. "How can I, who through my first sixteen years lived within and bound by the conventions of a homogeneous Roman Catholic rearing and community, explain how I am today and sustain how I have been conducting myself in any other way than because of who and how my husband is for me? Catholic girls do not behave as I am behaving!" Now her husband was in personal psychological crisis. How could she sustain her own life! She derived from woolgathering and woolspinning with me sharpened awareness that her socio-dramatic performance was inspired not so much, in fact, by her husband's inspiration as by her own personas. The cliche: "Behind every famous man stands a strong woman of great resourcefulness" applies to each of us individually. Behind a strong and able socio-dramatic performance are our personas realizing their needs and interests through the performances of their public personas. This woman teased out of here-to-fore unconscious self awareness, recognition of various personas who began emerging into sharp definition from early childhood. This woman retrieved many memories of how her mother subtly cultivated thinking attitudes in her that were not harmonious with standard Catholic Old School thinking. The mother slipped books to her on the sly that encouraged adventure and independent thinking. My client uncovered in her exploration with me two personas evolving parallel to one another, one who through reading became a woolgathering adventuress, the other a social critic reading people rather than books, in the sense of an investigative reporter writing in the Dear Diary of her mind.

However essential woolgathering and woolspinning are in gathering material for the next move in the theater of every moment, and granting the powerful effect the play of personas have upon this process, acting impulsively on woolgathered and spun produce can work havoc on stage.

A scene comes to mind. The restaurant hostess is trying to seat customers as best she can. We have already waited in line for some time. There are five of us, and it is only eight in the evening, Oregon time. Eight o'clock is not remarkably late for time in the city. People who have arrived after we have arrived are seated first! Parties of two and three. I catch the hostess and say, "It is eleven o'clock for us!" I explain that we arose at four in the morning New Hampshire time in order to get to Boston's Logan airport in time to wait out a delayed departure for Denver and Portland. "So we have been up since one a.m. your time. Not our time. Our time was four a.m." Should I wonder that the hostess looks at me wildly? How can she cope with who and how I am right now when she has a job to do? Who cares what I am woolgathering and spinning? This may not seem to be the same kind of deep daydream, the same medium to deep trance woolgathering, that I was alluding to to begin with. But it is! It's still woolgathering! In my entranced state, I am incorporating other figures into my psycho-dramatic daydreaming. I am letting my woolgathering run unbridled, including supposing the hostess doesn't care. What is wrong with her that she isn't reading my thoughts and rushing to our rescue? She looks at me wildly! I have broken the rules. What can getting personal do to change the situation! The hostess should drive a party away from their table before they have finished their dinner? Would I be interested or even impressed were she to slip away from her hostess role to disclose to me what her day has been like? Not at all! Realizing my folly, snapped out of pursuing my foolish performance by my eldest daughter, Sarah, a professional chef, I repair into the more appropriate socio-dramatic role performance of patient customer. Now I retrieve presence of mind. I am out of personal trance. I am no longer woolgathering and spinning.

Sarah, a troop of personas characters in her own right, just as exhausted as I am, knows when and how to show her personal colors and when to keep them under cover. Sarah snaps at me to hush up. Now she spies a table that can accommodate our party, a table she guesses the hostess has not seen, she assumes a low profile public persona presentation as fellow restaurateur, and with precisely correct staging, secures the hostess's attention. Sarah to the Hostess: "We have a table available for this party of four." Sarah's performance has effectively induced the hostess into trance. The hostess responds to Sarah. Sarah is invited by the hostess to seat "her" party! A little while after we are seated the hostess comes to our table, looks closely at Sarah and says: "You must be in the restaurant business! You are very good. That was an impressive move!"

As figure skaters in competition demonstrate their command of school figures before incorporating these figures into creative dance, so we are wise to "practice" and gain command of social roles and rituals informing the socio-drama of everyday life before staging the psycho-dramatic expressions of our woolgathering and spinning.

Slipping From Outer to Inner Terrain

As Isis searched the world for the dismembered parts of her beloved Osiris, and in recovering them, re-membered them, so it is open to each of us to uncover veiled indications of deep aspects of our selves, and in recovering ourselves, remember who and how we are.

This is the journey Sigmund Freud assisted his patients in through free association and in the exploration of their dreams and spontaneous slips of the tongue. This is the investigation that is facilitated through Gestalt Therapy, and through Ericksonian hypnotherapeutic trance-work. This is the play that is fostered through Persona-work. And this uncovering is available to all of us quite naturally and without deliberate intent whenever we allow room for woolgathering and woolspinning as we allow ourselves to become lost in reverie, absorbed in our reading, compelled by a movie, and drawn into following associations that "come to mind," as we share with one another the adventures of the day.

Exploring inner terrain, the geography, topography, history, and culture of the inner life is prompted often by attention to external landscape.

I am writing while the rest of my family sleeps a little longer. The five of us are playing tourist from Portland, Oregon, to San Francisco. Four of us flew to Portland from New Hampshire for my sons graduation from Lewis and Clark College.

We hit the Pacific coast southwest of Portland just before dinner last night. During our previous five days we had explored inland Oregon in and east of Portland. Now, for the first time, we folk from Atlantic coast country saw the Pacific Ocean. And we were thrilled! My twenty-six year old daughter, Sarah, appeared to me to take on the most pronounced personal change. Her manner assumed the features of a little girl. The beach along which we walked was a beach-in-and-of-itself, a unique place in the world she had never seen before, and, a place immediately familiar to her as it drew from within her a piece of her personal inner landscape. From the beach she found and brought for herself and for me pieces of lava through which harder-than-lava pebbles had worn, and in being worn down themselves, had formed here and there through the lava, ever diminishing concentric cone shaped holes from surface through center to under-surface. So beautiful! So intriguing! A metaphor in stone? I wonder! Even as life gets to us, and we are worn through and through again by rough encounters, we have it within and about us to suffer this wear and sculpting at the surface and into our deepest inside places, and turn out remarkably reshaped in time. It seemed to me that Sarah was prompted by this Pacific beach place into trance in which she wandered along her inner landscape beach place, along which her eyes stumbled upon archaeological artifacts out of her own experience that touched and delighted her immensely. Exploring the surface of external landscapes prompts entrance into inner landscapes, where, in turn, Sarah found her selves and stories in clearer definition. Exploring external landscapes calls forward the suchness, the "thusness", of one's deepest knowing.

I once heard theologian Paul Tillich propose that eternity intersects our experience-in-time vertically through the present moment. And I hear that Albert Einstein held that time is not ultimately linear—that the future, past, and present defy chronological reduction. Could it be that my daughter-as-she-existed-on-her-inner-landscape-beach along the Pacific beach, in trance prompted into being one of her inner persona-children of the past, found a lava object symbolically reminiscent and simultaneously intimating yet-to-occur for her events further shaping herself as subject and object of her own experience?

The name by which one of my clients introduced herself was not, she informed me, the name by which she was legally and legitimately identified in and by the world. The name she offered me was the name she chose for herself as this name had come to please her. This name was the name of one of the girls in the book *Little Women*. And, during her early adolescence, when reading *Little Women*, upon stumbling upon this name, she was drawn by it, compelled by it, and knew, as she said to me, "in her heart of hearts," that this name had to be her name! Years after she had found what she had to believe was her true name, she sought through an agency to find her biological parents. They reported to her in due course that they had not only located the record of her mother's death, as well as the where-abouts of her biological father, they had also located her record of birth and the name her parents had given her. She had been given up to adoption by her biological mother when she was three and a half and had, after a period of time in an orphanage, been adopted, and legally re-named by her adoptive parents. The name that struck her so in reading *Little Women* proved to be the name her biological parents had given her, a name she had been effectively pressed "to forget". Within the context of the outer terrain of her public life she knew nothing of her true name. And yet, in reading a book available to her from the outside world, she was lured through the boundary between consciousness and non-conscious-ness onto her inner terrain, and there she re-membered some of her true self.

I see some clients in my City office, others in a lodge situated just a few steps downhill from my country home. There, on my hillside property, we keep dogs and cats, ducks and geese, chickens, hogs, and horses. Clients enjoy the sights and activity of the animals very much in view from within the lodge.

As I am writing, I am drawn back in time to a very interesting event. I am in that lodge in session with a man who is struggling in dismay over a second failed marriage. We have been talking of the ouroborous, that mythic serpent that lives recursively, consuming its own tail, ever consuming what it has been consumed by in the past, ever avoiding anything beside itself that may trouble and perturb its own system. This man is worrying over his ouroborian susceptibilities, the fear that he will repeat his sorry tale in yet another relationship. He wants to grow, to become more aware, change the kind of experience he has of himself. He is talking earnestly; I am listening carefully. I see a flash of color outside the window just over his left shoulder. The flash of color is so startling, I wonder what it was. A scarlet tanager? I saw my first tanager two summers ago deep in my woods when I was yarding pine logs in preparation for building a barn. Scarlet tanagers are a rare treat! I interrupt him. "Ray! I think there's a scarlet tanager out the window behind you. I want you to see it. I want to see him again." Ray and I lean on the back of the couch he has been sitting on. One minute goes by. Another passes. I worry. Am I setting him up for a disappointment? Great! Just what he needs just now. The tanager reappears! He lands and perches on the limb of an oak very near by. He is magnificent. He remains there for a couple of minutes. Wonderful. We are enthralled. Now he flies away. We return to our seats. We sit quietly. Our session is coming to a close. As Ray gets ready to leave, he tells me that he will have been to Seattle for a few days by the time he sees me again the next week. I encourage him to take the Seattle harbor boat tour. He hopes he can. Ray leaves.

A week passes. We are in session. Ray has a mischievous look about him. I know something's up. "I arrived in Seattle early in the evening," he tells me, "settled in, slept well. The workshop went well the next morning. At noontime, we were recessed for a couple of hours. We were encouraged to enjoy some of Seattle. I wasn't looking for anyone in particular to go with. We all drifted out of the room and down to the lobby. By the time I was on the street outside of the hotel, I was one of several in a drift-together group. Half way down the block, Peter, I was struck by the weird notion that we were waddling along like your gaggle of geese. Honking. We honked as we paraded down the block. I knew I was in trouble, thinking about things like this! I couldn't shake the idea that we were all a silly gaggle of geese. Then what's worse, I realized I had just looked over my shoulder. For about the third time! What was possessing me to look over my shoulder? I was looking for a scarlet tanager! I was looking for a scarlet tanager in downtown Seattle! Now I knew I was nuts. And having to confess that I was enjoying feeling nuts.

"Now the thought occurred to me that I had noticed something back there behind me. But I couldn't remember just what it was. so I slipped away from the rest. I had to do it without being noticed. I knew that if the others noticed me slipping away, they'd honk at me. Well, I managed without their notice. Walking back the way we had come, I saw what I had noticed, an old woman tending a vegetable and fruit stand across the street. I found a place where I could watch her without being seen. Her hands fascinated me. So much in the earth, they looked like the earth alive. Something about her, about all of her struck me. A scarlet tanager. She was a scarlet tanager!

"Peter, did you know that scarlet tanagers come in various forms and sizes? After a while I stepped away from that spot, and followed my nose through the streets of downtown Seattle. And I saw other scarlet tanagers, Peter. They are everywhere!

"I'm seeing differently now. I'm seeing beyond the familiar. I have changed this week. I do not feel I am as I was last week. I am becoming what I have been seeing. I guess what I have been noticing outside of myself that I haven't noticed before is myself in forms I haven't recognized before."

As I look at Ray, I am struck with how he is now not what and who and how he was last week only less so. And he is not what and who and how he was last week only more so. He is different in kind. He is transforming as he is fascinated by and as he consumes what is around him. And his discoveries in the terrain outside and about him, are leading to fascination with and discoveries of what has figured within the terrain of his inner life. Consuming novel information and becoming transformed by what he is assimilating has become his emerging tale, and the tail end of the old story he had been recycling in one relationship after another.

Finis